WHERE THE WEST ENDS

Michael J. Totten

Michael J. Totten is a foreign correspondent and foreign policy analyst who has reported from the Middle East, the Balkans, and the former Soviet Union.

He's a contributing editor at *World Affairs* and *City Journal*. His work has also appeared in the *New York Times,* the *Wall Street Journal*, *The New Republic*, *Slake: Los Angeles*, *Reason*, *Commentary*, the *New York Daily News*, *LA Weekly*, the *Jerusalem Post*, and Beirut's *Daily Star*.

His first book, *The Road to Fatima Gate*, won the Washington Institute Silver Book Prize in 2011. He won the 2007 Weblog Award for Best Middle East or Africa Blog, he won it again in 2008, and was named Blogger of the Year in 2006 by *The Week* magazine for his dispatches from the Middle East. He lives with his wife in Oregon and is a former resident of Beirut.

Visit his blog at www.MichaelTotten.com

ALSO BY MICHAEL J. TOTTEN

The Road to Fatima Gate
In the Wake of the Surge

WHERE THE WEST ENDS

MICHAEL J. TOTTEN

First American edition published in 2012 by Belmont Estate Books

Cover design by Kathleen Lynch
Edited by Whitney Lee

Manufactured in the United States on acid-free paper

FIRST AMERICAN EDITION

Totten, Michael J.
Where the West Ends
ISBN-13: 978-1475183641
ISBN-10: 147518364X

For Sean

Contents

PART THREE - THE CAUCASUS

PART FOUR - THE BLACK SEA

I was in Jerusalem, standing before an eighteen-foot separation barrier between Israeli and Palestinian territory, when it hit me—that concrete wall is a civilizational boundary. The Israeli side is either part of the West or similar to the West; Arab civilization begins on the other side. That border may be the only place on earth where Western civilization suddenly stops and another abruptly begins. Everywhere else, the West falls away in degrees.

On the part of our planet between Turkey and Russia, and between the Balkans and the Caucasus, the West mixes and co-exists with various eastern civilizations and forms something else—not one thing, but different things in different places, depending on what's being blended.

This book is a journey through thirteen nations, all but two formerly communist. All are far from my home.

I was born and raised in Oregon and that's where I live now. Jets flying in over the ocean are coming from Asia. The beach is but a leisurely drive from my house. Beyond it is nothing but water for thousands of miles. North America's Pacific Rim is the western edge of the West. In the east, the West fades slowly like twilight.

PART ONE

THE MIDDLE EAST

One

Back to Iraq

"An adventure," the great travel writer Tim Cahill once wrote, "is never an adventure when it happens. An adventure is simply physical and emotional discomfort recollected in tranquility." I have never taken a trip that more aptly fits that description than when my best friend Sean LaFreniere and I drove to Iraq on a whim.

It was stupid of us and the trip was unrelentingly miserable, though in my defense the idea was not solely mine. Sean was my accomplice and we suffered together.

I lived in Beirut at the time. He lived in Copenhagen, where he was studying for his Master's in architecture. I invited him to Beirut, but he said he would rather see Turkey, so instead we met in Istanbul. Neither of us had any idea that we would end up driving all the way to Iraq. Why would we? Hardly any tourists visiting Turkey even think of it. Istanbul is one of the world's greatest cities while Iraq is—well, it's Iraq.

Sean's plane was a day late due to an airline snafu, and he arrived exhausted and grumpy. "I need a drink," he said. "Is it even possible to get a drink in this country?"

"This is Turkey!" I said. "You can get a drink in even the smallest mountain village in Anatolia." He knew that already, but he was tired and had forgotten. I had been to only one Muslim country that bans alcohol, and that was Libya. It's available most other places.

"Come on, Sean," I said. "Let's get you a drink."

We washed down bloody steaks with smoky red wine in a brick and stone building that was older than our own country while a man in a tuxedo masterfully played the violin. I dearly wished I could have been there with my wife. The restaurant's atmosphere was achingly romantic and I hadn't seen her for months. Sean missed his wife, too. Angie, like my wife Shelly, was back in the United States.

But Sean and I had a man's trip ahead of us. He and I both love hitting the open road in a car, especially in foreign countries. It is not our wives' style. When he and I are in the mood for a road trip, we go alone.

I let Sean decide the itinerary since I'd been to Turkey before and he hadn't. The city of Izmir on the Aegean coast is spectacular, but we only had three days before he had to return for exams and I had to catch a flight to Tel Aviv. So the plan was to visit Gallipoli and Troy which were much closer.

We hurtled down the highway from Istanbul toward Gallipoli. That road heads west in the direction of Greece and Sicily. On the way we argued about whether Turkey was Eastern or Western. In the twenty-four hours since he had arrived, he decided it was mostly Western. I played Devil's Advocate and said it was Eastern, though what I really think is that it's neither and both.

Many visitors to Istanbul are surprised that, aside from the mosques on the skyline, it looks much more European than Middle Eastern. They shouldn't be. Although part of the city is on the Asian side of the Bosphorus strait, most of it is in Europe. It was the eastern capital of the Roman Empire and endured as such for centuries after the western half, with Rome as its capital, first declined and then fell. It was not until 1453 that the city, then named Constantinople and the capital of the Byzantine Empire, was conquered by Turkish Ottomans out of Asia. The Ottoman Empire then ruled over most of the Middle East and much of Europe's Balkan Peninsula for hundreds of years. The empire was Islamic and ruled by a caliphate, but it was also, simultaneously, trans-civilizational.

Many Europeans in Bosnia and Albania converted to Islam during this time, but the Turks couldn't resist becoming a little Westernized by incorporating Europeans into their realm. Turkey is thoroughly

Western compared with its cousin Turkmenistan, which isn't at all. The same phenomenon partly explains why Russia today has Eastern aspects to its culture due to its conquering of lands in the Far East and why Mexico and Peru are culturally part Aztec and Incan despite being the former colonies of Western imperial Spain.

"Be careful out there!" Sean's Danish friends said, as though Turkey were teeming with Islamist fanatics who wanted to kill him. "Isn't it dangerous?" one of his professors said. "Don't let anyone know you're American or living in Denmark!" Little did this educated man know, Istanbul is safer than Copenhagen.

Danes were right to be a little concerned, though. The Danish newspaper *Jyllands-Posten* had recently published a batch of cartoons of the Prophet Muhammad that Muslims all over the world considered "blasphemous." Frenzied mobs sponsored by the Syrian government set Denmark's embassies in Beirut and Damascus on fire. One hundred and thirty nine people, almost all of them Muslims, were killed during various protests worldwide.

Istanbul looked and felt more Western than Sean expected. It felt Western to me, too, since I had just arrived from the Arab world. I was still in Devil's Advocate mode, though, so it was my job to make the case for Turkey being Eastern.

"Remember," I said. "This country borders Greece and Bulgaria. But it also borders Iraq."

I could all but hear the gears turn in his head.

"That's right," he said and put his hand over his mouth. He knew he shouldn't say what he was thinking, but he removed his hand and said it anyway. "Holy shit, we could drive to Iraq."

The instant he said it I knew that we would, indeed, drive to Iraq. Who cares about Troy when we could drive to *Iraq*?

I have known Sean most of my life. I should have known, then, that it's impossible for us to rent a car in a foreign country and only drive a few hours, that he and I would almost certainly end up more than a thousand miles and a whole world away from where we innocently planned to visit over the weekend. He is the only person I grew up with in Oregon, with the possible exception of my brother, Scott, who would see any appeal whatsoever in driving from a pleasant and heavily-touristed part of the world to one of the scariest countries on earth.

But Sean didn't yet know what I knew. I had just flown over Turkey's Anatolian core in an airplane on a clear day from Lebanon. All of Turkey east of the Bosphorus ripples with mountains. And when I say mountains, I mean *mountains*. Huge, steep, snow-covered monsters that rise from the earth and the sea like impassable walls. Turkey is a miniature continent unto itself. (Hence the name Asia Minor.) You can't blow through that land in a car like you can if you stick to I-5 in California.

I wanted to do it, though. Badly. How many people have ever decided to spontaneously take a road trip to Iraq from Europe after they were already in the car and driving in the other direction? We were heading toward Greece, not the Tigris. We had no visas. No map. No plan. And no time. Sean had to be back in Copenhagen in three days for his exams. Pulling this off would be nearly impossible. Nothing appealed to me more.

I pulled off the road and stopped the car so I could think.

"We're going to make this work," I said.

Why go to Iraq? Because it is there, because it is different, and because no one else wants to. Because adventurous travel and unusual human experiences make our lives better. Istanbul is spectacular and Paris is even more so, but visiting a place like Iraq engages the senses and the mind on a much deeper level even if it is unpleasant. It's not like going to another planet, exactly, but it's new enough and *strange* enough that it makes me feel like a kid again when everything was hard and had to be learned. Iraq is so different from my native Oregon that almost everything about it is utterly fascinating. Istanbul is Eastern enough and exotic enough for it to be interesting for a short while, but at the same time it's enough like the West I grew up in that it begins to feel mundanely familiar within a few days, if not hours. A sudden arrival in an utterly alien culture is as intoxicating as a narcotic.

I called my wife and told her what I was up to. I also called a friend of mine who worked for the Council of Ministers in Erbil, the capital of Iraq's autonomous Kurdish region just across the Turkish border. I had visited Iraqi Kurdistan just three months earlier as a journalist, so I knew some people. And I needed to know: would it be possible to get tourist visas on arrival at the border?

"Michael!" my Iraqi friend said, disappointed that I even asked. "You know the Kurds won't give you any problems."

Iraqi Kurds, unlike Iraqi Arabs, are some of the most pro-American people in the world.

"Sorry," I said. "The border is more than a thousand miles away. I don't want to drive all the way over there in winter unless I'm sure we can get in."

"Of course you can get in," he said. "You are always welcome in Kurdistan."

"Can I call you from the border if we have any problems?" I said.

"Michael!" he said. "We will not give you any trouble. The only people who might give you trouble are Turks."

I didn't think the Turks would care if or how we left Turkey. They might care once we tried to come back, but Sean and I had multiple-entry visas.

It soon dawned on Sean that we were actually going to Iraq. (Even though we would be in the tranquil and friendly Kurdistan region as opposed to war-torn Fallujah.) We were no longer talking about it, but doing it.

"Would you take your wife there?" he said.

"Of course," I said. "It's really not dangerous. Shelly wished she could have gone with me when I went there before."

Iraqi Kurds have never been at war with the United States. Nearly every man, woman, and child was relieved when Saddam Hussein's regime was demolished. Their part of the country suffered no insurgency, no kidnappings, almost no crime, and even less terrorism.

It was a minor drag that Sean and I wouldn't get to see much of Turkey except from the car. Gallipoli isn't the most interesting place in the country, but it was the site of a crucial World War I battle and the inspiration for one of the most moving speeches of Mustafa Kemal Ataturk, modern Turkey's founder.

"Those heroes that shed their blood and lost their lives," he famously said of the buried British dead, "you are now lying in the soil of a friendly country. Therefore rest in peace. There is no difference between the Johnnies and the Mehmets to us, where they lie, side by side here in this country of ours. You, the mothers who sent their sons from faraway countries, wipe away your tears. Your sons are now lying in our bosom and are in peace. After having lost their lives on this land, they have become our sons as well."

The only things we didn't have that we needed were a decent map and a good night's sleep.

We crossed the surging Dardanelles by rain-spattered ferry and landed on Turkey's Asian shore in the charming town of Canakkale.

Gallipoli was just on the other side of the water. A monumental set piece downtown was made of big guns from the battle.

I asked the clerk at the hotel desk if he knew where I could buy a map.

He didn't. I wasn't surprised. Maps are generally harder to find in the Near and Middle East where a startling number of people don't know how to read them.

"Do you have any idea what's the best road to take to get to Turkish Kurdistan?" I said. Sean and I did have a map; it just wasn't a good one. We couldn't tell from the low granularity which route was best.

He didn't answer the question. Instead he said, "I don't like Kurds."

"What's wrong with Kurds?" Sean said.

"I don't like their culture," the clerk said and twisted his face. "They're dirty and stupid."

Sean and I just looked at him and blinked. He seemed like such a sweet kid when he checked us in.

I had a brief flashback to a conversation I had with a Kurd in Northern Iraq a few weeks earlier. "Istanbul is a great city," my Kurdish friend said. "The only problem is it's full of *Turks.*"

"What do you think of Arabs?" Sean said.

"Eh," the clerk said. "We don't like them in Turkey. We have the same religion, but that's it. They cause so many problems. You know."

Sometimes it seems like everyone in the Middle East hates everyone else in the Middle East. Arabs hate Kurds and Israelis. Turks hate Arabs and Kurds. Kurds hate Turks and fear Arabs. (Intriguingly, Kurds love Israelis.) Everyone hates Palestinians.

Not all people are haters. I know plenty who aren't. But every culture has its baseline prejudices that individuals either opt into or out of. It's exhausting. Sometimes I just want to shake people and say: *Keep your old-world ethnic squabbling out of my face, willya please? Jesus, no wonder there's so much war around here.* Even so, Middle Easterners are the most friendly and charming people I've ever met.

Sean and I tried to go to sleep early so we could leave at first light. I stared at the ceiling and remembered my flight over the spectacularly mountainous country. *We're screwed,* I thought. *There's no way we can drive across that landscape to Iraq and back in three days from where we are now.*

And I was right.

Sean and I woke at dawn and headed south from Canakkale toward the ancient ruins of Troy. We wouldn't have time to hang out there, though, or anywhere else for that matter, if we wanted to make it all the way to Iraq and back to Istanbul on time.

We weren't in the car for a half-hour before we saw the turnoff.

"We have to stop," Sean said.

"No time," I said.

"It's Troy!" Sean said. "We can't just drive past it."

I pulled off the road. Vicious dogs ran straight at the car. If I hadn't slammed on the brakes I would have killed them. This happened over and over again while driving through Turkey.

We parked in the lot and paid twenty or so dollars to get in.

"Hurry," I said to Sean. "Grab your camera and go."

Somebody built a wooden yet somehow cartoon-looking "Trojan Horse" and stuck it directly outside what would have been the gate to the city had it not been reduced to rubble by time, neglect, and erosion. Sean ran toward it while I snapped a quick picture.

"Run," he said.

We ran—literally, ran—through the entire ruined city in under ten minutes. It's amazing how small the place is. This tiny little town, no bigger than a dinky modern-day village, left an imprint on history and literature completely out of proportion to its actual size. Too bad we had no time whatsoever to contemplate any of it.

We ran back to the car. I damn near killed the dogs again on the way back to the main road. Do they snarl and charge at everyone who drives past? It's a wonder they're still alive.

I unfurled a brand-new map we picked up from a tourist information office. It looked like the best bet was to drive down to the Aegean Coast toward Izmir, a city we initially deemed too far away from Istanbul to visit in time. We couldn't possibly get all the way to Iraq and back in the two days we had left, but we kept going anyway. If by some miracle we could figure out how to get there on schedule, we'd have no time to do anything but have lunch and leave. We were driving 2,000 miles round-trip—to Iraq of all places—just to have lunch.

I drove us toward Izmir as fast as the coastal road would allow. The Aegean Sea sprawled out on the right. The view was extraordinary. Greece was on the other side of that water. I could see it. There were more islands between us and the Greek mainland than I could count on two hands. While beautiful, the view was also discouraging. Greece is a long way from Iraq. It's more than a thousand road miles away. And yet there it was.

The way south toward Izmir was a nightmare of slow-moving traffic around tight bends in the road and through coastal resorts. Izmir was at most five percent of the way to Iraq from Istanbul. We had driven almost half a day and still hadn't made it even that far. There was no way we could make it to Iraq in even a week at that speed.

"We need to head inland and get off this road," I said.

"The mountains will kill us," Sean said.

"The coast is killing us. We have to chance it."

I turned off and headed toward the heart of Anatolia. At first the road was encouraging. Then we got stuck behind truckers doing 20 miles an hour.

"Told you this was a bad idea," Sean said.

"The coast was a bad idea, too," I said. "We're pretty much screwed no matter what."

We pressed on into hard driving rain, which slowed us down even more. I wanted to blow up the slow trucks ahead with a rocket launcher. *Get out of the way, get out of the way, we're making terrible time!* Eventually the rain cleared, revealing a punishing road toward a gigantic mountainous wall.

"Oh my *God!*" Sean said. "We never should have turned inland."

He was right. I screwed up, but it was too late.

"We'll head back to the coast when we can," I said.

We didn't make it back to the coast until dark. This time we were on the Mediterranean. Rain washed over the road in broad sheets. In a third of our available time, almost no progress had been made at all toward Iraq.

We both woke up with a virus. My throat burned when I swallowed. My entire body, from the top of my head to the bottoms of my feet, was wracked with a terrible fever ache. We had so far to go and almost no time to do it. At least we were out of the punishing mountains.

But we were back on the punishing coast. A twisty little road hugged the shore which rose up so sheer from the Mediterranean it was impossible to drive more than 30 miles an hour without plunging shriekingly over a cliff.

"Now you see why I wanted to get off the coast!" I said.

Sean nodded silently. There was no way to win. You just can't drive across Turkey in a normal amount of time unless you take the autobahn linking Istanbul and Ankara. We were so far from that road, though, that it was very near hopeless.

I tried to sleep in the passenger seat while Sean took the wheel. There would be no more stopping to sleep in hotels. We would have to drive straight for the rest of the trip.

Without time to stop at restaurants, we were forced to eat terrible food. We had soft drinks, potato chips, and other crap from convenience stores attached to gas stations that carried the same kind of salty, sugary snacks sold in similar stores in the United States.

Once we tried to pop into a little food stall at night. Then we saw what was being cooked on a stove: a nasty green-brown substance bubbling in an unspeakable cauldron. We both turned and walked right out the door.

"I can't deal with that right now," I said.

"It looks like Orc food," Sean said.

In troglodyte country, where some people live in caves tunneled into the ground and the cliffs, an old man stood by the side of the road selling bananas.

"Want some bananas?" I said.

"Yes!" Sean said.

I pulled off the road.

"Quick, get those bananas," I said.

Sean rolled down the window and handed the old man a dollar. In return we received a handful of bananas. Real food at last.

We passed through great-looking towns that I cannot tell you the names of. Turkey is packed with wonderful places that hardly anyone in the States ever hears about.

The virus was killing me.

"We need a pharmacy," I said.

"No time to stop," Sean said.

"If we're going to drive all day and all night we can't be feeling like this," I said. "We'll drive off the road and kill both of us."

We stopped at a pharmacy and bought medicine.

We also stopped at an Internet café. Sean and I wouldn't be able to take our rental car across the border into Iraq. If we wanted to make our way to the Iraqi city of Duhok, someone would have to pick us up. So I sent an email to one of my fixers and tried to hire him for the next day. I asked him to please send someone else to meet us if he couldn't do it himself.

Sean and I got back in the car. A few hours later we could stop at another Internet café, check the email again, and continue to work on our Iraqi logistics. We didn't yet know that there would be no more Internet cafés. We'd be flying blind from then on.

I felt amazingly irresponsible for trying to put together an Iraqi itinerary at the last second from the road while sick and with no time.

"If no one picks us up," I said to Sean, "we'll have to hitchhike or flag down a taxi."

"Hitchhike in Iraq?" Sean said.

"Sure," I said. "It's the Kurds in Northern Iraq. They're cool."

Sean didn't say anything. I knew how dubious what I suggested must have sounded.

"Are you okay with that?" I said. "Will you cross the border if no one is there to pick us up? We'll figure something out. Trust me. Trust the Kurds. Trust the universe. We'll be fine."

"Alright," Sean said and threw his hands in the air.

We continued the punishing drive along the coast, in the rain, malnourished, sleep-deprived, and wracked with a terrible illness. It was unspeakable.

"Holy shit, look at that!" Sean said as we drove past some hotels on the side of the road.

"What?" I said.

"A sea castle," Sean said. "Wait, you'll see it again in a second."

I saw it when we cleared the bank of hotels.

"Holy shit!" I said and pulled off to the side of the road.

An otherworldly sea castle appeared to literally float off the coast of the Mediterranean. I had never even heard of this thing.

"Wow," Sean said. "Look what they have! This country is just amazing."

"Yep," I said. "We need to come back here and visit it properly."

"Let's go, let's go," he said. "It's getting dark."

It was, indeed, getting dark. The cold medicine we bought at the pharmacy seemed to have no effect. We were both sick as dogs and had no time to stop at a hotel to sleep it off.

BANG. We got a flat tire. I pulled onto the shoulder.

"So much for Iraq," Sean said.

"Wait," I said. "We might have a spare."

I popped the trunk. We did have a spare! It was a real spare, too, not a near-useless "donut" that can fall off at speeds faster than thirty miles an hour. The only problem was we had no jack.

Sean and I walked across the road and ducked into a store that sold yard tools. The owner did not speak a word of English. Darkness was falling. Sean drew a picture of a blown out tire on a pad of paper. The man indicated he didn't sell tires. I grabbed the pad of paper and drew a picture of a car propped up on a jack.

The man called a friend of his who showed up on a motorcycle with a big bag of tools. Without saying a word or even looking at us he jacked up our car and changed the tire for us in two minutes. I handed our savior twenty dollars.

"Thank you so much!" I said. He rode away on his bike.

And then we were off. The whole flat tire incident only took half an hour. What incredible luck. We just might make it to Iraq after all.

We drove all night, taking turns at the wheel in the dark. I could tell when we finally left the Mediterranean and approached inland Turkish Kurdistan after the silhouettes of palm trees vanished and I could see semi-desert features at the edge of the headlight range. Most traffic slacked off by this point. Towns grew poorer and farther apart. Syria was only a few miles off to our right. Turkey didn't look remotely like Europe any more. That much was obvious even in the dark. We were deep in the Middle East now.

"I can't drive anymore," Sean said. "You have to do it."

I got behind the wheel and drove as far as I could until three o'clock in the morning.

"You have to drive now," I said. "I'm going to go off the road if I drive any farther."

"I can't drive anymore," Sean said.

I stopped the car and got out. My teeth instantly chattered. It was absolutely frigid outside. If we napped on the side of the road we would shake inside our coats. My entire body still throbbed with fever ache. I needed a bed.

"We can't sleep now," I said as I got back in the car. "You have no idea how cold it is here. We need to find a hotel."

But we were in the absolute middle of nowhere. All I could see were rocks and scrub in the headlights.

I drove slowly so I would not kill us. We found a low-rent Turkish trucker motel. What looked like 900 trucks were outside.

"I'm stopping here," I said.

"I don't want to spend the night with a bunch of loud truckers," Sean said. The parking lot was awfully noisy.

"There's nothing else out here," I said. "It's either the truckers, the cold, or I kill us on the side of the road."

We went into the trucker motel in the middle of the Turkish wasteland on the road to Iraq. It was exactly as grim inside as you would expect. A twitchy man on the night shift checked us into a room.

"Sozpas," I said. *Thank you*, in Kurdish.

"Are you sure you're speaking the right language?" Sean said. "Are we really in Kurdistan?"

"I don't know," I said. "I think so, but I'm not sure. Anyway, he did not seem offended." He probably was, however, surprised. The Turkish government had only recently begun to relent in its draconian suppression of the Kurdish language.

It was four o'clock in the morning. We set our alarm clocks for six. Two hours later we woke. I felt exhausted and needed to sleep for a week. My eyes burned from the light. But I felt great at the same time. My fever had broken. And it was time to head into Iraq.

Sean and I dragged our sorry, exhausted, malnourished selves to the car at 6:30 in the morning just a few hours northwest of the Turkish-Iraqi border. For the first time we had a look at our new surroundings in daylight.

Turkish Kurdistan is a disaster. It is emphatically not where you want to go on vacation.

One village after another had been blown to pieces by tank shells and air strikes. Military bunkers, loaded with sand bags and bristling with mounted machine guns, were set up all over the place. Helicopters flew overhead. An army foot patrol marched toward us alongside the highway. Twenty-four soldiers brandished rifles across their chests. I slowed the car down as we approached so I would not make them nervous. I could see the whites of their eyes as they stared, deadly serious, at me through the windshield. Neither of us dared take their pictures. Those soldiers were not just hanging out and they were not messing around.

The civil war in Eastern Turkey didn't look anything like it was over. I could tell just from driving through that the Marxist-Leninist Kurdistan Workers' Party (the PKK) was still active. How else to explain the full-on siege by the army? The Turks' treatment of Kurds has been horrific since the founding of the republic, but the separatist PKK seems hell-bent on matching the Turks with the worst it can muster, including the deliberate murder of Kurdish as well as Turkish and foreign civilians.

The highway ran right alongside the Syrian border for a stretch. Turkey had walled off the deranged Baathist regime of Hafez and Bashar al-Assad with a mile-wide swath of land mines wrapped in barbed wire and marked with skulls and crossbones. At one point we could look right into a Syrian town in the distance where Kurds lived in possibly worse conditions than even in Turkey. While many, if not most, Turkish nationalists have a near-ideological hatred of Kurdish nationalism, the Arab nationalist regime in Damascus is worse. At least the Turkish government is elected and the Kurds get to vote. The Assad regime is a totalitarian monster that stripped many Syrian Kurds of their citizenship solely for the "crime" of not being Arab.

From a distance it appears that the biggest problem in the Middle East is radical Islam. Islamism surely is the worst of the Middle East's exported problems, but up close the biggest source of conflict seems to be ethnic nationalism and sectarianism, at least in the Eastern Mediterranean where no state is homogenous. The crackup of the Ottoman Empire has yet to settle down into anything stable. Arab nationalism, Turkish nationalism, and Kurdish nationalism everywhere create bloody borders and internal repression. And that's just for starters. Lebanese went at other Lebanese for fifteen long years. Sunni and Shia death squads mercilessly "cleansed" whole swaths of Iraq of the other. Syria's Alawite minority was using the state to violently suppress the Sunni majority.

Every Kurdish village I saw still standing in Eastern Turkey looked grim and forlorn compared with those I had seen in Iraq. The only places in Turkish Kurdistan that looked pleasant, from the main road at least, were those where no people lived, where the army hadn't dug in, where there was no visible poverty, where there were no blown up buildings, and where you did not look across minefields toward Syria.

Sean and I soon came upon the city of Cizre that straddled the Tigris River on its winding way to Iraq. I was glad we didn't spend the night there. It didn't look like a war zone, as parts of the countryside did, but it did look sketchy and miserable. Most businesses were shuttered behind filthy metal garage-style doors. Apartment buildings that looked like low-rise versions of communist public housing units in the former Soviet Union sulked behind crumbling walls. Utterly gone was the quasi-Victorian architecture of central Istanbul, the lovely classical Ottoman-era homes of the mountain interior, and the typically Mediterranean look and feel of the southern coast.

Sean documented the misery with his camera while I drove until I saw, just up ahead, a flatbed truck loaded with armed men who looked like guerrillas.

"Quick, put down the camera," I said. "Don't take a picture of *those* guys."

They wore keffiyehs on their heads. Only Arabs and Kurds wear keffiyehs. Turks never do, at least none that I've seen. These guys were heavily armed and sloppily dressed. They obviously were not Turkish military. They may have been PKK fighters or they may have been what the Kurds call *Jash*.

The Jash, or donkeys, are "very well paid Kurdish mercenaries that the Turkish government use against the PKK," said a man I know in Iraq's Kurdistan Regional Government. "Many Turkish soldiers aren't well trained (in most cases don't have the courage) to fight a guerrilla war in the uncontrollable Kurdish mountains. To save the lives of their soldiers, the Turks hired some local Kurds and paid them very well to fight the PKK on their behalf. During the 1980s Saddam's regime did the same. He hired locals, mostly escapees from military service, and gave them money and arms. But after the 1991 uprising all of the Iraqi Kurdish *Jash* failed Saddam and helped the [Kurdish fighters] as they liberated the Iraqi Kurdistan towns and cities one after one."

As I slowly drove onto a bridge over the Tigris, I noticed that every driver in oncoming traffic stared at us nervously. The vibe on the streets was palpably paranoid even from inside the car. It's so easy to misunderstand what's going on in a strange foreign land, especially when you don't walk around and talk to people, but it was clear that the situation in Cizre in early 2006 was not good.

N o one is allowed to drive a passenger car from Turkey into Iraq. Only trucks are allowed to cross over. And the truck inspection line stretched for miles.

So Sean and I left the rental car and our non-essential luggage in a gravel lot near the customs gate. We stuffed everything we needed— passports, cash, phone numbers, etc.—into our backpacks and started walking. I sure hoped my Kurdish fixer sent somebody to pick us up. We had long been out of email contact, however, and there was no way to know until we got to the other side.

As we approached the first building we were instantly mobbed by a crowd of gritty middle-aged men.

"Taxi."

"Taxi."

"You need a taxi."

"We're walking across," Sean said.

"You can't walk across," a man said. "Give me your passports." He stuck out his hand. "Come on, give me your passports."

"Who are you?" I said in my *don't-fuck-with-me* voice as I sized him up head to toe. He smelled distinctly like trouble.

"I'm a police officer," he said.

Liar, I thought. Did he think we were stupid? He wore shabby clothes, not an officer's uniform. And he had the obvious personality of a shake-down artist or braying carpet shop tout.

"Come with me," he said.

I trusted that he knew the border procedure, but I would not hand him my passport. He led Sean and me into a small room in a trailer where a real police officer sat behind a desk. The officer asked for our passports. We handed them over, he wrote down our names, then handed our passports back.

"Here," our 'guide' said. "Get in this taxi." He opened the back door of a yellow taxi.

"Why?" I said.

"Just get in," Sean said, annoyed with my resistant attitude. He got in the back. I climbed in after him. Two strangers, both of them men, hopped in with us. One had horrible pink scars all over his face and his hands.

"Why do we need a taxi?" I said. "I'd rather walk."

"No one can walk across this border, my friend," our fake policeman-driver-guide said. "It will cost fifty dollars."

"*Fifty dollars?*" I said. "For what? For a one-minute drive down the street? Come on."

Sean put his hand on my shoulder. He was feeling much more patient than I. I was sleep-deprived and cranky, and I had been shaken down in Egypt and Jordan recently and was in no mood for more.

"Did you notice what happened back there?" Sean said to me quietly. "We jumped to the front of the line and no one complained."

He was right. There *was* a huge line of people waiting for taxis. Mr. Fake Police Officer Man yanked us right to the front. I decided to cut him some slack. Yes, he was ripping us off. But he was also speeding things up.

We pulled up to the side of a building. The man with the horrible pink scars on his face got out.

"Follow that man," our driver said. "He knows what to do."

We followed him to a drive-thru type window and handed our passports to the border official. He stamped us out of the country and we were set.

"Do you know why that man's face looks like that?" Sean said on our way back to the taxi.

"No," I said. "Do you?"

"He's Iraqi," Sean said. "Those scars are burns from chemical weapons. I've seen photos online. I know that's what happened to him."

We drove through a wasteland of devastated buildings, piles of scrap metal and box cars, an unfinished international highway, and derelict drive-thru gates that presumably were closed after the deranged behavior of Saddam's regime required a shutdown of the Turkish side of the border. After a quick hop over a one-way bridge we were inside Iraq. The Iraqi side was cleaner, more orderly, more prosperous, and far softer on the eyes than the Turkish side. I swear it felt like the sun came out and the birds started chirping as we left Eastern Turkey behind.

An Iraqi Kurdish guard stood in front of the customs house wearing a crisp professional uniform.

"Choni!" I said. *Hello*, in Kurdish.

Everyone in the car flashed him our passports. He smiled and waved us past a sign that said "Welcome to Iraqi Kurdistan Region."

Inside the immigration office a bad Syrian soap opera played on TV. We were told to sit down in the waiting area after turning in our passports at the front desk. A young man brought us overflowing glasses of hot sticky brown tea on little plates with dainty spoons.

"Well," Sean said as he nervously flicked his eyes around the room. "We're here."

Indeed, we were. A portrait of keffiyeh-wrapped Kurdistan Regional Government President Massoud Barzani hung on the wall.

The customs boss came out from behind the desk and walked up to us.

"What do you guys do?" he said. "Are you NGOs?"

"You won't believe me when I tell you," I said.

He raised his eyebrows.

"We're tourists," I said.

He laughed. "Welcome to Kurdistan! How long do you want to stay?"

"We're just here for the day," Sean said.

He laughed again. "How long will you be here, really?" he said. "Two weeks? A month?" He spread out his hands.

"I swear to God," I said, "we are going back to Turkey today. I've been here before. Sean hasn't. We were just in the area and I want to show him Duhok."

He smirked at us, indicating he was willing to play along with what he thought was a ruse. "Welcome," he said. "Welcome."

"Sozpas," I said.

"Thank you," Sean said.

"You need to learn Kurdish," the man said to Sean. "Your friend will teach you Kurdish!"

"We're only going to be here for one day," I reminded him. He laughed and shook his head. "I only know a few words of Kurdish myself."

"What else can you say?" he said.

"Choni. Nosh," I said. *Hello* and *cheers*. "A few other things."

He grinned and patted both of us on the back. "Welcome, my American friends!" he said. "Have a wonderful time while you're here."

The whole thing was just weird. I don't quite know how to convey how surreal it is to leave a country that would like to join the European Union and enter a country that is a poster-child for war-torn catastrophe and have everything dramatically improve all at once. But that's how it goes these days when you cross from Turkey into Iraq. The ethnically Arab part of Iraq was at war with itself, with terrorists and insurgents, and with the United States, but the Kurdish region was pro-American, violence-free, and sedate. Even though Sean had never been there before, he, like me, breathed a sigh of relief at our arrival in a tranquil place at peace with itself.

No ride waited for us at the border. Our rental car was parked back in Turkey. I had no way of knowing whether my fixer had arranged for someone to meet us and drive us into town because I hadn't been able to get back on the Internet since I sent the request. If someone was waiting for us, how were we supposed to find him?

We walked into the nearby city of Zakho to see if we could find someone who seemed to be looking for us. Zakho is a small town, but it's huge if you're looking for a complete stranger who may or may not be looking for you.

And it's strange-looking. While Zakho looks reasonably clean and moderately prosperous, it doesn't look normal, not compared with Western cities, and not compared with Middle Eastern towns either. All the new buildings—and there are lots of them—are architectural oddballs. They have lots of glass, which made them look modern and fresh, but most of the details are jumbled together in an incomprehensible mishmash that their designers think looks good, but doesn't. And the materials are cheap. The glass is thin and the doors don't swing properly on their hinges. The materials found in the floors, walls, ceilings, roofs, and doors appear to be the cheapest on the market.

The construction companies that build these modern but weird rickety structures are Turkish. Sean and I later recognized the style instantly as similar units started appearing in the formerly communist world. Sean, as a student of architecture, found the style unappealing but fascinating and dubbed it "Turkitecture."

He and I walked around this "Turkitecture" town hoping to find someone who was looking for us to drive us into Duhok. The first time I arrived in Northern Iraq, at the airport in Erbil, I tried to blend in as much as possible. Iraq wasn't a place where I wanted to look like an obvious American, not even in Iraqi Kurdistan. This time, though, I tried to radiate as much American-ness as possible. *Hey! Look at us! We're Americans! Is anyone around here looking for two Americans who need a ride?*

More than a dozen men approached us.

"Taxi?"

"Taxi?"

"Duhok?"

"Someone is picking us up," Sean said, even though we didn't know if it really was true. It could have been true.

Not a single person spoke any English, but they seemed intrigued and excited when they found out we were Americans.

One man led us over to a soldier standing guard next to a gate.

"Hello?" the soldier said. "You speak English?"

"Yes," I said. "Hello."

"Where are you from?" he said a bit coldly. His uniform was clean, pressed, and professional.

"We're Americans," I said.

His eyes turned to saucers. "Americans? Welcome!" he said. "How can I help you?"

"I think someone is supposed to pick us up and take us into Duhok," Sean said. "But we don't know where to find him."

"Is there a place where people usually meet their rides on this side of the border?" I said.

"I don't know," the soldier said. "But the American military is here. Perhaps they can help you."

He led us through the gate and across a parking lot next to a restaurant. "Over there," he said and gestured around a corner. "Walk that way and you will find your fellow Americans."

Sean and I started walking.

"Huh," I said to Sean. "I didn't meet any American soldiers when I was in Kurdistan before. This should be interesting."

The reason I didn't meet or even see any American soldiers in the Kurdish region before is because there were only 200 of them. The war was long over in Kurdistan and Americans had little to do there. No insurgents lurked in the alleyways and shadows to kidnap us or blow anything up. On the contrary, the overwhelming majority of Iraqi Kurds wished Americans would build big permanent bases. The general attitude in this part of the country was radically at odds with the prevailing mood in Fallujah and Baghdad.

Sean and I walked past some parked civilian cars toward a compound of some sort. A pink-faced twenty-something who looked like a grown-up Iowa farm boy leaned over the engine of a truck under a propped-up hood with a wrench in his hand.

"Hey, man," Sean said.

"Ah, hey, guys," he said as though there was nothing remotely unusual about two unshaven Americans with backpacks ambling on over. "What's up?"

"We just got here from Turkey," I said. "Someone is supposed to pick us up, but we don't know where to find him. Is there Internet access anywhere around here? If I can check my email there might be more detailed instructions waiting for us."

"Hmm," he said. "There used to be a wireless Internet café around here, but they closed it down a couple of days ago." Who *they* were wasn't clear.

"I'm Michael, by the way," I said.

"And I'm Sean," Sean said.

"Tony," he said and shook my hand like he wanted to break it. "Good to meet you guys."

Sean shook his hand.

"There's a restaurant right over there," Tony said and pointed. "Lots of people meet up there when they come over the border."

"Perfect," I said. "We'll check it out. Thanks!"

Sean and I walked to the restaurant and looked around for anyone who looked like they might be looking for somebody else. A waiter brought us some tea. We tried to look as obvious as possible and made eye contact with everyone there. After twenty minutes or so we decided it would be best to find a taxi. No one seemed to be looking for us. In just a few hours we would have to go back to Turkey. We didn't have all day to wait around for someone who might not even show up.

I tried to pay the waiter who brought us our tea, but he flatly refused to take any money.

"Sozpas," I said and put my hand over my heart.

Sean and I walked up to the taxi stand outside.

"Choni," I said as we approached a group of men standing around. "Does anyone here speak English?"

"I speak English," a man said. "Do you need a taxi?"

"Please," Sean said. "We want to go to Duhok."

"Any of these men can take you," the man said. Twelve or so guys looked at us with hope.

"Do any of them speak English?" I said. "We would like to hire a driver all day who can also act as a guide."

"I don't think so," the man said. "They only speak Kurdish and Arabic." He addressed all the drivers in Kurdish. Presumably he asked if any spoke English. None apparently did.

The boldest of the drivers stepped forward. He appeared to be around sixty years old and wore a black and white keffiyeh on his head.

"Let's just go with him," Sean said.

"Where do you want to go?" the English-speaking stranger said.

"Duhok," Sean said.

"Where in Duhok?"

I had an idea.

"Let's go to the University of Duhok," I said. "We should be able to find somebody there who speaks English who we can hire as a translator and guide for the day."

"Okay," Sean said.

"Thank you so much," I said to the man who helped us out.

"Welcome to Kurdistan," he said as he waved goodbye.

We hopped in the back of the taxi. The driver spoke to us in Kurdish. We tried talking to him in English. It didn't work out.

"La etkellem Kurdi katir," I said. *I don't speak much Kurdish.* I said it in Arabic. Our driver smiled and shrugged.

He drove us for five minutes on the four-lane highway toward Duhok and Mosul. Then he abruptly turned off onto a minor road into a wilderness of bare mountains and scrubland.

Sean elbowed me. "Is this the right way?" he said under his breath. "This doesn't look good."

"I don't know," I said. "I've never driven from Zakho to Duhok."

I hated to agree with Sean about this, but I did. It didn't look good. Where the hell was he taking us?

"Don't we want the main road?" Sean said to the driver, though of course it was useless. We had no language in common. At least that freed us to talk about him amongst ourselves.

"How much should we trust him?" Sean said. "You told me we can be kidnapped in this country for only a thousand dollars."

I had, indeed, told him that in the past. But that was a problem in Baghdad, not in or around Duhok.

"That only happens down in the red zone," I said. "No one ever gets kidnapped in Kurdistan."

I knew it was true, but I was not happy to be having that conversation. I trust the Kurds. But showing up in even the safest part of Iraq is enough to get my survival instinct dialed up to eleven. At least I had been there before. It must have been much worse for Sean who had not yet been inside Iraq for an hour.

"What do we do if he takes us to a bad place?" Sean said.

Fight him, I guess. It would be too late, though, once we figured out he had taken us to a bad place.

"Just make sure he sticks to the mountains," I said. "Mosul is down in the plains. As long as this road hugs the mountains, we're still on the way to Duhok."

I was annoyed at myself for feeling paranoid. I was the one who had earlier said we could hitchhike in Northern Iraq.

A half-hour later our driver took us back on the main road to a Kurdish army checkpoint. He turned the car toward the mountains and Duhok, not toward the plains and the terrifyingly blood-soaked city of Mosul.

"I guess that was a shortcut," Sean said.

"I guess so," I said. "He's fine. We're fine."

As we pulled up to the checkpoint our driver said something in Kurdish to the soldiers. I heard the word "Americhi." *American.* The soldier waved us through.

Two minutes later we arrived at the gate to the University of Duhok on the outskirts of the city where, hopefully, we could meet some new friends. We needed a guide. I spent all of four hours in Duhok the first time I went to Iraqi Kurdistan so I could not be our guide for the day. I didn't know my way around the city at all.

This was the Middle East where hospitality is so legendary it has become a guidebook cliché. And we were in the land of the Kurds, who, unlike most Arabs, had genuinely warm feelings for Americans. Someone would help us. All we had to do was show up.

Sean and I stepped out of the car, paid our man twenty dollars, and walked toward the front door of the main building where snazzily dressed young men and women gathered around. What better place to find a little friendly assistance than where the young and educated gather to study and hang out?

Thirty or forty students loitered with backpacks slung over their shoulders and books tucked under their arms. I figured we could just stand there for a minute or two and see if anyone felt like approaching us, but no one did.

"Let's go talk to that guy," I said to Sean and gestured toward a garrulous-looking barrel-chested young Kurd wearing glasses and a tie and joking with friends. "He looks friendly enough."

"Hello!" I said to the young man who would, in fact, be our guide later that day. "Do you speak English?"

He looked startled.

"Yes?" he said. "Can I help you?"

Heads turned all around at the sound of spoken English.

"Yes, hi," I said and shook his hand. "We're Americans here for the day. We just came over from Turkey. Someone was supposed to meet us at the border and pick us up, but we couldn't find him. We're hoping somebody here can tell us where we can go to hire a driver and translator."

"Of course, come with me," he said and led Sean and me through the front door. "A translator works on staff in this building."

"Excellent," Sean said.

"I'm Michael, by the way," I said.

"And I'm Sean," Sean said.

"Kiman," he said and shook our hands again. "Welcome to

Kurdistan."

Kiman spoke to the receptionist. As it turned out, she said, the department's translator had the day off.

"Do you know where else we can find one?" I said to Kiman. Just then I noticed that a rather large crowd of students had gathered around. Sean and I were now the center of attention.

"I'm sorry," Kiman said. "I don't know."

"How about the press relations office of the KDP?" Duhok is a stronghold for Massoud Barzani's Kurdistan Democratic Party.

"I don't know that either," Kiman said. "I'll tell you what. I have class in an hour. I'll be free at two o'clock. I can show you around myself after that if you like."

That would mean Sean and I would have two hours without a guide. I looked at Sean.

"What do you think?" I said.

"I don't know," Sean said. "What do we do for two hours?"

"We could take a taxi downtown and go to the souk," I said. "Then we can come back here and meet him."

"Okay," Sean said.

"Great," I said to Kiman. "We'll pay you the money we were going to pay the guy who was supposed to pick us up this morning."

"No, no, no," Kiman said. "You cannot give me money."

"We were prepared to pay money anyway," I said.

"You are my guests," Kiman said. "I will be happy to show you around. What do you want to see?"

"Just the city," Sean said. "We don't know where we're going and we don't know what we're looking at. I'm studying architecture and would love to see some new construction."

Kiman, kind soul that he is, wouldn't let us take a taxi downtown. He drove us himself in his brand-new SUV.

I leaned out the window and snapped a photo of an enormous Kurdish flag painted on the side of a mountain. Unlike the flag of many Islamic peoples, the Muslim crescent was eschewed for a blazing yellow sun, the symbol of the Kurds' pre-Islamic pagan Yezidi religion.

"I have to ask," Sean said. "I know what Mike says, but…are we safe here?"

"Um," Kiman said. "Not really, no. You have to be very careful."

What the hell? We weren't safe in Duhok? Since when? The car was momentarily silent. I tried to figure out what to say to convince Sean that we were fine without acting like I knew Duhok better than someone who lived there.

"Here, you are safe," Kiman said, as though he realized what he just said could be misunderstood. "Duhok is safe. Kurdistan is safe. Just don't go south."

He dropped us off near the souk in front of an Internet café.

"I'll meet you back here in two hours," he said.

Sean and I said our thanks and goodbyes and wandered around downtown Duhok.

Although the aesthetic is different, the freshly constructed outskirts of Duhok are as modern as suburban Columbus, Ohio. Many of the buildings are made in the cheap "Turkitecture" style so prominent in Zakho, but they're modern. Downtown is more interesting. It's older. It feels more authentically Middle Eastern and is a place where the old and the new co-exist. Elderly people wear traditional clothing, including head wraps, while the young dress more or less like Westerners. Brand-new cars share traffic with hand-pulled and donkey-towed carts.

I knew I would once again write about Iraqi Kurdistan, at least for my blog if not for a magazine or a book. Sean planned to give a presentation at school about Iraqi Kurdistan's architecture and reconstruction. But the truth is we went there mostly as tourists. So we did what tourists do. We took pictures of each other in our far-flung location and decided we should buy souvenirs for our friends and families.

The souk had none of the usual tourist gimcrack for sale like so many other traditional eastern markets because hardly any tourists ever set foot in even the safest parts of Iraq. This was a place designed by locals, for locals. It was basically a rickety outdoor mall made of tiny stalls with a tin roof over everything to help keep some of the warmth in during the winter and the blazing sunshine out during the summer.

Spice vendors sold intoxicatingly fragrant coriander, cumin, nutmeg, and cardamom. Others sold bright bolts of cloth for making clothing, pillowcases, or sheets. Hand-crafted perfume and massage oil were available in unlabeled bottles. Fresh fruit was piled up in the farmer's market even though spring hadn't technically arrived yet. Asian carpets were not hard to find, but they tended to be of the cheaper machine-made variety since Iraqis, even in Kurdistan, tended to have less money on hand than those who lived in more stable parts of the region.

If we were going to shop and buy anything, though, we'd need Iraqi money. So we walked up the front stairs of a hotel and asked the man behind the counter if we could buy some dinars from him. The hotel was a boutique one. Most of the hotels in Iraq are boutique in the sense that they're run by individual families rather than large corporations. No international chain hotels operated anywhere in the country, and the smaller "boutique" hotels were hardly a step above hostels. This place was nowhere near as nice as the fake knockoff "Sheraton" in Erbil, but it still beat the dump of a place run by the local government in the city Sulaymaniyah, the inappropriately named Suli Palace.

The power went out in the middle of the hotel owner's sentence, but he neither paused nor flinched. It happened several times every day all over Iraq. The country's electrical grid was a decaying Third World catastrophe and under attack from insurgents. Residents lived in the dark more often than not. Hotels had their own generators, but the cheaper hotels used the municipal grid as often as possible, so the power went out momentarily at the beginning of each blackout. This sort of thing was a major drag in Kurdistan, but it was the least of Iraq's problems in other parts of the country where kidnappings and car bombings were rampant.

Now that Sean and I weren't on the road, we could sit down in a restaurant and eat a proper meal. We found (what else?) a kebab place.

"Welcome my cousins!" the host said as we walked in the door. He shook our hands and slapped us on the back. The restaurant was full. There was nowhere for us to sit. Whether we liked it or not, though, we were Americans and we received special treatment.

The host walked over to a table where two young men sat and kicked them out to make room.

"No!" Sean said.

"That isn't necessary," I said.

"Please, please, sit down," the host said.

"Do you want to join us?" Sean said to the guys who were given the boot.

"Please," I said and gestured for them to sit. There was room enough for four at the table, but they wouldn't have any of it, not because they didn't want to sit with other people, but because they wanted to make sure foreign guests were comfortable. That actually made us uncomfortable, but that's how it goes in Iraqi Kurdistan.

We ordered two kebabs. The waiter brought *eight*, along with enough vegetables and hummus to feed half of Duhok. He only charged us for two. We could only eat three.

A large table cleared out and in came a gaggle of Kurdish soldiers. They belonged to the Peshmerga, which means *those who face death* in Kurdish. Half the men in the restaurant stood up as the soldiers piled their weapons on the table. Everyone greeted them warmly. If any place in the world has a genuine people's army, this is it. I've never seen such heartfelt love for soldiers as I've seen in Northern Iraq, not only because they provide general security by walling off the violent parts of the country, but also because they waged a successful guerrilla, but not terrorist, war against the army of Saddam Hussein.

Sean and I still had another hour before it was time to meet Kiman so we went to the Mazi Mart grocery store. That's what people do for entertainment in Kurdistan; they go to the grocery store. At least in 2006, the Kurds had none of the usual sorts of diversions like movie theaters. They had the grocery store, though things other than food were also sold there: TV sets, washing machines, clothing, and sundry other items. The grocery store was like a miniature mall. You could see young people wandering around there on dates.

Sean and I both photographed milk cartons, sticks of butter, boxes of Froot Loops, and cans of 7-UP. Everyone stared. *What's so interesting about the grocery store that they're taking pictures?*

We took pictures because Americans in general, and not just the two of us, were happy to see that the Kurdish region of Iraq was in some ways a normal place. Sean even took pictures of the laser scanner in the checkout line. Hardly anything in Duhok looked like home—not the traditional architecture, not the cheap and unusual "Turkitecture," not the traditional clothing, nothing—but that laser scanner in the checkout line took both of us back to Whole Foods and Safeway. It was one of the only things in the entire country that reminded us of home.

Kurdistan is emphatically not European or Western. Yet part of Kurdistan is in Turkey and part of Turkey is in Europe. And the Kurds, for the most part, are not only more politically pro-Western than Arabs, they're more politically pro-Western than the Turks who belong to NATO.

We met two American soldiers in front of the store. They sat on a park bench outside. Iraqi Kurdistan is perfectly safe, so they did not carry guns. They did not wear body armor or helmets. I did not catch their names, but I was being more of a tourist than a journalist and I didn't want to weird them out by writing their names down. One wore a moustache. I'll call him Mark. The other was blonde. I'll call him Jake.

"Hey guys," Sean said.

"Ah, hey, what's up?" they said and stood up to shake our hands. "What are you guys doing here?"

"We're tourists," I said.

"No way," said Jake.

"Yep," Sean said. "We drove here for the day from Istanbul."

"I've been here before," I said, "as a journalist. I wanted to come back and Sean wanted to check it out. We had a few days, so what the hell."

"Where are you guys from?" Mark said.

"We're from Portland," Sean said. "Although Mike has been living in Beirut and I'm living and studying in Denmark."

"We're from Seattle," Jake said.

"My wife says Portland is having some pretty rough weather right now," Mark said. How odd to hear a weather report about what's going on at my house from a guy in Northern Iraq.

"Are you here on R and R?" I said.

"Yeah," Jake said. "It's a bit embarrassing right now because of what happened recently."

"Why, what happened?" Sean said.

"Well, you know," Jake said. "Lots of us come up here to take a break. A few guys don't deal with decompression after combat quite as well as they should."

"Can you tell us what happened?" I said.

Mark and Jake looked at each other.

"I'd rather not," Mark said. "Just understand that only a small minority don't know how to behave."

Sean and I later decided we wished we had witnessed whatever bad behavior these guys were talking about. We might have been able to put a stop to it if we said, "Hey, knock that shit off," at them in American English, especially if I said I'm a journalist. Then again, maybe not. I've been in war zones, but I have no idea what it's like to lose it while decompressing from combat. Perhaps it's a good thing we missed it.

"How's it going down there, anyway?" Sean said.

"Are you optimistic, pessimistic, or somewhere in between?" I said.

"I'm pretty impressed with the Iraqi army right now," Mark said. "They're coming along much better than we expected. They're great. The police are another story, though."

"They're tribal and corrupt," Jake said. "It's awful. There isn't much anyone has been able to do about it yet."

"The Kurds seem to like us," Sean said. "What do the Arabs think?"

"It depends," Mark said. "Some of them like us, some of them don't. A lot of them are conflicted."

"I understand where they're coming from," Jake said. "They've had enough of the occupation, but they're afraid. I don't blame them for being tired of us. When we drive our military convoys down a two-lane street we take up the whole road and force all the other cars to get out of our way. We do it because we have to, for our protection, but I hate having to do it. I don't want to force people out of our way, and no one likes being forced out of our way."

"The Kurds are further along right now," Mark said. "Some of the Arabs still don't get the freedom and democracy thing like the Kurds do. I just want to say to them: *Haven't you seen what it's like in the north? What, exactly, is it that you're not understanding?*"

Some Arabs knew what it was like in the north. Huge numbers of laborers were heading up there where they could earn better wages and live in a more secure environment. They're taking low-end jobs that the Kurds of Iraq no longer want. Arab Iraq was becoming to Kurdish Iraq what Mexico is to the United States.

"You guys have one hell of a job," I said.

"I just want to say thanks for what you're doing here," Sean said and shook both of their hands.

"Thanks, man," Mark said. "I really appreciate your saying that."

"We better go," I said. "It's time to meet Kiman downtown. A pleasure meeting you two," I said to Mark and Jake. "You guys be safe down there."

Sean and I hailed a taxi and went back to the Internet café near the souk. Kiman pulled up in his SUV at the exact moment we arrived.

"Hello my friends!" he said as he rolled down the passenger side window.

It's hard to convey what it's actually like meeting Iraqi Kurds. Fleshing out the dialogue doesn't capture the feel of it. Americans and Kurds don't just get along because we're temporary allies of convenience in the Middle East. The connection is deeper, personal. Kurdish culture and American culture might as well be from different planets, yet somehow, oddly enough, Kurds think much like Americans do. They think in straight lines, not circles. They rely on logic and reason more than emotion. More than anything else, they yearn for freedom and the right to be masters of their own destiny. We have similar values despite our extraordinarily different cultural backgrounds. I find it easier to develop a rapport with Iraqi Kurds than with people from any other country I have ever been to. It's instant, powerful, and totally unexpected.

Independent war correspondent Michael Yon noticed it, too. "Meetings with Iraqi Arabs sometimes seem more like talking with the French," he wrote. "We are not enemies. But, generally speaking, there is no real personal connection. At best, our collective personalities just don't seem to 'click.' Yet by recognizing the sovereignty and inevitability of each other, we manage to cooperate toward our common interests, while not going to war when we disagree. But with the Kurds, like the Poles or the Brits, there is an easy and audible click. We have mutual goals, mutual enemies, and, also importantly, we actually like each other."

I hopped in the back of Kiman's SUV and let Sean take the front since I had seen more of the city than he had.

"Where do you want to go?" Kiman said.

"Well," I said. "We've already seen downtown. How about some of the new neighborhoods on the outskirts?"

"I'm working on an Islamic architecture project at the university," Sean said. "I realize the new construction around here isn't necessarily Islamic, but it's in an Islamic country and I should see it."

"As you like," Kiman said as we pulled away from the curb.

"Thanks so much again," I said, feeling a bit awkward that I was going to pay someone for this service but now had it for free.

Duhok is not a large city. Perhaps 750,000 people live there. Somehow it feels even smaller. I wouldn't say it's a backwater, but it's not a cosmopolitan capital either. There's something strangely Utah-like about Iraqi Kurdistan, not only because it's situated in a desert among mountains—unlike the greener, flatter, and occasionally palm-treed parts of Iraq where the Arabs live—but because of its conservative, though not fundamentalist, down-home common sense attitude.

"What do you think of George W. Bush?" Sean said to Kiman.

"He's controversial," Kiman said. "A lot of people don't like him. But I don't care about that. American presidents are all the same from our point of view. We love Bush for freeing us from Saddam, but we would love any American president."

"How many hours of electricity do you get here in Duhok?" I said. The grid seemed a little more solid than what I was used to in Northern Iraq.

"We get about twelve hours a day," Kiman said.

"Twelve hours!" I said. "That's pretty good. In Erbil they only get two."

"We buy it from Turkey," Kiman said. "We're supposed to get twenty-four hours, but we don't."

The new construction in Duhok is amazing. Aside from a few standard apartment buildings, almost all the new homes are, at least on the surface, comparable to middle class, upper-middle class, and even elite houses in the United States. The materials tend to be cheaper, making the homes a bit lower in quality, but they're huge, and, while a bit gaudy, are at least not depressingly plain. They're also extremely colorful. Duhok is unlike even the other Kurdish cities in Iraq, not to mention the Arab cities, in that it's colorful. Even from a distance the city has a pleasing aesthetic character thanks to the reds, blues, greens, yellows, and oranges of the buildings and houses. Every other city I've seen in the country is uniformly the color of sand. Despite Duhok's semi-ramshackleness in the old city center, the colors, all the shiny new glass, and the craggy mountains surrounding it in every direction make it aesthetically delightful in ways no other city anywhere in the country can even come close to. If you squint hard enough at it from a hilltop, it looks a little like Italy.

The first time I visited the city on a day trip from Kurdistan's capital Erbil it seemed like such an innocent place. After seeing the rough hell of Turkish Kurdistan, though, and realizing that the Kurds in Iraq had it even worse under Saddam, it did not seem so innocent anymore. Iraqi Kurds struck me as deeply, profoundly, mature. It took so much work, blood, and sacrifice to build what they have. And they built it from nothing on the ashes of genocide barely a decade after the Saddam regime massacred hundreds of thousands.

Iraq is the only country in the world where Kurds wield any power. Their autonomous region is sovereign in all but name. They're ground down under the majoritarian boot everywhere else. For the most part they wield their power responsibly, though government corruption is still just atrocious and they haven't yet fully emerged from a traditional society into a completely liberal and modern one. A Kurdish journalist was recently thrown in prison after a fifteen minute show trial for blasting the Kurdistan Democratic Party in a newspaper column. He was later released, but he's not out of trouble yet. The Kurdish quasi-state wants to be liberal, but still doesn't quite understand how or what that means.

Even so, they've made more progress in the region than almost anyone else. And they did it in a mere fifteen years. From the Mouth of Hell to…the Utah of the Middle East. By force of sheer will against extraordinarily long odds.

Sean and I wanted to stay, but we couldn't. He and I already had to patch scratchy phone calls to the Turkish Airlines office and change our flight dates out of the country, and if we didn't get back to Istanbul—and fast—he'd miss his exams in Copenhagen. So we said our thanks and goodbyes to Kiman and headed back to the border crossing at Zakho.

We thought our adventure was over, that all we had left was a drive on the autobahn back to Istanbul. We should have known, though, that getting out of Iraq and back into Turkey would not be so easy. Even if we knew what a horrendous pain that process normally was, there was no way to predict what lay ahead.

G etting into Iraq was easy. Getting out of Iraq and back into Turkey was not.

Sean and I went back to the crossing gate an hour or so before night fell. We hoped to get back to our car and make a little progress toward Istanbul before the light in the sky completely went out.

"Hello again!" I said to the customs official who, earlier that morning, thought we were lying when we said we would return to Turkey the very same day. "Told ya we wouldn't stay long."

"Hello my friends!" he said and laughed. "Good to see you."

He asked us to sit in the waiting area. Once again, a young man brought us sticky brown tea in clear glasses on little plates with dainty spoons. Another bad Syrian drama played on the TV set in the corner.

"I suppose you need our passports," Sean said while stirring his tea.

"Why?" the official said.

"Don't we need exit stamps?" I said.

"You can't go back," he said.

"What?" Sean said.

"What do you mean we can't go back?" I said.

My face flushed and my heart leapt into my throat. Sean damn near panicked. Was this guy joking? It would be a first order disaster if we couldn't get back into Turkey. Our rental car was parked just on the other side of the border. Most of our luggage was inside. We both had planes to catch the next day.

Would we have to fly out from Erbil? There is only one commercial flight a week from Erbil to Istanbul. We would have to wait in Iraq for a week—a whole week—without any cash in a country that has no international banks or ATMs and accepts no credit cards. We would have to figure out some way to get ourselves onto that plane without any money. Then, after we got back to Istanbul, we would have to rent yet another car and drive all the way back to the Iraqi border again to pick up the first car and the luggage. I felt like I was going to be sick.

"We need to get out of here!" I said and tried to explain what *you can't go back* meant to us.

"Just go down the street," he said. "It's only fifty meters or so. You enter Kurdistan here and go back to Turkey over there."

I felt like the perfect idiot. Iraqi Kurdistan may be safe—especially compared with Baghdad—but the place isn't yet normal and it makes me twitchy. Sean loudly exhaled and put his hand over his heart. I instantly felt fifty pounds lighter.

We walked to the exit gate, still rattled by our ten seconds of misunderstanding. Now that we had our little false alarm scare, I desperately wanted out as quickly as possible. I wouldn't be able to relax until we were back in Turkey with our car and could control what happened next.

It was time to flag down a taxi. I assume the reason no one is allowed to walk across in either direction is that it makes cross-border traffic easier for both sides to keep track of. Anyone seen walking is obviously sneaking.

Our driver Himdad drove us past a long line of cars with passengers waiting to get their exit stamps from Kurdish security officials.

"Did you see what just happened?" Sean said.

"Yep," I said. "We went right to the front of the line again." Getting special treatment because I'm an American makes me uncomfortable. I don't really want it and I certainly don't expect it, but this time I was glad. We barely had enough time to drive back and needed to get out of there.

A Kurdish Iraqi border official stopped us and asked for photocopies of our passports. We didn't have any photocopies. He demanded photocopies anyway and refused to budge.

Himdad knew what to do. He took our passports and walked off somewhere to make copies. He came back. The border official kept us waiting for what seemed like forever.

"How long will it take to cross the border?" I asked Himdad. He understood almost no English at all. I had to point to my watch and pantomime the rest of it.

"Three," he said and made a circular motion with his finger.

"*Three hours?*" Sean said.

He must have meant three minutes. It was only a one-mile crossing.

I pointed at my watch. It read six o'clock. Himdad pointed at nine o'clock.

"Shit!" I said. "We don't have three hours." We really didn't.

"We're screwed," Sean said. "We'll never make it back to Istanbul in time."

"I guess we just won't get a hotel tonight," I said and sighed. "We'll have to drive all frigging night again. It will suck, but we'll make it. We have to."

Once the border official—finally!—let us go, Himdad drove onto the bridge over the reedy Tigris River that marked the border between the two countries. A long line of cars was ahead of us. We sat still on that bridge for what seemed like forty-five minutes without moving an inch.

"Crap!" I said. "This is really taking forever. I'm going to try to sleep now so I can drive when we finally get out of here."

Himdad could tell we were stressed. He pointed at the line of cars in front of us. "Problem," he said.

"Yes, problem," I said.

"One hundred dollars," he said, "no problem."

Sean and I looked at each other. We could bribe our way across for one hundred dollars? Without waiting in this godawful line?

"Should we do it?" I said.

"Do we have a hundred dollars?" Sean said.

"I do," I said. "I have a wad of fifties in my pocket."

Himdad and I got out of the car and walked to the front of the line. Most drivers had turned off their engines. Many people were sleeping. Everyone knew we would be there for a very long time, time Sean and I just didn't have. It looked like we would spend more time sitting in line on the bridge than we spent in Iraq.

A young Turkish soldier saw us approaching. He pointed his rifle at us and screamed something in Turkish.

Then he lowered his rifle and laughed.

I nervously laughed right back at him.

He and Himdad had a conversation in Turkish.

"You are American?" the young soldier said.

"Yes," I said and shook his hand. "Nice to meet you."

"One moment," he said and walked toward a compound of some sort. He returned with a much older officer who looked like a colonel.

"You are American?" the colonel said.

"Yes," I said. "Hello."

He stared at me in shock and with disgust, abruptly turned around, and stormed back to the compound.

"Problem," Himdad said.

We walked back to the car. The colonel wasn't interested in any bribes. Himdad and I had clearly offended his professionalism. It wasn't my idea, I wished I could tell him. *I don't know how this works. Sorry! This creep seemed to suggest it was normal.*

"Problem," Himdad said to Sean when we got back to the car.

"An officer there wasn't having any of it," I added.

"Other problem," Himdad said.

What now?

He pointed at himself and said, "Peshmerga, no problem," referring to the Iraqi Kurdish authorities. Then he pointed at himself again and said "Turkey, problem."

What the hell? The Turks have a problem with him? Why didn't he say so when we first got in the car?

"What's the problem?" Sean said.

"Cigarette," Himdad said and pointed at himself. "Many cigarette. Turkish. Problem."

I had no idea what he was talking about.

He peeled back the lining on the passenger side door of his car, pointed inside, said "many cigarette" again, then "Turkish" and "problem."

"He got busted smuggling cigarettes," I said. "Now the Turks won't let him in."

"Yes," Himdad said and nodded.

"Great," Sean said. "Why does he have this job?"

Himdad got out of the car, popped the trunk, and pulled out fifteen cartons of cigarettes. Lovely! He was smuggling again with us in the car.

"Take cigarette," he said.

"What?" I said, even though I knew exactly what he wanted.

He held up five fingers on this hand and said, "No problem." Then he held up six fingers and said "Problem."

He pointed at himself and held up five fingers. Then he pointed at Sean and held up five fingers. Then he pointed at me and held up five fingers and said "No problem." Then he pointed at himself, held up six fingers, and said "Problem."

I knew what he meant. Each person was allowed to carry five cartons of cigarettes across the border, but no one was allowed to carry six. He wanted me to carry five cartons and he wanted Sean to carry five cartons.

"No problem," he said again.

But it was a problem.

"Problem!" I said.

"Yes, problem," Sean said.

"No problem," Himdad said.

No one has given me more trouble in the Middle East than people who drive for a living. No matter which country they're in, they are the most obnoxious and least principled people a typical person will have to deal with on a regular basis.

Himdad already said the Turks have a problem with him because he's a known smuggler. For all I knew his face was on a poster in an office on the other side. That's more or less what he seemed to be telling us.

Sean and I had entrance stamps and exit stamps in our passports only six hours apart. That looks suspicious all by itself. Ten minutes ago I infuriated the colonel by trying to bribe my way across for a hundred dollars, making us look even more suspicious. We didn't look anything like model American citizens. The last thing we needed was to add smuggling to our list of demerits.

What were we supposed to do now? Sit on the bridge for hours and wait to be interrogated all night?

I thought of that stupid 1970s movie *Airplane* where the captain kept harassing a ten-year old kid.

Hey, Joey. Do you like movies about gladiators?

Hey, Joey. Have you ever seen a grown man naked?

Hey, Joey. Have you ever seen the inside of a Turkish prison?

I did not want to see the inside of a Turkish prison.

Himdad handed Sean five cartons of cigarettes and pointed at his backpack. Sean looked at me without a word.

"I don't know," I said. "What do we do?"

If we didn't carry five cartons apiece Himdad would be busted for smuggling again before we even got back into Turkey. Then what? He was our ride. Would we get in trouble, as well? Aside from stupid tourists like us, who on earth goes into Iraq for six hours? Who tries to bribe their way across the border? People who are up to no good, that's who.

Presumably Himdad knew what was legal and what wasn't since this was his "job." So perhaps we would be wise to just do what he said and hope for the best. If we were interrogated on the other side we could explain to the authorities that we were smuggling under duress. Himdad didn't tell us what he was up to until we were exactly, precisely, in the middle of the no-man's land between Turkey and Iraq, after the Kurdish Iraqi authorities had already stamped us out of the country, when it was too late to turn around and hire a different driver. The man was a championship asshole for roping us into his scheme.

Sean wearily stuffed five cartons of cigarettes into his backpack. I stuffed five cartons into mine. It felt like surrender.

We sat in the back of the taxi, pissed off and worried about what would happen next. The line of cars still wasn't moving. It could be ten hours before we got to the other side. Then Lord only knows what would follow.

The good news was that Himdad barely understood English. We

could plot our own moves right in front of him.

"We should take these cigarettes and throw them into the river," Sean said.

"Are you serious?" I said.

"Yes. Throw them into the river. He can't stop us. Then it will be done."

"Hmm," I said. "But then we have to sit in this car with him for several more hours. We have no idea how he'll react."

I didn't like Sean's proposed solution, but I did like the fact that he was trying to come up with one. It got me thinking. I had felt checkmated by Himdad. Sean's idea, extreme as it was, proved that Himdad hadn't won yet. We could turn right around and check-mate him ourselves.

"Here," I said and clandestinely handed Sean a fifty dollar bill. "Take that to the front of the line. Wave it in somebody's face and ask if we can hitch a ride across the border. I don't want to do it myself because the colonel might see me. He won't recognize you."

Sean took the money, got out, stretched, and slowly started walking to the front of the line as though he had nothing better to do.

Himdad offered me a cigarette. "No, thanks," I said. He lit his own cigarette and puffed away contentedly, having no idea that Sean and I were plotting to ditch him on the bridge, leaving him to smuggle his contraband alone.

A few short minutes later I saw Sean walking back to the car with a spring in his step. He looked happy, like he was trying to conceal hidden glee.

"Quick," he said as he got back in the car. "I got us a ride all the way at the very front of the line."

"Excellent!" I said. "Now we just need to get these cigarettes out of our backpacks without him seeing."

I slowly and quietly started to unzip my backpack. Himdad turned around and offered Sean a cigarette. He saw what I was doing. This wasn't going to work.

"Take his cigarette," I said to Sean, "and see if you can get him to walk somewhere with you. I'll unload all this stuff while you keep him distracted."

Sean got out. "Want to take a walk?" he said to Himdad and gestured for him to get out of the car. Himdad happily got out. Sean slowly walked Himdad away from the car. I saw him squint and point at something off the side of the bridge in the darkness. Himdad also squinted and looked. Perfect.

I pulled all ten cartons of cigarettes out of our luggage. It took longer than I expected. Sean had so many zippered compartments in his backpack where various cartons were hidden and buried.

Sean and Himdad returned just as I set our backpacks in the street next to the car. There was no turning back now. It was done.

Himdad saw our stuff outside the car. He looked at me with a startled expression.

I pointed at my watch. "Problem," I said.

Then I handed him the fifty dollars we "owed" him, pointed toward the front of the line and said "taxi." Presumably he would understand that Sean had just found us another taxi. Then I showed him the ten cartons of cigarettes in the back seat of his taxi so he would know we weren't ripping him off.

"My friend," he said and grabbed my arm.

"Problem," I said and tapped my watch again. "Problem. I'm sorry." I put my hand on his shoulder so he would think there were no hard feelings.

He wasn't happy. Now he had fifteen cartons of illegal cigarettes. He couldn't cross with them all without getting arrested. He would have to throw them into the river himself. But that was his problem and his fault. I couldn't let myself feel too bad about it, especially since he tried to trap us in his criminal enterprise.

Sean and I started walking. Himdad yelled something at us. Sean and I ignored him and kept walking.

"Our passports!" Sean suddenly said.

Oh, that's right. Our passports were on the dashboard of Himdad's car. We would have to go back.

I turned around and braced myself. Himdad was running after us with our passports in his hand. Thank God he was a good sport about all of this. He could really have screwed us over.

"Thank you," I said as Sean took the passports from Himdad. "Thank you."

He smiled at us now as though he understood and was over it.

Sean and I hopped in our new taxi at the very front of the line.

"Hello!" I said to the driver and shook his hand. "You aren't smuggling anything, are you?"

"Eh?" he said as he shook his head in incomprehension. He didn't speak any English. It didn't matter. He knew what it meant when a fifty was waved in his face, and that's what counted.

Two minutes later it was our turn to pull up to the customs house. That may have been the best fifty dollars I ever spent in my life.

A soldier gestured for Sean and me to get out. Another came over and spoke to us in perfect American English.

"Can I see what's in your backpacks?" he said.

"Of course," I said, elated that the contraband was no longer in there.

"You speak excellent English," Sean said.

"Well, I should," the soldier said. "I'm from Long Island."

"You're from *Long Island*?" I said.

"Long Island, *New York*?" Sean said.

"Born and raised," he said.

"What on earth are you doing here?" I said.

"I'm Turkish," he said. "My parents are from here. I'm just doing my military service for my country."

The soldier from Long Island led Sean and me into the interrogation room. Every person who crosses that border is required to spend some quality time there with the army.

A second soldier in that room also spoke perfect English, this time with an Australian accent.

"Where are *you* from?" I said, already gobsmacked that the first Turkish soldier was from New York.

"Melbourne, Australia," he said.

These two were not at all who Sean and I expected to meet in that room. I was worried about the colonel who understandably suspected that I was up to no good. Instead we were "interrogated" by two dudes from the West who looked like they would rather be shooting pool and drinking some beers.

Turkish Kurdistan is a disaster. It's in far worse shape than Iraq. The thought of Turkey joining the European Union seemed ludicrous to me now. Yet here were two born and raised Westerners guarding the frontier. The only possible way I'd meet anyone from the United States or Australia guarding the Iraqi side of that border is if the American or Australian armies took over the job.

"What's it like down there in Iraq?" said the young man from Long Island. "Is it scary?"

"Well," Sean said. "It's actually kind of nice in the Kurdistan region."

"It's a lot nicer than most people expect," I said. Neither Sean nor I wanted to say the Iraqi side is *superior*. Better, I thought, to give them the truth subtly so they wouldn't think we were hostile or full of it.

We spent a long time in that interrogation room, drinking hot tea, laughing, and swapping stories with our new Turkish friends from the West. They were the absolute last people I expected to "grill" us. They seemed as happy to see us as we were to see them.

"You guys better get going," said the young man from Melbourne. "We've kept your driver waiting for a long time."

"Oh that's right," Sean said. "Our poor driver."

Our poor driver wasn't the only one who suffered. The entire line of cars on the bridge had to just sit there.

We all shook hands warmly and said our goodbyes. I had a bounce in my step on the way back to the car. I could hardly believe how nicely our crossing turned out after how badly it started, but the East is full of surprises.

Sean and I weren't the only ones amazed by who we ran into in the ass end of Turkish Kurdistan.

On the dark empty highway a Turkish military patrol pulled us off to the side of the road. We were never stopped on our way into Turkish Kurdistan. On the way out, though, the army wanted to know who everyone was and what they were doing.

I pulled the car over as soldiers bearing rifles surrounded us. I rolled down the driver's side window and reached for my passport. A uniformed officer barked something at me in Turkish. I didn't understand any of it.

"Hello!" I said. "Do you speak English?"

He jerked his head back, clearly startled, squinted his eyes, and said something else to me in Turkish.

All the soldiers wore deadly serious facial expressions and held their rifles ramrod straight across their chests. We could have been terrorists or gun-runners for the PKK, and they were not messing around.

I handed him my passport. "We're Americans!" I said, playing up the oblivious aw-shucks tourist persona for all it was worth.

"How ya doin'?" Sean said and gave them all a big grin.

"*Americans?*"

"Yeah, hey, what's up?" Sean said.

The soldiers looked at each other, looked at us, looked at each other again, and busted out in big laughs. They could hardly believe two American tourists were tooling around blasted-up Turkish Kurdistan, in the middle of the night, just a few miles from Syria and Iraq, in a rental car, with luggage piled up in the back, when five seconds before they were worried we could be terrorists.

The East is full of surprises.

PART TWO

THE BALKANS

Two

A Dark Corner of Europe

"If Yugoslavia was the laboratory of Communism, then Communism would breathe its last dying breath here in Belgrade. And to judge by what [Slobodan] Milosevic was turning into by early 1989, Communism would exit the world stage revealed for what it truly was: fascism, without fascism's ability to make the trains run on time." - Robert D. Kaplan

Y ou bombed my country." These were nearly the first words I heard after clearing passport control on arrival in Belgrade, the capital of Serbia, from a taxi driver who flagged me down inside the airport. "Fifteen countries bombed my country."

I didn't know what to say. Sean was traveling with me again and he didn't know what to say, either.

"Why are you here in Serbia?" the driver said.

"We're tourists," I lied. I didn't want to say I was an American journalist on a trip through the former Yugoslavia with an end destination in Kosovo. Serbia's last war of ethnic cleansing was fought there. It only ended when NATO, led by the United States, bombed Serbia's tyrannical leader Slobodan Milosevic into submission. That was 1999. Kosovo declared independence from Serbia just three months before I arrived in the spring of 2008. A mob of Serbian nationalists answered by firebombing the American embassy.

"If people ask what two tourists are doing here," the driver said, "where you are from, you say you're from Holland."

From a distance the latest news out of Belgrade made the place look like a reactionary Middle Eastern capital on a bad day, but this was still Europe. How dangerous could Serbia possibly be? Tensions were higher than at any time since the 1999 war, but I refused to lie about where I'm from.

Sean and I tossed our bags in the trunk of the taxi and collapsed into the back seat. It was midnight and there was no traffic. I figured the ride into town should cost around twenty dollars, though I also expected the driver would rip us off and charge something like forty. The exchange rate wasn't posted anywhere in the airport, so I had pulled out a wad of bills from an ATM. I knew better than to withdraw and spend foreign currency without knowing how much it was worth, but I was too exhausted to care after crossing ten time zones in twenty hours. We paid 4000 Serbian dinars and only later found out that meant eighty dollars for a fifteen-minute cab ride.

"I cannot go to America," our driver said as he hurtled us at top speed down the freeway and weaving in and out of his lane. "America will not give visa. America closed to us in Serbia."

"Sorry," I said. "It's probably because of the war. Thank God that's over." Firebombing our embassy didn't help, but I wasn't going to antagonize a man who almost certainly wasn't one of the arsonists.

He was a Serb, but he looked like a Turk. Ethnicity in the Balkans, as in the Middle East, has nothing to do with biological characteristics. Expanding and contracting empires of both the East and the West have mixed up the gene pools everywhere in both regions. American-style racial categories make no sense there. An Orthodox Christian in the former Yugoslavia who speaks Serbo-Croatian as a first language is a Serb no matter where his ancestors may have lived hundreds of years ago. And that's true whether he attends church or not. Religious belief as such is no more relevant to ethnicity in the Balkans than it is inside Israel. Dark-eyed or dark-skinned Slavs are even more common in Serbia than white-skinned or blue-eyed Arabs are in North Africa and the Levant—and the Arab world has more white-skinned and blue-eyed

Arabs than you might think if you've never been there to see it. Blue-eyed Arabs are often the children of Crusaders. Dark-skinned Slavs tend to be the descendents of Ottoman Turks.

Sean is my oldest friend, and we're accustomed to taking road trips together that our friends and family think are ill-advised. Ever since our on-a-lark road trip to Iraq we're always asking each other where we're headed next. When I decided to visit Kosovo to write about the world's newest country, he and I planned to drive there together from Serbia, from which the world's newest country seceded, and to do so through Bosnia, Croatia, Montenegro, and Albania.

Most of the city's hotels are in so-called New Belgrade. They are overpriced, far from the city center, and surrounded by communist-era monstrosity architecture. Downtown is better. It looks and feels like a proper European environment. So instead of staying in an overpriced five-star hotel in a communist-looking neighborhood, we stayed in a run-down hotel in a five-star neighborhood.

The Hotel Royal was established in 1886, but you wouldn't know it from the look of the place. It couldn't have been upgraded much, if at all, since the fall of the Berlin Wall.

I did not want to know where the disgusting stains on the carpet came from. Sean kept banging his head on the poorly affixed reading lamp next to his bed. Shower curtains were missing most of their rings and only stretched halfway across the tub anyway. An ankle-busting open drain in the bathroom threatened bare feet at all times. Beds were too hard, too short, and too narrow, yet the stiff sheets still barely fit. The screen on the TV was smaller than the one on my laptop. There was no cable or satellite, and there were only two volume control settings: too quiet to hear and loud enough to irritate the neighbors even at noon. Towels were hardly more absorbent than rubber sheets.

Everyone should stay in a hotel like this once in a while so they can appreciate the relative luxury of Motel 6. Compared to this place, a room at the Hilton is nicer than Buckingham Palace.

We walked the streets of old Belgrade after midnight and searched for whatever cafés or bars were still open. Sean said at once the city reminded him of his trips to Moscow and St. Petersburg, though Serbia's capital is a bit more prosperous and less sketchy.

A karaoke bar on the corner would not have been our first choice of hangouts, but it was one of the few places still open late on a holiday weekend. We stepped inside. Beautiful and fashionably dressed young Serbian women and men sang songs in their native language with their arms around each other, empty shot glasses and crumpled packages of cigarettes before them on the tables. Except for the bartender we spoke to, no one in the establishment could tell we weren't Serbs. The atmosphere in the bar was one of energetic and joyous camaraderie. I was happy to be there. Serbia didn't feel remotely sinister and I chuckled to myself as I remembered our taxi driver's warning.

"I could live here," Sean said. I was tempted to agree as I took a swallow of my locally brewed beer. Belgrade was my kind of place—intriguing and troubled, yet attractive, cultured, and fun.

We later found a Turkish-themed bar in a basement, and I reconsidered somewhat.

This place was quiet. Two young men brooded over beers in a corner and two young women at the bar laughed at the bartender's jokes. The other tables were empty. I was surprised to find an Istanbul-like establishment in a country so violently anti-Islamic, but old Turkish style is warm and sophisticated and the Serbs have good taste.

"We should order some of their plum brandy," Sean said as we leaned against the bar.

"You mean *slivovitz*?" I said.

Everyone heard us, dropped their conversation in mid-sentence, and stared. Their looks weren't hostile, exactly, but they were not friendly.

"Can we get some slivovitz?" Sean said to the bartender.

"I'd also like a beer, please," I said.

The Balkan Stare abated, and the bartender smiled. He seemed happy that we knew their national drink and wanted to have some. The handful of Serb patrons switched to talking about us instead of staring at us.

Not until we sat down with our drinks did I remember an obvious and very important fact for the first time since we landed. Americans are not only the ones who bombed Belgrade. American soldiers are currently stationed in Kosovo, which Serbia officially considers its territory. From the Serb perspective, we were occupying their land. Most of Yugoslavia dismembered itself, but from Belgrade's point of view, Americans were instrumental in the dismemberment of Serbia, which is something else entirely.

It was a strange twilight zone feeling and it didn't seem real. I've only seen American soldiers in the U.S. and Iraq. Europe is often thought of as a post-historical paradise, yet a place that looks like a banged-up version of Vienna got what was basically the Saddam Hussein treatment.

I sipped from my shot glass of *slivovitz*. It tasted of sweet plums and fire, but mostly of fire.

Roughly ninety percent of Kosovo's two million inhabitants are ethnic Albanians; seven percent are Serbs. Of the Albanians, about three percent are Catholic, while the rest are at least nominal Muslims. The Serbs, meanwhile, are Orthodox Christians. Against this backdrop, many observers interpreted the Balkan wars that tore Yugoslavia to pieces during the 1990s as an inevitable resurgence of ancient hatreds in a post-Communist ideological vacuum.

But the truth is that Serbian nationalists, led by Slobodan Milosevic, deliberately crafted their own ethnic nationalism as an ideology to replace Communism, seeking to retain power and seize as much territory as possible as the Yugoslav federation unraveled. On June 29, 1989, just a few months before the Berlin Wall fell, Milosevic delivered a thunderous speech to throngs of budding Serbian nationalists in the Kosovar village of Kosovo Polje. Exactly 600 years earlier, on the nearby Field of Blackbirds, the Turks defeated Serbian ruler Tsar Lazar in an epic battle, ending the sovereignty of Serbia's medieval kingdom and beginning its absorption into the Ottoman Empire. "No one will ever beat you again," Milosevic promised his audience.

Contrary to the conventional wisdom, ethnic conflict was relatively new to the area. "There have been many battles and wars in Kosovo over the centuries," historian Noel Malcolm wrote in *Kosovo: A Short History*, "but until the last 100 years or so none of them had the character of an 'ethnic' conflict between Albanians and Serbs. Members of those two populations fought together as allies at the battle of Kosovo in 1389— indeed, they probably fought as allies on both sides of that battle."

Nevertheless, Milosevic used the ancient grievance, along with others both real and imagined, to kindle Serbian nationalism. Three months after his speech at Kosovo Polje, he revoked Kosovo's political autonomy and imposed an apartheid-like system on its ethnic Albanian majority. Three wars followed in the breakaway republics of Slovenia, Bosnia-Herzegovina, and Croatia, and then a fourth of ethnic cleansing in Kosovo at a time when the United States and NATO were in no mood to tolerate any more violent destabilization in Europe. NATO bombarded Yugoslav targets for two and a half months in 1999 until Milosevic capitulated and relinquished control of Kosovo to NATO and Russia.

Serbia is mostly Christian, but it's hardly less Eastern than Turkey. (Recall that Christianity is itself a Middle Eastern religion by origin.) Serbia did not belong to the Western half of the Roman Empire with Rome as its capital. It belonged, instead, to the Eastern half of the empire whose capital is now Istanbul. The dissolution of medieval Serbia, and its annexation by the world of Islam, deeply traumatized the Serbian national psyche. The recent crimes of Slobodan Milosevic and his band of like-minded war criminals shouldn't obscure that, even though they were not justified by it.

Most of the Balkan Peninsula was part of the Ottoman Empire for hundreds of years. It did not belong to the West. It was the northern-most region of the same political entity that included much of the Arab world, and it was anchored there for longer than the United States has so far existed. The region of the South Slavs is European by geography and in most ways by culture, but for the last half-millennium much of it has been ruled by Easterners and Muslims more often than not. For hundreds of years Belgrade was governed by those who also ruled Mecca, Medina, Jerusalem, Cairo, and Baghdad.

Serbia didn't much take part in the Renaissance, which spread from Italy through much of Europe (less so to Ottoman lands). Serbia was beyond the reach of Napoleon and his code, which laid a strong foundation for the rule of law. Serbia was likewise less affected by the Western European Enlightenment. It was subsumed at the time in Islam and the world of the East.

The Ottoman Empire disintegrated at the end of World War I, but many of its unstable former pieces—from Israel and Cyprus to Lebanon and Iraq—are still at war with themselves and with each other. The unraveling of Yugoslavia was a European echo of the sectarian communal warfare that ripped through the formerly Ottoman lands in the Middle East.

The Balkan Peninsula is, in some ways, the Middle East of Europe. And why shouldn't it be? Most of it was part of a Middle Eastern empire for hundreds of years.

Sean and I met one of Belgrade's most famous writers, Filip David, at a café downtown across the street from a park. You may know him as the writer of the award-winning film *Cabaret Balkan* (or, *The Powder Keg* in its original Serbo-Croatian), a disturbing Altman-esque kaleidoscope of intertwined stories set in Belgrade on the eve of Yugoslavia's violent demise.

He wanted to get one thing out of the way before Sean or I asked him anything.

"I opposed from the first moment the Milosevic regime," he said, "from the beginning of the 1990s. I was in non-government groups and organizations that were opposed to Milosevic and the nationalistic policies of Serbian power."

He did not, however, spend time in prison. "Milosevic," he said, "was very clever. He let dissidents stay free so he could always say to people outside Serbia: *here is democracy*. You could see these small groups, but they were without any real influence. I did lose my job. For twenty-five years I was the head of the drama department at Belgrade TV."

Belgrade TV, at the time, was the only Serbian channel. It was Slobodan Milosevic's very own *Pravda*. Now, though, Serbia has many channels. And even during the Communist era under Josip Broz (Marshal) Tito, Western newspapers and magazines were available.

Serbia's election that year produced a better result than David expected. Boris Tadic's pro-European Democratic Party earned less than 50 percent of the vote, but still garnered a bigger share than any of the individual nationalist parties. Serbian nationalists outnumber internationalists overall, but they are disorganized and no longer start wars.

"Milosevic is dead," David said, "but his ideas and Serbian nationalism are still very strong."

That's certainly true. Serbia's full-blown nationalist parties—the Radicals led by Vojislav Šešelj, who is currently in the dock in the Hague for war crimes and genocide, and Milosevic's old Socialist party—are supported by roughly half the population. A smaller base of support for Vojislav Kostunica's more moderate party, which is still nationalist and anti-European, places Serbia's supporters of Westernization and liberalization in the minority.

Tito was liberal and lenient as far as communist dictators go, but Serbia's nationalists are by far more extreme than any others in Europe. As Paul Berman put it in the *Boston Globe*, "the best communism led to the worst post-communism." The likes of the French National Front, led by Jean-Marie Le Pen, may wax nostalgic for the extremist actors of yesteryear, but the head of Serbia's Radical Party is headed by present day war criminals who plotted and carried out genocide against both Muslims and Catholics not during World War II, but *after* the Cold War.

"What put Yugoslavia together was communism," David said. "There was an ideological base. There were communist parties in Serbia,

Croatia, everywhere. But after the fall of communism, after the fall of the Berlin Wall, they lost their ideological base. Milosevic was a real communist, but also a pragmatist. He knew what to do to keep his power. At first he was against nationalism."

"You mean after Tito?" I said.

"After the fall of the Berlin Wall," he said. "But communists in Serbia had to fall also. So very soon Milosevic became a Serbian nationalist. You must understand that Serbian nationalism is also a totalitarian ideology."

"It's not that hard to go from one totalitarianism to another," Sean said.

"He was not really a nationalist," David said, "but he had to do this to keep his power. The problem with Serbs then was that Serbs controlled the Yugoslav Army. At that moment he went all over Yugoslavia and raised the issue of nationalism. He was sure that because the Serbs in the Yugoslav Army controlled everything, he could control Yugoslavia. He then began to attack Croatia and Bosnia. The army was already there. That was the beginning of the end of Yugoslavia."

The *dénouement* was a long one. The end of the end of Yugoslavia only came to pass three months earlier when Kosovo declared its independence.

"I'm on the political committee of a small party," David said, "the Liberal Democratic Party. In the opinion of some people, especially outside Serbia, this is the only party that's based on the real situation. We say Kosovo has separated, it is now a new state, and we should have good relations with them."

"You recognize this?" I said.

"Yes," he said. "One hundred thousand Serbs still live there, so we have to have good relations with Albanians. But we're only a minority here in Serbia. Maybe six, seven, or eight percent of people agree with us. The people in Kosovo, the Albanians, don't want to live in Serbia. Before the Milosevic regime we had no connection to Kosovo. They had their own parallel institutions. They were already outside Serbia. I am sure that some of our politicians are happy that it has separated, but officially they speak differently."

"You mean, privately they're happy?" I said.

"Yes," David said.

"They've removed the problem," Sean said. "It's been cut loose."

"Kosovo was only part of Serbia after the First World War," David said. "It was not forever even though they say it was forever. Myths are based on emotions, not on facts. Hitler has one very important sentence in *Mein Kampf.* He said his National Socialist movement was not based on facts, but on emotions, and that no facts can destroy it. I asked myself, *how did things change in Nazi Germany?* With a complete catastrophe. We haven't had one. And I don't want one because I live here."

A large number of Europeans have been anti-American for most of America's history. The worst of it, though, comes from Western European elitists. Eastern Europe is different, as Secretary of Defense Donald Rumsfeld bluntly pointed out with a now infamous quip in 2003. At the time, Germany was run by Gerhard Schroeder and France by Jacques Chirac, two congenitally combative and at times bigoted leaders who even *campaigned* on anti-American platforms.

"You look at vast numbers of other countries in Europe," Rumsfeld said to the foreign press corps, "they're not with France and Germany.... They're with the US. You're thinking of Europe as Germany and France. I don't. I think that's old Europe."

New Europe, in Rumsfeld's analysis, was the eastern half, the post-communist half. Most of Eastern Europe really is more pro-American, but not all of it. Serbia is on the "new" eastern side, but geopolitically it's even farther east than it is geographically. Anti-Americanism runs much deeper there than it does anywhere else in Europe outside of Russia—if Russia even counts as European at all, which it does at most only by half. Serbian anti-Americanism is partly based on recent and current grievances, but also on conspiracy theories and paranoid Soviet phantasmagoria. It is a much nastier beast than anything you'll find in the cafés of Paris.

"What do most Serbs think of Americans now?" I asked Filip David.

"Very bad!" he said and laughed. "There is very messy propaganda, you know. There is no private opinion here, only public opinion. During Milosevic they said for four years that there was no alternative to war. And after Dayton, the next day, they said that peace has no alternative. Everyone changed his or her mind overnight. The influence of the media is very strong. And now they say Americans are our enemies."

"They actually use the word *enemies*?" I said.

"Yes," he said. "You also have some kind of stereotypes. The first is that there is an international conspiracy against Serbia, and that behind it are Americans and Jews with *The Protocols of the Elders of Zion*."

"Oh, you're kidding," said Sean. He spent six months in Denmark while I was in Lebanon, and he never heard that kind of talk there.

"Really," David said. "They say Jews control America."

Sean couldn't help but laugh at the absurdity.

"And the second," David said, "is that all independent journalists and non-government members are traitors who are paid by the West. These two stereotypes exist now, in this moment. I am against this, you know, because I am Jewish."

"Is that a problem for you here?" I said.

"It's an attack on international Jews," he said, "not Jews here, because, you know, in Serbia there are only 2,000 Jews. A lot of people who attack Jews and are anti-Semites have never met any Jews. In this moment, we have over 100 anti-Semitic books. A lot of them are reprinted books that were written during the Nazi occupation of Serbia during the Second World War. They are trying to explain how it's possible that Serbia lost all its wars. They are saying that it's an international conspiracy. And people believe it. It's true that in the American administration you have lots of Jews. But they are Americans, they act like Americans, not like Jews. I think so."

"And the honest truth," Sean said, "is there aren't that many."

"Most are Christians," I said.

"Henry Kissinger," David said. "Richard Holbrooke, Wesley Clark."

General Wesley Clark was NATO's Supreme Allied Commander of Europe when the U.S. went to war against Milosevic. What was left of Yugoslavia at the time might best be thought of as a rump Serbian Empire. Nothing was left of it but Serbia, tiny Montenegro, and pulverized Kosovo. Yugoslavia was derisively described by some of its citizens as *Serboslavia* even before the rise of Milosevic. It wouldn't be reasonable to expect many Serbs to admire Wesley Clark, but slagging him for being a Jew seemed a bit much.

"Wesley Clark was born a Jew and adopted by some family," David said. "It's not important whether it's true or not. People here say someone is a Jew when they don't like him."

Wesley Clark does have a paternal Jewish great-grandfather. That doesn't make him Jewish according to Jewish law, where Judaism is inherited through the mother instead of the father, but it does make him Jewish according to Hitler's definition and, apparently, according to the Serbian definition as well. When General Clark ran for president in the Democratic primary in 2004, the American media let this factoid languish in obscurity because hardly anyone in the United States would find it interesting or even relevant.

I didn't know any part of Clark's background was Jewish until I heard it in Serbia, and I initially thought it was nonsense. I had to check. Belgrade's communist-constructed propaganda industry has been manufacturing lies about its enemies for years. (Republican Senator Bob Dole was widely accused of being a secret Albanian Muslim, for instance.) When you throw *The Protocols of the Elders of Zion* into the mix, it's a good idea to fact-check what you hear—which is good advice everywhere in the Balkans, not just in Serbia.

"Everybody tries to make their identification with Palestine or with Jews to explain what happens here in Serbia," David said. "People very often can't understand what happens here. During Tito's regime there wasn't any kind of anti-Semitism. Tito had good relations with Israel.

But with the rise of nationalism everywhere we have the rise of anti-Semitism everywhere. In Slovenia they have maybe fifty Jews, but they have problems with anti-Semitism when there are problems with the economy."

So what do average Serbs think about Israel?

"It's mixed," he said. "Sometimes they praise Israel and say we too must defend ourselves with arms. But other times they say we are like Palestinians and that Israel is an extension of the United States. But it's also not so simple because Palestinians are Arabs. And they don't like Arabs because Arabs are Muslims. That's why I say there is so much confusion here about political life, cultural life, and economic life. You can be very surprised by what people say here, and the next day they will say the exact opposite."

"Is there any talk that if you joined the European Union that the economy would take off?" Sean said.

"Yes," David said, "but these are facts. People in the Democratic Party are saying so, but others are saying they would rather us be very poor and have our dignity."

"That's very much like the Arabs," I said. I know of nowhere that places more cultural and political importance on dignity than the Arab world, even at the expense of peace and prosperity.

"Yes," David said. "In some ways."

"I don't mean to be offensive when I say that," I said.

"If you have no facts, you play on dignity," David said.

"But you know what?" Sean said. "Cash buys a lot of dignity."

"Without cash you have no dignity," David said. "You know, when we were under sanctions we had so much inflation. You can't imagine. If I didn't send a letter to my friends in the morning, in the afternoon it cost in the millions. It was the highest inflation in the world during Milosevic. In shops you couldn't buy anything. They were completely empty. But because we are an agricultural country, we could eat. Pensions were less than one deutschmark per month...less than one. Money completely lost its value. If I had my pockets full of money, I couldn't even buy cigarettes. You can't imagine that kind of situation. It's like living in some absurd galaxy."

Neither Sean nor I had been to Belgrade before, and Filip David offered to take us on a walking tour. We set out from our downtown café toward Belgrade TV, David's old employer before Milosevic fired him and before the headquarters was bombed by NATO.

He showed us the Serbian parliament building, Orthodox churches, the old Marx and Engels Square from the communist days, and other various landmarks. I saw virtually no evidence that Belgrade had ever been bombed. Serbs suffered much more elsewhere during the Yugoslav wars. In Croatia, for instance, they were ethnically cleansed from the Krajina region in one of the most under-reported atrocities of the war.

"During the bombing here," Sean said, "how bad was it?"

"I have very contradictory feelings," David said. "On one side, I knew, I was sure, that Milosevic wouldn't resign without bombing. The resignation of Milosevic was a result of the bombing. On the other side, I was with my family here, my boy, my girl, you know, and they were afraid. My son lived 100 meters from Belgrade TV, which was bombed, and I lived 200 meters, and I begged him to stay with me because we knew it would be bombed that night. He said no. He passed all these buildings that were bombed and he saw that the Americans were very precise."

"But it's still dangerous," I said, "precision bombing or not."

"Sometimes they bombed the wrong thing," he said, "but here in Belgrade they were very precise. It was not the kind of bombing as in the Second World War where they were bombing everything. They said what they were going to hit before they hit it. But it became very dangerous because they bombed all the official buildings and then they didn't know what to do next if Milosevic wouldn't resign. But Milosevic stopped at the right time."

The bombed-out Belgrade TV station building wasn't far from our starting point. It stood out as one of the few remaining buildings damaged during the air campaign. It seemed to be left as a showpiece. It's hard to say, though, if it was left in its condition to wave the bloody shirt against the United States or against Milosevic.

Part of it remains standing. It's six stories tall with a pitched roof and looks like it was cut vertically in half with a gigantic buzz saw, with one half carted away and the other left gaping and exposed to the elements.

"We predicted it would be bombed because it was a massive propaganda mission," David said. "And I was very sorry because sixteen people who were innocent in that building were killed."

"People chose to stay in it?" Sean said.

"No," David said. "It was not by choice. The conclusion was that if people were killed, we would have an argument against the West. The man who was the general director at that moment is in prison because he gave orders to put people there."

A memorial to the dead is placed across the street from the decaying hulk. All sixteen names are engraved in the stone. Above the list of names is written one simple question: Why?

But the truth is that everybody knows why. Civilians killed by Americans make for great propaganda. Journalists, even Western journalists, predictably complied and blamed NATO even though the building was struck at two o'clock in the morning when it should have been empty. Totalitarian regimes routinely use human shields as a matter of course, but it occurred to few at the time that Serbian authorities might want to cynically parade the corpses of their own innocents in front of the cameras, though this sort of grotesquery is *de rigueur* in the Middle East and should have been obvious.

"I feel like we're safe here," I said to David. "Is that true?"

"Yes," he said. "Generally. But sometimes you will have somebody say they don't like you if they hear you speak English."

I'd seen some looks of surprise and the occasional uncomfortable stare, but no one had been verbally rude to either Sean or me yet.

"Our taxi driver from the airport told us not to say we're Americans," Sean said, "but to say we're from Holland."

"That seems paranoid," I said.

"Maybe that was his impression," David said. "Or maybe he didn't want to say directly that he doesn't like Americans, but in that indirect way he said you are not welcome here. You may meet some people who say, *fine, you're Americans*, and others who say they hate Americans. But you could say you support the Radicals, that you came here to support Šešelj and Milosevic."

Sean and I laughed.

"What if we say we support Kosovo?" I said.

"That would be dangerous," David said.

Predrag Delibasic grew up in Sarajevo, in Bosnia, when Yugoslavia was still Yugoslavia. Ethnically he's half-Serbian and half-Bosnian, so today he fits just as well—or just as poorly—in each place. But he spent most of his life as a Yugoslav when the word still actually meant something. All his closest childhood friends were from different backgrounds. They eventually became the subjects of a documentary film he made called *Maturity Exam*.

He and his friends meet every day at the same café downtown for coffee and lunch. Members of the group hail from Serbia, Bosnia, Montenegro, Macedonia, and Kosovo.

"We are all friends," he said. "We don't care about ethnicity. But others, people around here...it's hard. The radish is too deep. It cannot be uprooted."

Many at the café didn't speak English, so Sean and I spent most of our time talking to Delibasic, who did.

"My best friend now is a Serb who married a Bosnian woman," he said. "Jovan Divjak, the Serb defender of the city of Sarajevo."

General Divjak was the highest-ranking Serb officer in the multi-ethnic Bosnian army during the war. His very existence shows that even then the liberal idea of a cosmopolitan and ethnically mixed Bosnia was still alive in the hearts and minds of some of its people. Not every Serb agreed with Slobodan Milosevic's and Radovan Karadzic's ethnic nationalist Greater Serbia project, and some fought and died to put a stop to it. Many were singled out and publicly executed by nationalist Serb forces for resisting and for refusing to fight Catholic Croats and Bosnian Muslims.

"Do you know who that man is?" Delibasic said and gestured behind him. "The man at that table there with the white hair?"

I looked to my right and saw who I thought he was talking about four tables down.

"The man sitting with the young woman?" I said.

"He was Tito's general," he said.

"Which general?" I said. Tito had, of course, more than one. "What's his name?"

"He is General Jovo Kapicic," he said. "His son owns this café. We are good friends."

One of the pleasures of traveling to the capital cities of small countries like Serbia is how easy it can be to meet important people even by chance. Sean and I didn't want to bother Tito's general, however, who was deep in conversation with a young lady, perhaps his granddaughter. We wanted to talk about Bosnia, where Delibasic grew up.

"When I was a kid in Sarajevo," Delibasic said, "some visiting Montenegrin nationalists asked me, *who are you*? I had no idea, and I didn't care. So I made up an answer. *I am Jewish!* I said. My mother said no, no, no. But I didn't know or care. My friends were Jews, Muslims, and Catholics. After I was told I wasn't Jewish, I said I was a Muslim. But that wasn't right either. So after that I've always just said I am a Yugoslav. If I could, I would take citizenship in Slovenia, Croatia, and Montenegro, as well as in Bosnia and Serbia. But I can't. I still call myself a Yugoslav, but the census-takers won't accept that as an answer."

Milosevic's isn't the only violent nationalist movement in Yugoslavia that Predrag Delibasic has personally had to contend with. He is old enough to remember World War II vividly, and he told Sean and me about his experience with the Ustasha—a fascist Croatian militia aligned with the Nazis.

"Armed and drunk Ustasha men came to our house when I was 13 years old," he said. "They demanded our papers and couldn't find them. My mother was very brave. She screamed at them and told them it was their fault because they messed up the house. The commander put a gun in her mouth. I grabbed the man's gun and said, *Kill me, not my mommy!*"

He and his mother were then taken to prison in Visegrad, just inside Bosnia near the Serbian border. They managed to escape and were smuggled into Serbia with help from a train conductor. His family reunited in Uzice where his father waited for him and his mother.

Later he joined Tito's Partisans. "I was a member of the Communist Party," he said. "But I was ideologically quiet."

He didn't ultimately fare any better with the communists than he had with the Ustasha.

"I was falsely accused of being a Stalinist," he said, "after Tito broke with Stalin in 1948. Only recently, almost sixty years later, did I finally receive a document explaining exactly why I was arrested."

As it turned out, according to the document, Delibasic was accused of being a Stalinist because he met with a visiting film student from Moscow.

"They sent me to Goli Otok," he said. "Tito's concentration camp."

Goli Otok was a prison on an island in the Adriatic that now belongs to Croatia. It's name means Naked Island. The island is mostly bare, as were its prisoners. "They made us march naked," he said, "and do forced labor."

"That must have made you re-think communism," Sean said.

"Yes," Delibasic said and nodded as he widened his eyes. "The camp was run by Tito's general."

"Which general?" I said. "*Him?*" The man with the white hair just a few tables down? Whose son owned the café?

"Yes," Delibasic said and gestured by nodding his head toward General Kapicic. The old gulag chief nursed his coffee only a dozen or so meters away. "It was the hardest time of my life. I could not believe that my beloved Partisans would build such an infernal place."

I could hardly believe he was friends with the general who ran it and who made him break rocks with a hammer just for meeting a film student.

A few minutes later, General Kapicic stopped by our table. Delibasic introduced Sean and me to him.

"He is a good friend to me," Kapicic said, "and now to you. He is a very smart professor and you should listen to him."

After the general left, I had to ask: "How can you be friends with him after what he did?"

"You heard what he said," Delibasic said. "I accept it and I don't hate anybody."

Three

The Mash of Civilizations

"The Balkans produce more history than they can consume." – Winston Churchill

"Sarajevans will not be counting the dead. They will be counting the living." - Radovan Karadzic, Bosnian Serb leader, war criminal

A gigantic poster of genocidal war criminal Radovan Karadzic hung on the outside wall of a communist-style apartment block on the outskirts of Belgrade.

"Get a picture of that," I said to Sean. I had the wheel and he had the camera.

"Too late," he said.

We were driving fast on a four-lane road out of Belgrade toward Sarajevo, the capital of Bosnia-Herzegovina, and were almost out of the city.

"That's okay," I said. "We'll probably see another one."

We didn't, however, see another one, not anywhere in Serbia or even in Bosnia's Serb-controlled separatist Republika Srpska. Europe's worst living political leaders still have a base of support among Serbs, but it's dwindling.

Old Belgrade is beautiful, sophisticated, stylish, and fun, but outer New Belgrade looks exactly as junky and communist as I expected it would. Neither Sean nor I had any idea what to expect from Serb villages aside from the fact that they're in no way as cosmopolitan as the capital is. Small Serb towns and villages—especially in Bosnia's Republika Srpska—were the least friendly places for any Americans brave enough to visit the former Yugoslavia while it was violently coming apart at the seams in the 1990s.

The countryside beyond the city limits is flat agricultural land that looks more or less like the American Midwest. Sean and I could have been in Iowa or Illinois. Bosnia, we knew, would be much more rugged, and we'd be there in less than two hours.

"We have to stop before we reach the border," Sean said. "I still have thousands of Serbian dinars." (The dinar, by the way, is the name of the currency used in many Arab countries, including Iraq. It's named after an early Islamic coin , reinforcing in yet another small way my notion that the Balkan Peninsula is in some ways the Middle East of Europe.)

"Just exchange them in Bosnia," I said.

"You can't exchange them in Bosnia," he said. "You can't exchange dinars anywhere outside Serbia."

"You can't?" I said. "Are you sure?"

He was sure. And he had a wad of dinars worth almost $200, so I pulled off the highway into a small town that looked just barely large enough that it might have a bank.

"Want to find a bar and drink some *slivovitz* with the locals?" I said. I was kidding slightly, but only slightly.

"Hmm," Sean said. He didn't know if he wanted to down *slivovitz* with drunk villagers or not. I wasn't sure I really did, either.

We both wondered how well we'd be received if we sidled up to a bar in the Serbian countryside and asked for shots of *slivovitz* in American English. With only a single exception, everyone we met in Belgrade was perfectly friendly and pleasant despite Serbia's sometimes primitive anti-Americanism. But when was the last time the average drunk villager ran into the people who recently bombed his country?

Sometimes I'm not sure what to make of even the primitive anti-Americanism, let alone the moderate variety. I later met an Albanian woman in Kosovo who frequently travels to Belgrade. "I go there all the time," she said. "I have friends there. I'm not paranoid about it. We go out and have a good time. But in the back of my mind I remember they are Serbs. One night I met a Chetnik guy." The Chetniks were Serbian nationalist and royalist paramilitary units that fought against the Ottomans in 1904 and again during the two world wars. Some of the most vicious Bosnian Serb death squads during the Yugoslav wars of the 1990s also called themselves Chetniks. "He couldn't believe it," she continued, "when I said I was from Kosovo. He said, *Oh, I killed you during the war*. I yelled at him. I screamed at him. But at the end he wanted to marry me."

Our randomly selected small Serbian town had but a single main street. Maybe we would see a bank and maybe we wouldn't.

"There," Sean said. "On the right." They did have a bank. "Park."

There was nowhere to park in front, so I found a place a few hundred feet down the road.

A badly dressed man in his fifties who had not shaved in days stared holes through me and walked toward our car. Sean paid him no mind, flung open his door, and started toward the bank by himself. I guessed that meant I would stay with the car.

Scruffy Guy came up to my driver's side door. I looked around. Was I illegally parked? Was I in front of his house?

I stepped out of the car. He said something to me in Serbian.

"Do I need to move my car?" I said.

He pointed to my license plate and jabbed his open hand at me as though I owed him money.

"I am not giving you money," I said. He wasn't a parking attendant or a cop.

He pointed at the license plate again.

"Beograd," I said. "The car is from Beograd." That was obvious from the letters "BG" on the plate. "So what?" I knew he couldn't understand me, but I had to say something.

He demanded money more aggressively this time.

"No!" I said.

Scruffy Guy spat out an insult in Serbian and shuffled off. I impatiently spun the key ring around my index finger while waiting for Sean to change his money when Scruffy Guy grabbed the arm of a younger man on the sidewalk, turned him around, and pointed menacingly at me as though I was a hated witch or a leper. He said God-only-knows-what in Serbian. The word "foreigner" was probably in there somewhere, but I can't be certain. The younger man narrowed his eyes at me briefly, then contemptuously brushed off Scruffy Guy and walked away.

Scruffy Guy wanted money or worse, and he wanted some help from his townsfolk. So he pointed his finger at me and yelled something awful in Serbian. Heads turned from every direction. I had no idea what to expect, and I prepared to jump back in the car and lock the door if I had to.

I no longer had any interest whatsoever in drinking *slivovitz* in a run-down bar in this town with these people.

Nobody approached me, though. All eyes turned from me to Scruffy Guy, whose reputation in town—I'd be willing to bet at this point—was worse than the reputation of travelers like Sean and myself. His fellow citizens were initially startled by my presence, but they seemed to have no interest in doing or saying anything to me. Scruffy Guy was clearly frustrated by his inability to gin up a big scene.

Still, I faced hostility the *instant* I stepped out of the car. So I was relieved when Sean returned.

We crossed the border into Bosnia on a small village road in agricultural country. No cars were ahead of us in line at the remote crossing, and none were behind us. The border police at each gate on our way out of Serbia and on our way into Bosnia stamped our passports without saying a word.

Bosnia didn't look or feel like a new country at first since Serbs lived on both sides of the border. We had merely crossed from Serbia into the Serb-controlled Republika Srpska. This region of Bosnia was an ethnic patchwork during the Yugoslav days, but has since been ethnically cleansed of Catholic Croats and Muslim Bosniaks.

Sean and I tried our best to follow the map from the border to Tuzla, a city outside the Republika Srpska, where we could easily find the main highway to Sarajevo. Almost every road sign, though, used Cyrillic letters, the alphabet of Russia. Neither Sean nor I recognized most of them.

Most road signs in Serbia proper are written in both the Cyrillic and Latin alphabets, but the Serbian government in the Republika Srpska couldn't bother with that courtesy even though the majority of their fellow Bosnians use Latin letters. I didn't see a single road sign anywhere in the Republika Srpska that pointed toward Sarajevo in any language or alphabet. All signs, instead, pointed to Belgrade or to small nearby villages as if Srpska was in Serbia rather than Bosnia.

We were lost. Thanks only to the location of the sun in the sky did I eventually figure out that I had screwed up and that we were heading north toward Croatia instead of south toward Sarajevo. We needed to stop for directions, so I pulled into the parking lot at a gas station.

"Let's both go inside," I said and braced myself for another hostile encounter. Bosnian Serbs tend to be more nationalistic than those in Serbia proper, and we already had a few issues there.

The station owner didn't speak a word of English, but he understood where we needed to go. He pointed at the map and used hand signals to give us directions to Tuzla. He was perfectly pleasant and charming, but another man coldly sized me up from head-to-toe and let his eyes linger on my watch. I smiled at him as though he hadn't just done that, but he kept up the Balkan Stare until Sean and I were back in the car.

Hey," Sean said after another hour of driving. "There's a mosque." On the hill to our left was the first Muslim village we had seen since we entered Bosnia almost two hours before.

"It looks like a nice little town," I said. It was just off the main road to Tuzla and Sarajevo, yet we both wanted to take a look and compare it with the Serb towns we had been driving through all day. So I turned off and drove up the hill. Serb towns in the Republika Srpska were mostly nondescript and a bit on the trashy side. Would the Muslim towns be nicer or worse? I had no idea.

The instant we entered the village I saw bullet and shrapnel holes in the walls.

None of the Serb towns or villages we passed through bore a single scar from the war that I could see, but the minute I saw a mosque — bang, just like that—I found myself in what had very recently been a war zone. I'm accustomed to seeing this sort of thing in the Middle East, but this was Europe.

Bosnia is a far cry from Iraq, though. Half the people we drove past on the village road were women. In an Iraqi village, all or nearly all would have been men. Women rarely leave the house in most Arab villages. None of the women we saw in this Bosnian Muslim village wore an Islamic headscarf. In Iraq, all or nearly all village women wear head-to-toe black abayas.

So far this was the most outwardly secular Muslim village I had ever seen. But, as I would later discover, it was typical of Muslim villages in Bosnia, Kosovo, and Albania. Europe's indigenous Muslims—as opposed to its immigrant Muslims from Pakistan, the Middle East, and North Africa—are no more likely to be religious than Europe's indigenous Christians these days. Many, if not most, are Muslims in name only. Religion appeared to have faded in Bosnia as much as it has in France.

There was little to see in the small village, but I wasn't sure we were still on the correct road to Tuzla. So I pulled into a car repair shop and rolled down the window to ask.

A man stepped out of the shop and frowned slightly when he saw the license plate on the car. Here we go again.

"Hi!" I said and tried to sound as American as possible. *We aren't Serbs*, was what I meant to convey. *We are not the people who blew up your house. We're from a country that kinda sorta helped you a tiny bit during the war.*

The man smiled. He didn't speak English, but he understood when

I told him we were driving to Tuzla and he confirmed that we were heading in the right direction. So we continued driving toward Tuzla, in Bosnia proper outside the Republika Srpska.

Wherever I saw mosques I also saw destroyed houses.

There was pain and suffering on all sides during the war. No faction was innocent. I take seriously the following written by Rebecca West in *Black Lamb and Grey Falcon* shortly before the outbreak of World War II: "English persons...of humanitarian and reformist disposition constantly went out to the Balkan Peninsula to see who was in fact ill-treating whom, and, being by the very nature of their perfectionist faith unable to accept the horrid hypothesis that everybody was ill-treating everybody else, all came back with a pet Balkan people established in their hearts as suffering and innocent, eternally the massacree and never the massacrer."

Nevertheless, it's obvious just from driving around that the Muslims of Bosnia *really* got hammered hardest the last time around. I don't mean to pick on the Serbs, but the visual evidence, as well as the documented evidence, is just overwhelming.

According to the *Bosnian Book of the Dead*, more than 97,000 people were killed on all sides and two-thirds of them were Bosniaks. Eighty percent of the civilians killed were Bosniaks.

The Serb towns I saw in the Republika Srpska were not the charming little villages on postcards from Europe, but the Muslim towns had clearly gone through an utter catastrophe. They were clean now, and the houses had been repainted, but bullet holes and husks of shattered houses were strewn all over the landscape.

Ottoman-style mosque minarets were also common, of course, as was cheap Turkitecture.

"Welcome to Turkey," Sean said. "We're in Turkey."

We weren't, of course, in Turkey, but Bosnia was part of Turkey's vast empire for hundreds of years. The similarities didn't surprise either of us in the slightest. There would hardly be *any* Muslims in Bosnia if it hadn't been for the Ottoman Empire's expansion into the Balkans.

Turkey is politically and culturally secular to an extent, but the Muslim parts of Bosnia are noticeably more so. If it weren't for the mosque minarets on the skyline, there'd be no visible evidence that anyone in these villages and towns were Muslims at all.

S arajevo can be startling for first-time visitors. Shattered buildings, walls riddled with bullet holes, and mass graveyards are shocking things to see in a European capital in the 21st century. The war in Bosnia-Herzegovina was more violent than the others in the former Yugoslavia, and it shows. If I believed in ghosts I'd say Sarajevo must be one of the most haunted places on earth. At the same time, the reconstruction and cleanup work is impressive. The destruction gave me a jolt, but at the same time I was slightly surprised I didn't see more of it.

Bosnia is a troubled country with a dark recent past, but it is no longer the war-torn disaster it was. Sarajevo was under siege for almost four years by Bosnian Serb forces on the surrounding hilltops who fired mortar and artillery shells and sniper rounds at civilians, but it's over now and it has been over for more than a decade. Most damaged buildings have been repaired, and many neighborhoods look like nothing bad ever happened there.

Though much improved, Sarajevo is still a bewildering place for visitors trying to get a handle on things, much as Lebanon was the first time I traveled there during the twilight of Syria's military occupation. Out-of-date books and simplified media reports for distant foreign consumption can only help so much in these kinds of places, I'm afraid. There is a great deal of local detail rarely covered by foreign correspondents and not yet recorded by historians that can only be absorbed through immersion.

"Maybe in twenty years Bosnia will be nice again," said a Bosnian I know who now lives in Oregon.

"I *love* Sarajevo," an Albanian woman in Kosovo later told me, "but I was there recently and saw on their faces that they are unhappy, more than they were a few years ago. You could see it and feel it."

On the other hand, Sean and I met a man named Avdo in the spectacularly beautiful and meticulously restored Turkish Quarter who said the situation is bad but getting better. His biggest complaint wasn't about politics, but the exorbitant price of real estate.

Whether it's getting better or worse, I can't say. Serbian writer Filip David's basic diagnosis seems to be right, though. "In Sarajevo it is not a good situation," he said in Belgrade the day before Sean and I left Serbia for Bosnia. "My friends who are Croatians and Muslims are not satisfied. It doesn't function. Serbs, Croatians, and Muslims in the [government] can't agree on *anything*."

Bosnia-Herzegovina is ethnically divided between Orthodox Serbs, Catholic Croats, and Muslim Bosniaks. No group commands a numeric majority. Muslims (including nominal and atheist "Muslims") make up a plurality of the population at just under one half. But everyone is a minority. The country is also politically divided between the Serb-controlled Republika Srpska and the rest of the country. Bosnia, Herzegovina, and the Republika Srpska aren't three separate regions, however. Republika Srpska itself divides both Bosnia and Herzegovina. The map is a mess, and so is the country.

It doesn't feel like a mess on a brief visit, though, the way Baghdad does. The Bosnian war was ferocious—much worse than Iraq's while it lasted—and seeing Sarajevo in reasonably good shape was a welcome reminder that terrible wars end. I could not have imagined Sarajevo looking the way it does now in the middle of the 1990s.

Some of my friends and family thought I was a bit strange for wanting to see Bosnia, even though the war has been over for more than ten years. The truth is that Sarajevo is great for cultural and historical tourism. Belgrade is sometimes described to would-be travelers as an undiscovered jewel of the Balkans. It's true that the place is a bit underrated for what it has to offer, but that goes at least double for Sarajevo. Serbia is still known for extreme politics, but that won't affect visitors. Bosnia's former reputation as being *go-there-and-die* dangerous is a much harder one to live down no matter how out of date.

It's a beautiful place. And it is worth going to see. Sarajevo's old city center is unique. Half of it looks and feels like Ottoman-era Turkey, the other like the defunct Austro-Hungarian Empire. There aren't many cities in the world where in less than five minutes you can walk from an Eastern urban environment to another that is unmistakably Western. Sarajevo reminded me of Beirut in both bad ways and good. Bad because, like Beirut, parts of it are still shot full of holes. Good because, also like Beirut, there are sizable numbers of mosques and churches in a city that has been at a civilizational crossroads for centuries.

Before the war, the percentages of Muslim and Christian inhabitants of the city were more or less even, with Christian Serbs and Croats together just barely eking out a majority. The war changed the demographics, though. Sarajevo is mostly Bosniak now. It's not that Serbs were ethnically cleansed. Many of the people who still live there are Serbs. Rather, ideological Serbian nationalists left to be among the like-minded in the Republika Srpska. The city sadly no longer is the same kind of living example of inter-religious tolerance and co-existence that it once was, or at least pretended to be. Nationalists like Slobodan Milosevic, Radovan Karadzic, and their ilk made sure of that.

Aside from some of the architecture, however, Sarajevo doesn't look or feel even remotely like a Muslim-majority city. In this way it resembles Istanbul, only from outward appearances it is even more secular. Bosnians tend to be less demonstrative about religion than Turks, and both are less demonstrative in general than Arabs. Bosnia is also in Europe where God, if not dead, is mortally wounded.

I saw very few women wearing Islamic headscarves. Alcohol is no less available than it is anywhere else in Europe—or in Turkey for that matter—for those who want it. It is not even in the same time zone as a radical Islamist environment. Sarajevo, like Beirut, is a city with both Western and Eastern characteristics, but unlike Beirut, it is one hundred percent European.

Sean and I stayed at the Holiday Inn, a hotel made famous by war correspondents in the mid-1990s. The thing looks like a modernist cube from the 1970s, though it was built in the 1980s. It fits in rather well in a part of the city near the center that is dominated by other modern buildings. Some are generically international while others look explicitly communist. Nothing near the Holiday Inn will ever appear on a pretty postcard. I wished we'd stayed in the Turkish Quarter, a neighborhood of such outstanding tiled and cobble-stoned charm that it eclipses every place I've seen in Turkey itself.

The war never left my mind in Sarajevo. Something that struck me at once is how narrow the old part of the city is. Serb snipers took up position in houses on the tops of the hills and fired at anyone they saw moving, including, of course, fellow Serbs who decided to stay. The infamous "Sniper Alley" was right outside our hotel. The geographical compactness of the city—you can walk from the bottom of one hill to the other side in just a few minutes—meant the snipers were always close. If you can see the hills, the hills can see you, and the hills loom beautifully but ominously over everything.

That night I dreamed I was trapped there during the siege, scrambling to find a place where I couldn't see hills.

B osnia might one day split into three. Serbs live in their own area as do Croats and Bosniaks. Sarajevo is one of the few multi-ethnic places remaining, but even it has a Bosniak majority now.

Dividing it up peacefully, equitably, and in a way that would satisfy everyone is impossible. Partitioning unevenly mixed countries, especially those, like Bosnia, with so many mixed families, is a nasty business. Kosovo's break with Serbia was a lot cleaner than what could be done in Bosnia or what could be done anywhere in Iraq south of the Kurdish autonomous region. James Longley captured the gruesomeness of the idea well in his documentary film, *Iraq in Fragments*. "Iraq is not something you can cut into pieces," a small child says. "Iraq is a country. How do you cut a country into pieces? With a saw?"

It's on the minds of some in Bosnia, though, and Kosovo's declaration of independence makes the question more complex than before. All Bosnians are Slavs, whether they're Serbs, Croats, or Bosniaks. The only thing that divides them is religion. The religious boundary even separates those who are not religious.

Serbs are Orthodox Christians with a geopolitically Eastern orientation. Croats are Catholics with a geopolitically Western orientation. Bosniaks are Muslims who seem confused about their geopolitical orientation, unsure if cities like Istanbul and Mecca should be at the center of their world or if it should be Brussels. The result is that Bosnia is yanked apart in at least three directions at once. Atheist Serbs in Bosnia feel a pull toward Belgrade and Moscow. Atheist Croats feel a connection to Rome. Even many atheist Bosniaks can't help but feel tied to Istanbul in some ways. Can a country even survive if it sits at the crossroads of three separate civilizations? Yugoslavia couldn't, so why should Bosnia?

Sean and I met with Samir Beglerovic from the Faculty of Islamic Studies in Sarajevo and asked him what he thought.

"What does the Muslim community of Bosnia think about the independence of Kosovo?" I said.

"Kosovo had the worst position in ex-Yugoslavia before the 1990s," he said, "so there is support for them. In the beginning all Kosovo wanted was to be a republic within Yugoslavia. They didn't allow that, so then they wanted independence, and finally they got it. People from Bosnia—Muslims and Croats—are supporting this."

"Does anyone here who isn't a Serb support the Serbian side?" I said.

"There was some talk," he said, "[about whether or not] it was good for Bosnians for Kosovo to seek independence now. They say that now, by giving Kosovo independence, Serbia is sending a clear sign to the Republika Srpska that they can do the same thing to Bosnia."

While it may seem reasonable to let the Serbs in Republika Srpska leave Bosnia if they want to for the same reason many think it is reasonable to accept Kosovo's independence from Serbia, there are grounds for rejecting the idea, and not just because it would be messy. There are also issues of justice.

"Forty-nine percent of Bosnia is Republika Srpska," Beglerovic said. "But from eighty percent of it people were killed and expelled from their lands. This is territory they won by war, nothing more."

Kosovo never expanded its borders through war inside Serbia before the declaration of independence, but the Bosnian Serb Army and affiliated paramilitary units used mass-murder and ethnic cleansing to create geographically contiguous territory purged of Croats and Bosniaks.

European countries imposed an arms embargo on all of Yugoslavia during the war, severely degrading the Bosnians' ability to defend themselves since the Serbs controlled the regular army and the Bosnians had to build one from scratch. The Serb forces had most of the weapons, and the embargo preserved the imbalance of power. Desperate for assistance, the Bosnians accepted "help" from around a thousand Arab veterans of the anti-Soviet insurgency in Afghanistan in the 1980s who volunteered to fight a "jihad" against Serbs.

As it turned out, the Arabic *Mujahideen* from the Middle East had no more effect on the war in Bosnia than they had when they ran off to Afghanistan. In each place they were basically tourists with guns who made little or no impact on the outcome of the war, or even the outcome of major battles. Some of these characters stayed in Bosnia, though, where they still live today.

Bosnia has a bit of an Islamist problem then, partly as a consequence of the so-called Afghan Arabs, but also from Saudis and other rich Gulf Arabs who swooped in after the war ended to rebuild damaged mosques in their own severe Wahhabi style and to impose a rigid interpretation of religion in a region with a relatively open and liberal European tradition.

I asked Beglerovic about it since he lives there. He belongs to a theologically moderate order of Sufi mystics and is therefore detested by Wahhabis as much as Christians, Jews, and other so-called "infidels" are.

"We have a problem and I think it is obvious," he said. "In the beginning, during the war, mostly people didn't realize what was going on. They had their priorities—how to survive, how to do this, how to do that. And after the war I think the majority didn't recognize what was going on. We have seen some changes; we have seen some things we didn't know about before—different approaches, different attitudes. There is something we didn't have before in Bosnia-Herzegovina. Mostly they were targeting the common people, not intellectuals as much. They were students that had gone to study in other countries in the East, and when they had received their MA or Ph.D. they came here to Bosnia."

"Do you think it is a big problem," I said, "or a small problem?"

"It depends," he said. "As far as individuals are concerned, we have to accept everyone, but regarding organizations and movements we have to be very careful."

"What is it exactly that the Wahhabis are trying to do here?" I said. "Are they trying to make Bosnian Muslims more conservative, or do they have a bigger agenda?"

"They say, *We have to Islamize you*," he said. "That's the notion they are using, to *Islamize*. They think that even the practicing Muslims— that means going to mosque, praying—they think they are not good enough, that they have to be better. And also that our perception of Islam is wrong."

"What is your perception of Islam according to them?" I said.

"I don't know what they think," he said. "They say it is full of innovations, things you cannot find in Islam. We made it up or got it from the interactions with the non-Muslims living here in Bosnia-Herzegovina and especially from Europe. So it is a religious position, the Islamization. *You are not Islamic enough, we have to Islamize you more*."

"What is it about your version of Islam that they don't like specifically?" I said.

"Every segment of it," he said. "Meaning our clothes, we are dressing like Europeans, the way we look. We don't say you have to wear a beard or that it has to be long. It's also the literature we are using because mostly we are leaning on the traditional scholars of Islam while they are leaning on the so-called reformers. There are lots of things. The logical aspects of Islam, the interior and exterior of the mosques, everything. Almost everything we do is wrong. It's very hard to recognize why and from where they get this kind of attitude."

I know exactly where they get this attitude. It comes from the 18th century religious scholar Muhammad ibn Abd al-Wahhab who was born and raised in the Diriyah region of Saudi Arabia. He sought to "reform" Islam by purging it of everything impure, innovative, and modern. His reactionary fundamentalist school has been slowly growing in popularity in the interior region of Saudi Arabia and has been expanding outward from there for some time, mostly as a result of Saudi petro-dollar-fueled "charity" work in other parts of the world, not only in the Arab Middle East but in non-Arab countries like Bosnia and even the United States.

"How popular are they here?" I said.

"We don't have statistics," he said. "That's our major problem. We don't do statistics. After the war, 1997 and 1998 were hard years here in Bosnia. The first shocks came to you—you do not have a job. If you want to repair your house, repair your apartment, send your kids to school, go to school yourself, you need money. Therefore you need a job, and they were hard to find. So in the beginning people were mainly disappointed with the new aspects of life in post-war Bosnia when everyone was expecting that the government would support people somehow and we wouldn't be having trouble with food and schools. And then there was this group that came in and started criticizing anyone who had any important position in the community, the government, or the political parties. The best way to recognize their strength may be from the newcomers on the Web sites, because in the print media they don't have much space. We now have very strict regulations."

"Today?" Sean said.

"Yes," Beglerovic said. "In Bosnia-Herzegovina the Regulatory Newspaper Agency, the RAK…radio stations and TV stations have to get a license from them. They are monitored. And in the beginning if you do something wrong, first you pay, then you can be banished. There are a lot of inter-religious and nationalist...let's call it bad words."

"So if you incite amongst the public," Sean said, "the government will be upset with you."

"Yes," Beglerovic said. "There are some standards we didn't have before."

"This is a problem for the Wahhabis?" I said.

"For everyone," he said, "but also for the Wahhabis because you are asking about them. The only space they can get is on Web sites."

"What do Bosnian Muslims think of NATO and the United States?" I said. "I know most Serbs don't like us, but what about your community?"

Albanians in Kosovo love the United States for saving them from mass-murder and ethnic cleansing. Bosnians, though, were left to twist in the wind and face Serbian guns alone for years with very little assistance. I would not expect Bosnian Muslims to feel the same way about Americans that Kosovar Albanians do, but some help is better than nothing, and it has not gone unnoticed.

"We consider NATO the only way for feeling secure in our land," Beglerovic said. "And it's said that the only friend we have is the United States. So that's why each time someone like Richard Holbrooke says that Bosnia could be a place for Al Qaeda, it scares us. It can mean that we lose our only friend."

"It won't happen," Sean said.

"Historically," Beglerovic said, "we had our friends in Austria and in Germany, but the only practical support we get is from the United States. I mean, okay, Germany accepted a lot of Bosnian refugees, and everyone helped in a way, but the most practical help is coming from the United States."

I have no idea where all this is going, if Bosnia will be okay or if it won't. Will the country split into pieces? Will there be more fighting? Will the Islamists become dangerous to those who live inside and outside the country? I can't say, and I won't even guess. I learned the hard way to be careful about predicting events in the Middle East, so I know better than to guess what will happen in always-complicated and hard-to-read Bosnia. There are too many unresolved problems and too many variables. But the fact that it resembles, in some ways, a Yugoslavia writ small did not leave me feeling as optimistic as I would have liked. History there isn't over. That's all but certain.

Four

The Road to Kosovo

Sean and I wished we could linger in Sarajevo for weeks, but we were time-pressed to hit the road to Kosovo. Our route was a circuitous one that would take us the long way round through Croatia, Montenegro, and Albania. When I scrutinized the map I realized the distance between these places was much larger than he or I realized when we planned our trip from afar, so we ended up checking out of the Holiday Inn and heading toward Croatia a day early.

We drove past a bizarre-looking mosque built in a post-modern style outside Sarajevo.

"I want a picture of that," I said and pulled the car into the driveway. We got out. A Muslim man left the building and glanced downward at the license plate and muttered something rude-sounding in Bosnian.

"Hi," Sean said. "We're Americans." The man just walked on.

"What was that about?" I said.

"He just stuck three fingers at me," Sean said.

"Like this?" I said and made the *tri prsta*, the three-fingered Serbian nationalist salute.

"Yeah, that," Sean said.

"Why the hell would he do that?" I said.

The *tri prsta* means different things depending upon whom you ask, but they're all related in one way or another to Serbian nationalism. Predrag Delibasic, the half-Bosnian and half-Serbian professor Sean and I met in Belgrade, told us the three fingers stand for the Serbian Orthodox Church, the Academy of Science, and the Military.

"Maybe he thought we're nationalist Serbs," Sean said, "and he was mocking us?"

I don't know. Maybe he didn't really mean to jab three fingers in that exact way, and maybe he was just annoyed that I stopped the car in his path. Either way, I didn't like how so many people looked at the license plate to figure out who we were—or supposedly were—but I found myself doing the same thing to other people and their cars after I saw that they did it to us.

Sean and I drove up one of Sarajevo's big hills to get a look at the city from above. A defunct Austro-Hungarian military fort still sits up there and looks like it was used recently by at least one armed faction in the Bosnian war. We saw several mortar-sized holes in the walls.

I parked in front of some residential homes at the steps leading up to the fort. A group of young men sat at a table in the yard in front of the car.

"Hi!" I said in English and tried to sound as American as possible. "How are you guys?"

"Hello," one of them said.

I wanted them to know we weren't Serbs in case they looked at the license plate. I wasn't paranoid and thought it awfully unlikely that they would key the car or worse if they thought we were from Belgrade, but it only took one second's worth of effort to make sure they didn't.

"We need to stop in Mostar," Sean said on our way out of the capital toward Croatia. "We have to see the Mostar Bridge."

I wanted to see it, too. It's a famous bridge built by the Ottomans in the 16th century and it was recently rebuilt after being destroyed by the Croatian Defense Council during the war in 1993.

"We also need to get to Dubrovnik before dark," I said. "This might be the only time we'll ever get to see it, and I want some pictures."

Dubrovnik is a spectacular walled city on the Croatian coast near the Montenegrin border. We booked a hotel room in Montenegro and needed to leave for Kosovo first thing the next morning, so there would be no time to go back to Dubrovnik if we missed it during daylight.

Rather than put ourselves ever further behind schedule by stopping for proper food in a restaurant, we pulled into a gas station to stock up on road food. I hoped oranges, bananas, or *anything* that had some nutritional value would be available, but gas stations all over the world sell little other than junk food, apparently. They had peanuts and pistachios, but the rest of our stock consisted of cookies, potato chips, chocolates, and croissants. And the croissants were really just Twinkies from Turkey in the *shape* of croissants.

Sean and I wanted to speed through Bosnia and get to Croatia as quickly as possible, but the Opel we rented in Belgrade drove like it had a moped engine under the hood. Step on the gas in one of those things and nothing much happens unless you're at a dead stop on a flat road. Passing slow trucks was impossible if there was a bend in the road anywhere in the same time zone.

So we tooled through Bosnia at a moderate speed, passing mass graveyards, shattered houses, villages scourged by artillery fire, and other horrifying evidence of recent atrocities that stretched from one end of the country to the other.

In one otherwise beautiful town on the shore of a lake we drove past a mosque minaret with its top shot off.

"Let's drive to that mosque," Sean said. "I want a picture of that."

"No time," I said. "We have to get to Dubrovnik before dark."

"It will just take a second," he said.

"Would you rather photograph that mosque or Dubrovnik?" I said.

"It will just take a second!" he said again. "Just make a left here."

I made a left.

"You have a second," I said.

I gave Sean a hard time, but was quietly glad he talked me into it. I *wanted* to be talked into stopping at least once in a while. We were short on time, but neither of us wanted to only see the Bosnian countryside from the inside of a car.

Two blocks away from the decapitated mosque was an intact Serbian Orthodox church. At some point this town may have looked like a model of inter-religious co-existence, but it sure doesn't now.

"Okay," I said. "Let's get to Dubrovnik."

This time Sean got behind the wheel. I had done much of the driving and needed a break.

Bosnia is a troubled country, but it's also heartbreakingly lovely. It was hard to imagine such a terrible war erupting amid such breathtaking scenery. Sean nearly ran the car off the road when we drove through a canyon between Sarajevo and Mostar that was so deep and so sheer it might have been in the Himalayas or Andes. "My *God*," he said, "look at this place!"

I was glad he was driving or I might have actually gone off the road while gawking at the mountains and canyons.

Mostar is also stunning. Sean and I couldn't just drive through it without stopping, at least briefly. And besides, we were tired of road food. Potato chips and chocolate chip cookies could pass for lunch when we were in college, but not anymore.

So we sat at an outdoor café near the recently repaired bridge, ate Bosnian kebabs, and drank from bottles of locally brewed beer as the muezzin's haunting call to prayer echoed off the looming walls of the mountains.

Parts of Bosnia look and feel like Turkey, but Mostar looks and feels like no place other than Bosnia. It's what you'd get if the Middle East and the south of France blended so thoroughly together into something different and new that what emerged no longer resembled either. It's a beautiful place and, aside from the mosques and a few blown-up buildings that hadn't been fixed yet, it *felt* no different from anywhere else in Europe. Westerners who may be afraid to visit Bosnia for its wars or for its Islam, and who may worry that places like Sarajevo and Mostar might still resemble Iraq or hyper-conservative Saudi Arabia, have no idea what they are missing. I saw no hijabs or bearded fanatics, but plenty of liberated women and their hipster boyfriends drinking beer and wine and having a wonderful time. Bosnia, despite its troubled past, is benign.

"Let's go," I said. "Mostar is great, but the sun is going down and we don't want to miss out on Dubrovnik in daylight."

We weren't far from the Croatian coast. It was obvious that many Catholic Croats live in Mostar and in the surrounding region because as we moved toward the western edge of Bosnia, I saw lots of Croatian flags flying from houses and draped over electrical wires.

The Croatian coastline itself is extraordinary. Steep hills and mountains rise sheer from the shores of the sea. Wooded islands just off the coast make the view stunning in every direction.

The sun went down as the outskirts of Dubrovnik came into view.

"We're just minutes too late," I said and sighed. "Our pictures are going to suck." I almost said we shouldn't have stopped in Mostar, but it would have been a mistake to skip it. What we needed was more time.

Dubrovnik is a medieval walled city on the mountainous shore of the Adriatic. You can't fit a car inside the old city walls because the streets are too narrow. To get there you have to pass through a gate and descend several blocks down a perilously steep staircase. Once you reach the bottom, the city opens up into something straight out of the *Lord of the Rings*. No living humans build cities like this anymore. While visiting Dubrovnik it's hard to think people from generations long dead weren't superior to us in the 21st century, at least in some ways. They certainly had a more advanced sense of aesthetics and beauty. Dubrovnik, at least the old part of the city inside the walls, I daresay is perfect.

"This is the most amazing place I have ever seen," Sean said.

I instinctively thought to object. Paris is amazing. Istanbul is amazing. The old city of Jerusalem is amazing. Does Dubrovnik really beat all of them? But I couldn't bring myself to object. If Dubrovnik isn't the most spectacular place I've ever seen, it comes awfully close.

We both said "wow" around every new corner and wondered why on earth we waited so long to visit. And why did we spend so much time in Belgrade when we could have been *here*?

I would not have wanted to be there during the war, and neither would you. At the gate leading up to the old city walls is a map that shows every site that was bombed and how much it was damaged.

"Grad Dubrovnik," it says. "City map of damages caused by the aggression on Dubrovnik by the Yugoslav Army, Serbs and Montenegrins, 1991-1992."

Dubrovnik was listed by UNESCO as a World Heritage Site twelve years before the Yugoslav Army shelled and burned it. Aside from the map, however, I saw no evidence that it had ever been under siege. The reconstruction job in Sarajevo impressed me, but they have done an even better job in Dubrovnik. I saw not a single bullet hole, nor did I see even one tile or cobblestone out of place. The reconstruction of this city was flawless.

Many Croatians still nurse a grudge against Serbs—which is answered in kind by no shortage of Serbs—for what happened during Yugoslavia's violent demise. Some Croatians would like to secede not just from Yugoslavia but even from the Balkan Peninsula, and they have felt this way for some time.

Stjepan Radić, founder of the Croatian Peasant Party in 1904, argued that "Croats are not part of the Balkans, geographically, culturally, or politically." "To him," wrote historian Frederick Bernard Singleton, "as to many Yugoslavs today, the term Balkan is not a neutral geographical designation. It contains emotive undertones, implying backwardness, squalor, and ignorance. Radić saw Croatia as a central European country, with more in common with Austria, Hungary, and Czechoslovakia than with the former Turkish territories south of the old Sava-Danube frontier."

He saw Croatia as Western, in other words. So do I. Not that I would describe Belgrade and Sarajevo as wallowing in backwardness, squalor, and ignorance, but they clearly are in the distant orbits of Moscow and Istanbul while Croatia defiantly isn't. There is no Turkish Quarter in Dubrovnik, nor is there Cyrillic lettering.

The southern half of Croatia is, however, part of the Balkan Peninsula geographically. And Croatia was involved in two of the recent wars in the former Yugoslavia. Croats were victims of ethnic cleansing and mass-murder by Serbs, but they dished out the same treatment to Serbs and Bosniaks in Croatia and Bosnia. They can't liberate themselves from geography, nor were they able to exempt themselves from the rough and dirty politics of the region, led as they were in the brutal 1990s by Franjo Tudjman, a man who lorded over Croatia as if it were a banana republic.

"It is true that Mr. Tudjman was not charged because he is dead," wrote Judge Jean-Claude Antonetti at the international war crimes tribunal in The Hague, "but alive, he would be here on the accused bench."

Still, the minute Sean and I stepped inside the walls of the ancient city, I felt that at least *this* part of Croatia really is different even though it's at the southern extreme of the country and lies below the Danube-Sava-Kupa line that commonly defines the Balkan region. So far I had half-jokingly called Bosnia and Serbia "the Middle East of Europe," but I was only half-joking. Serbian politics uncomfortably resemble politics in the Arab world while Bosniaks share the religion of most of the Arabs.

Dubrovnik, though, looks and feels emphatically Western. I felt like I had passed through an invisible barrier in the dimension and had returned "home" the instant I walked through the gate. I can't tell you what, exactly, made me think of Dubrovnik as "home." I had never been there before, I knew little about what to expect in advance, and I stayed for such a brief period that I had no time to get past the disorientation and confusion of being in a strange new city and country. But I know what "home" looks and feels like when I freshly return to it from a different part of the world, especially while my heightened sense of stranger's awareness is still at its peak.

Historian Peter F. Sugar notes Dubrovnik's unusual history in the region in *Southeastern Europe Under Ottoman Rule, 1354 - 1804*. "The relationship between the little city-state and the large empire," he wrote, "is extremely interesting and *sui generis*. Dubrovnik was the only vassal state of the Ottoman Empire whose territory was never invaded during its long vassalage, in whose internal affairs the Ottomans never interfered, and whose status was ambiguous from the point of view of Muslim-Ottoman jurisprudence."

The city once rivaled Venice and it looked the part. Most churches in Croatia are Catholic. I felt closer to Italy on the other side of the Adriatic than I did to Bosnia even though Bosnia was less than five miles away. Far more tourists poked around Dubrovnik than I had seen in Sarajevo or Belgrade.

There was an elusive and indefinable *x-factor* about the place that was unmistakably Western and I couldn't pin down what it was. I do not know why, but it was somehow obvious to me that, unlike much of the Balkan Peninsula, Dubrovnik had not been significantly transformed by the Ottomans. Its cultural and political compass points only West. The East, even if it is the Very Near or Only Just Barely East, is just on the other side of the mountain, but it is at Croatia's back.

Sean and I spent mere hours in the city and never did see it in daylight. I've promised my wife that one day I'll take her.

Recently our mutual friend Seth Gallant took a road trip in Europe by himself. Sean and I both insisted he visit Dubrovnik, but it was far off the path he had planned for himself and he had a hard time believing anywhere in the former Yugoslavia could compete with the likes of Paris and Prague. Sean and I refused to relent, though, so Seth grudgingly added Dubrovnik to his list of cities to visit, not so much because he really wanted to go, but because he wanted Sean and me to shut up and leave him alone about it.

He sent us an email after he'd been in the city a couple of days.

"Dubrovnik is the most beautiful place I've seen in the world," he wrote. "Thank you for insisting I come here."

Montenegro didn't strike me as Western the way Dubrovnik did. Montenegro is just…Montenegro.

Its name in the local language, Crna Gora, means *Black Mountain*.

The Ottomans absorbed Montenegro into their empire, but it remained a largely autonomous island of Christianity in a sea of Muslim rule much as Maronite Catholic Mount Lebanon did. Its mountains—which are riotously green with thick forest—are so tall and so sheer that it must have been nearly impossible to send in soldiers to hold ground if their purpose was to put the country's people under the boot. Anyone who seriously contemplated the oppression of Montenegrins would have looked upward in terror at the towers of forest and rock and said *never mind*. The relatively light Ottoman presence was vanquished entirely at the end of the 17th century, hundreds of years before the Ottoman empire was dismantled at the end of World War I.

Sean and I couldn't see Montenegro yet, though, because we drove along the coast in the dark. We drove past some of the world's most spectacular coastline on a moonless night and missed it entirely.

Well, almost entirely.

The wall above the ancient city of Kotor shot straight up the side of the mountain ahead of us. It was illuminated with spotlights like a shimmering and luminescent vertical Great Wall of China.

I wished we could have slowed down to see Montenegro properly in the daylight, but we had to content ourselves with seeing just part of it the next afternoon as we took the narrow winding road up into Kosovo.

The country is tiny, but it seemed like it took us all night to reach our hotel on the twisting coast road.

"Where exactly *is* our hotel, anyway?" Sean said.

"It's just outside Bar," I said.

"Bar?" he said. "The town's name is Bar? I don't trust a city with only three letters."

Kotor. Budva. Ulcinj. Bar. Who outside the Balkans has heard of these places in Montenegro?

The only thing we really saw that night, aside from the illuminated wall over Kotor, was our hotel room. It looked like the inside of the *Brady Bunch* house with its retro 1970s era décor.

I unfolded our map to plot our route for the next day. If we cut short our sleep time we could make a quick detour around Lake Skadar in Albania before heading up into Kosovo.

"And we could have breakfast in Shkodra," Sean said.

"Shkodra," I said. (The city is also known as Shkoder.) "It sounds exotic and strange. Like a city named by Klingons."

Many cities and countries in the Balkans have strange-sounding names in their original languages. Most Westerners couldn't even name which continent they belong to if their names were not translated. Some are straightforward enough: Serbia is *Srbija*, Kosovo is *Kosova*, and Macedonia is *Makedonia*. But Croatia is locally known as *Hrvatska*. (I like that name, Hrvatska. It's fun to say, and it has more gravitas than "Croatia." I think we should all start calling Croatia *Hrvatska*.)

Montenegro is *Crna Gora*.

Albania is known by Albanians as *Shqiperia*. Its name means Land of the Eagles.

"I should call up my mother," Sean said, "and tell her we just left Hrvatska, we're in Crna Gora, and we're on our way to Shqiperia. *What?* she'd say. *Where the heck are you? I thought you were in Europe!*"

Neither Sean nor I knew the first thing about Shkodra, the mysterious-sounding place in the supposedly wild north of Shqiperia where tourists just do not go. Hardly anyone went anywhere in Albania until very recently. Most outsiders' mental maps of the place might as well have been marked with the words *Here, There Be Dragons*. All I knew then is that Northern Albanian had a reputation as the most lawless place in Europe after a devastating economic and political collapse in the late 1990s.

Robert Young Pelton's Web site *Come Back Alive* still warned would-be travelers about the region where Sean and I were going under his heading *Dangerous Places*: "In just a few short years Albania has had the distinction of changing from a country with the most paranoid and overcontrolled communist state ever to a country without a state. It was tricky, but Albanians have risen to the challenge to become Europe's most lawless people at the turn of the century....Being a foreigner, unless you happen to know a couple of the local banditos, you stand an excellent chance of being fleeced. The minute you walk in the door and open your mouth, the $ sign will start ringing for just about everybody there—except you."

We went anyway. And we went there with Belgrade plates on the car.

T he majority of ethnic Albanians in Kosovo were displaced by Serb forces during Slobodan Milosevic's ethnic-cleansing campaign in 1999, so showing up in Albania with a Serbian car only made our detour more potentially dicey than it already was.

If you drive from Montenegro to Albania you will first pass through the beautiful and prosperous ethnic-Albanian region that straddles the border. The Albanians of Montenegro were lucky, I thought as we approached the customs agents, to live under Josip Broz Tito's relatively lenient communist system in Yugoslavia instead of suffering the full-bore Stalinist regime of Enver Hoxha (pronounced HOE-juh) just a few miles away in Albania proper. Hoxha ranks among the most thoroughly oppressive tyrants in the history of the human race and made Tito's Yugoslav dictatorship look libertarian by comparison.

The most enduring physical legacies of Albanian communism are the remains of more than 700,000 military bunkers Hoxha's regime installed all over the country as part of his mass militarization of the society. Everyday civilians were expected to hunker down in these things with machine guns and fight an invasion from "bourgeois imperialists" or an internal counter-revolution. Hoxha's concrete pill boxes still litter the country in fields, in backyards, on the side of the roads, and even on beaches.

Post-communist Albania was an economic catastrophe, and what little progress had been made after the dismantlement of the regime came apart in the late 1990s when both the economy and the authority of the state unraveled. Albania—especially Northern Albania where Sean and I were headed—became by far the most dangerous and chaotic place in Europe.

"Bunkers!" Sean said.

Sure enough, just up ahead, perhaps only a mile or so past the border, were a handful of derelict cement domes. I pulled the car over. We got out to take pictures. A large group of children and their schoolteacher excitedly surrounded us.

"Hello! Hello!" the kids said. "Mister! Mister! What's your name?"

I felt like I was in Iraq—and I don't mean that in a bad way. You can't go anywhere in Iraq, especially not with a camera slung around your neck, without being mobbed by children. This never happened in Serbia, Bosnia, Croatia, or Montenegro, but it happened instantly upon arrival in Albania. Albanians struck me at once as very different indeed from the South Slavic peoples.

"There is a very nice view on top of this hill," the schoolteacher said to Sean. "Follow us up, I will show you."

So we followed the lady with the kids in tow up the hill above Hoxha's bunkers. Children grabbed my arm and excitedly asked my name as we climbed.

"My name is Michael," I said to a young boy. "What's yours?"

"Mario," he said and grinned.

"Mister, where are you from?" said a little girl.

"America," I said.

"Yay!" The kids cheered.

Albania is fanatically pro-American, almost absurdly so, which is perhaps a bit counterintuitive to many Americans since it is at least nominally a Muslim-majority country.

"You should have seen President Bush's face when he came to Albania," an ethnic Albanian man later said to me in Kosovo. "All over Western Europe he was met by protests, but the entire country of Albania turned out to welcome him. He was *so* happy. You could see it on his face."

Albanian pro-Americanism resembles that of Poland and Iraqi Kurdistan, but it's more expressive and emotional. The unspeakably oppressive communist regime pushed Albanians strongly into the U.S.-led Western camp, and the humanitarian rescue of Albanians in Kosovo from Slobodan Milosevic's tyrannical despotism bolstered that sentiment even more.

More kids tugged at me and wanted their pictures taken. I was overwhelmed and more than a little bit startled.

Slavs in Serbia, Bosnia, Croatia, and Montenegro are friendly people for the most part, but they are not exuberantly so, at least not to strangers. They are a bit friendlier than Western Europeans, perhaps, but their temperament is still European. These Albanians, by contrast, at least these children, were as ecstatically friendly as Middle Easterners whose hospitality and warmth are deservedly legendary.

The view from the top of the hill opened up to reveal a classic subtropical Mediterranean landscape of distant mountains, red tiled roofs, and tilled fields. It was hard to believe a regime that was just as odious as the Kim family dynasty in North Korea brutalized such a bucolic place so very recently.

We needed to get back in the car and head into the city of Shkodra for a brief coffee and breakfast before we ran out of time. Our rented car was due later that day in Podgorica, the capital of Montenegro, and we still had no idea how we would travel to Kosovo after dropping it off.

Shkodra, by European standards, is not doing well. It's ramshackle. Many communist-era housing blocks are still run down and drab, though some have been improved with coats of paint. Many of the traditional buildings that weren't bulldozed for the sake of "progress" are still rough around the edges. Cars weave all over the road as if their operators were still learning to drive.

"It looks like Mexico," Sean said.

In some ways it does. The traditional architecture is of the Mediterranean style, as are traditional (Spanish) buildings in Mexico. The styles aren't the same, but they are recognizably similar. And Albania's barely controlled chaos, at least in this part of the country, felt much more Latin American than European.

Balkan people are notoriously bad drivers, but after living in Beirut for a while I thought traffic everywhere in the former Yugoslavia was perfectly civilized. Albanians drive just like Lebanese—which is to say, more aggressively than drivers I have seen anywhere else in the world. Lanes don't exist. Stop signs are suggestions. The right of way goes to whoever hits the gas pedal first.

I admit to enjoying that kind of traffic. People in these countries only look like bad drivers at first to people from outside. What they are is aggressive, and their reflexes and awareness are much more sharply honed than those of people who routinely drive in tame and predictable traffic. It's fun to join in if you know how, but fatigue sets in much faster. You can't drive on autopilot in Lebanon or Albania. If you try you'll be jolted out of it in terror almost immediately.

How different this place is from Yugoslavia! I could not help but wonder: is Kosovo also like this, or has it been Yugo-ized? How much of what I was seeing was a product of the Albanian cultural character and how much was a delayed combustive reaction to Enver Hoxha's ridiculous tyranny?

Sean and I had no time to find food in Shkodra, so we decided to just stop for coffee at a small brightly painted café on a main road.

"Hello, hello!" two men said as I sat in a hard metal chair at the table next to them. They saw my camera and gestured for me to take their picture, so I did. As it turned out, it wasn't just the children of Albania who were outgoing and gregarious toward visitors.

My chair was right next to a generator. I have no idea what shape Albania's electrical grid is in, but seeing a plugged-in generator outside a café was not a good sign.

When it was time to pay our waiter for the coffee, I realized we had no Albanian leks, the national currency.

"Do you see an ATM around anywhere?" I said to Sean.

"You're going to go to an ATM just to pay for coffee?" he said.

"Well," I said, "I have some American money. Maybe they'll take that." I seriously doubted the waiter had any interest in currency from

Serbia, Bosnia, Croatia, or Montenegro.

I pulled an American twenty dollar bill out of my backpack and waved it at the waiter. "Will you take American money?" I said.

"I don't know how much that is," he said. "What's the exchange rate?"

"I have no idea," I said. I was going to ask him. "We just got here."

"The coffee is from house," he said.

"Are you *sure*?" I said. "Here, just take the twenty." I didn't expect anything for free and didn't mind overpaying if it would save me a trip to the ATM that would leave me saddled with extra currency I couldn't use.

"No, no," he said. "I can't take your money. The coffee is from house. Welcome to Albania."

It's too bad we couldn't have stayed longer. From the car it appeared Shkodra has a number of high-end restaurants and cool places to hang out, in addition to having the usual European consumer goods for sale alongside more basic shops that cater to people who don't earn much money. Shkodra is a city in transition, which is often the most rewarding kind of place to visit.

There are many statues of national heroes in town, and the one of Isa Boletini, who led battles for independence in Kosovo against both the Ottomans and the Serbs in the late 1800s, stood out for its brazen militancy. This guy was a barrel chested badass with an enormous moustache, a pistol tucked in his pants, and belts of ammunition draped over his shoulders. Albania is in Europe, but it's comically un-European in so many ways. And it's not even remotely Islamic. I hardly saw mosques, let alone headscarves. This place is the wild west of Mexico on the Med.

Sean and I drove north out of town to catch the road into Podgorica, Montenegro's capital.

"There's a lot more money in the countryside," Sean said, "than there is in the city. It looks like everyone with the money to build a new house would rather build it out here."

That seemed right. Shkodra wasn't a slum-ridden city, but it still looked a bit rough. The countryside just to the north looked solidly middle class and above.

More of Hoxha's crazy bunkers were in place near the Montenegrin border—a lot more. Whole lines of them stretched across the countryside from the road toward the mountains just alongside and parallel to the border with the former Yugoslavia.

Montenegro is a tiny country. Only half a million people live there today. The capital is home to fewer than 150,000. Of course Montenegro was part of the much larger and more muscular Yugoslavia when the bunkers were built, but it still struck me as patently absurd that all these pill boxes were set up along the border of such a moderate and non-expansionist country.

Sean and I waited in line behind two cars at the border. A handful of men stood around smoking cigarettes while waiting to get their passports stamped out. One glanced down at our license plate and went bug-eyed, reminding me that we rented our car in Belgrade. "You took a *Serb* car to *Albania*?" I'm pretty sure that's what he said. He might have said, "You're *Serbs* and you went to *Albania*?" I can't translate precisely, but it was one or the other.

"We're Americans!" I said in a cheery voice. "We rented the car in Belgrade, but we're Americans."

"Aha!" he said and laughed as if that explained everything.

"The price is one Euro per kilometer," said the taxi driver at Montenegro's international airport.

"You're kidding," I said.

"One Euro per kilometer," he said again. "It is the standard rate."

The drive from Podgorica, the capital, to Prishtina in Kosovo is around 300 kilometers.

"That's way too much money," I said. Sean and I would be paying the guy almost one hundred dollars an hour. It was not going to happen. It would be better to take a bus or buy a plane ticket than hire a taxi into

Kosovo if that's how much it costs. "We're going to have to discuss this," I said.

A Europcar employee met us at the taxi stand to pick up our returned rental car. He overheard our conversation with the driver.

"I can call a friend of mine," he said quietly and conspiratorially. "This guy is charging you too much money. "

"Terrific," I said. "Yes, please call your friend."

"Just don't tell this guy I'm calling someone for you," he said. "Tell him you'll take a bus or something."

So we found ourselves another driver who agreed to take us to Prishtina for less than half the amount we were first quoted. His name was Ratko and he spoke almost no English. His vocabulary was hardly better than my limited knowledge of his. Sean and I more or less gave up trying to engage him in conversation and just let him drive.

The road to Kosovo from Montenegro is more spectacular than even the road to Dubrovnik. Few places in the world can boast of such dramatic mountainous scenery. I signaled to Ratko that I wanted him to pull over for a second so I could photograph the heart-stopping canyon we were driving through, but he dismissively waved me off and pointed in the direction we were heading, telling me, I was pretty sure, that the view was even better ahead.

He was right. The road followed a small river at the bottom of a narrow canyon that looked even deeper than Hells Canyon, the deepest in the United States, on the Oregon-Idaho border. This Montenegrin scenery has no peer that I've seen anywhere in the world. It is so deep and so steep and so galactically *huge* that I can hardly imagine a better one anywhere. Now I could really understand why the Ottomans had such a hard time with this country. There's no way terrain like this could ever be conquered and held against the will of the people who live there. Taking Switzerland would be easier.

The dense and dark forests of inland Montenegro look the way the Mediterranean region in general must have looked before the deforestation that disfigures most of it now. So few people live in this country that even alongside the major highway into Kosovo is still mostly pristine wilderness. As far as I know, such Mediterranean forest doesn't exist anywhere else.

Sean tried to ask Ratko a few questions using simple words and improvised sign language. He made fists with both hands and placed them together. "Montenegro and Serbia," he said, then pulled his fists apart quickly to refer to Montenegro's declaration of independence from Serbia two years earlier. "Good or bad?" For a brief period what was left of the Yugoslav rump state called itself Serbia and Montenegro before the latter finally gave up on Belgrade like its cousins had and decided to go its own way.

"Good!" Ratko said.

Sean did the two-fisted maneuver again, only this time he said, "Serbia and Kosovo." He was trying to figure out what Ratko thought of Kosovo's declaration of independence from Serbia.

"Good!" Ratko said again.

So far, everyone Sean and I spoke to in the former Yugoslavia thought Kosovo's newfound independence was a good thing—including the Serbs we had coffee with in Belgrade. The Serbs we met, though, are cosmopolitan writers and intellectuals far out of step with most of their countrymen.

"Montenegro and the European Union?" Sean said. If countries as troubled as Romania could join the European Union, why not placid and prosperous Montenegro?

"No!" Ratko said. "European Union...big Yugoslavia."

I have a hard time imagining how a tyrant and mass-murderer like Slobodan Milosevic would ever be in charge of the European Union, but Ratko's skepticism still made some sense after the violent disintegration of the out-sized multinational federation he used to live in. The European Union is a strictly Western club, but it nevertheless includes member states that are drastically different from each other culturally, politically, and economically. There isn't a civilizational divide that rips through the heart of it the way there is in the former Yugoslavia, but it is unwieldy, spread thin, and in perpetual crisis.

After dinner at a restaurant in a cold valley far above sea level, I decided to nap in the car. I was tired and couldn't see the scenery in the dark, anyway. Sean woke me an hour later as we neared the Kosovo border.

"Mike," he said and shook me awake. "I think if we keep taking this road we're going to end up in Mitrovica. Isn't Mitrovica that dangerous city in Kosovo that we're supposed to avoid?"

"It's fine," I said. "The road goes up to South Mitrovica, but doesn't cross into North Mitrovica. North Mitrovica is the place we need to stay out of."

"Okaaaay," Sean said. He sounded skeptical, but I knew South Mitrovica was fine. North Mitrovica was the place to avoid.

The north side of town was a bad place for Americans because it's the most politically radicalized of the Serb cities in Kosovo and it's the most unstable and violent. Mitrovica used to be a relatively normal mixed Serb-Albanian city, but Albanians have since moved to the south side of the city, and Serbs live almost exclusively in the north across the bridge over the Ibar River that cuts the city in half.

Self-described Bridge Watchers—bands of political radicals, former paramilitary fighters, and garden variety troublemakers—had been standing watch on the Serb side of the bridge and harassing those who cross to the southern Albanian side. Sometimes those who attempt to cross were ganged up on by mobs and beaten up on the spot.

Rioting exploded throughout the Serb side the previous month when U.N. soldiers and police tried to clear out a courthouse occupied by Serbian nationalists opposed to Kosovo's declaration of independence. Tanks were sent into the streets. More than 100 people were wounded in clashes. A Serb demonstrator was shot in the head. A police officer from Ukraine was killed by a hand grenade. Kosovo north of the Ibar isn't Iraq, but it's also not a place Sean and I had any business going by ourselves at night. Every single person I checked in with about traveling to North Mitrovica—including American soldiers and police officers stationed in

Kosovo—warned me to stay out of there unless I was accompanied by soldiers from NATO.

But the road on my map only passed through South Mitrovica, the safe Albanian side.

"I think we're almost to the border," Sean said.

When we reached the last Montenegrin town before the border, Ratko found a civilian man on the sidewalk and pulled the car alongside him to get directions. The man on the street told Ratko which way to go and gestured left and right turns with his hands. Ratko then asked the man a question. The man laughed and shrugged and appeared slightly nervous on our behalf. Sean and I assumed Ratko asked if it was safe for us to drive into Kosovo, and the man on the street figured it *probably* was, but he couldn't be sure.

The road plunged rapidly in absolute darkness from the granite mountains of Montenegro toward the green valleys of Kosovo. There were no street lights, no city lights, no front porch lights, and no oncoming headlights. We were alone on a remote frontier road.

Towering Montenegro must make a spectacular backdrop to the west from Kosovo, I thought, and I anticipated looking back in our current direction in daylight from the new country below.

We quickly cleared Montenegro's customs and got exit stamps in our passports. Then houses reappeared suddenly in the darkness before we reached the entry point on the other side.

"I guess we're in Kosovo now," I said.

"Yes, Kosovo," Ratko said.

I felt a small flush of excitement. Here was the country where Europe's most recent conflict was waged. American soldiers were still stationed there to prevent another round of war and ethnic cleansing. In that way, it's the closest thing Europe has to Iraq.

But where was Kosovo's entry point?

Ratko's headlights illuminated a sign welcoming us to the Republic of Serbia.

"That's strange," I said to Sean. "Kosovo declared independence from Serbia, but they still haven't taken that sign down?"

"I'll bet that sign isn't long for this world," Sean said.

We saw the entry point up ahead. A gigantic Serbian flag hung on a pole next to the customs house.

"Oh shit," I said. "We went the wrong way. We aren't in Kosovo. We're in *Serbia*. This is the road from Montenegro to *Belgrade*, not to Kosovo." Ratko thought he could take us to Prishtina by crossing the bridge from North Mitrovica—the one place in the country even American combat veterans from the Iraq war told us to stay out of. Did he have no idea what he was doing?

A Serb policeman stepped out of the customs house. Ratko had been speeding down the mountain, and the officer held up his open hand for Ratko to stop and stared at him furiously for approaching the post at high speed.

"The road we were *supposed* to take," I said, "goes to *South* Mitrovica."

"We have to turn around and go back," Sean said.

"It's too late now," I said. "We're here. First we have to get past this border post."

Ratko stepped out of the car, spoke to the Serb policeman, and handed over our passports. I heard him say "Prishtina."

Great, I thought. *Now the Serb police know we're trying to get to Prishtina.* Most Arab states ban entry to anyone with an Israeli stamp in his passport. Likewise, Serbia bans entry to anyone with a Kosovo stamp in his passport. It was entirely possible that the border police would throw us out of the country before we could even get in now that Ratko told them what we were doing. I tried to imagine Americans traveling from Lebanon to Syria and telling the border police that they were on their way to Israel. It would not go over well. Had Ratko just unknowingly done the Balkan equivalent?

The officer took Ratko inside the customs house.

"They're yelling at each other," Sean said.

He was right. I could hear them. I sunk in my car seat and rubbed my eyes.

But Ratko came back a few minutes later with entry stamps in our passports. "Okay," he said. Then he drove us toward Kosovo. I looked at my map and figured out where we were. Kosovo was only twenty or so miles away.

"We have to say something about North Mitrovica," Sean said. "The police officer didn't warn him. He has no idea what he's doing."

"I know it," I said. I turned on the dome light, pointed at the map, and gestured for Ratko to pull over.

Ratko pulled over.

I didn't know how to tell him about the hazards of going through North Mitrovica. He hardly understood any English at all. So I traced the road on the map with my finger, and when my fingertip reached Mitrovica I made a slashing motion across my throat.

Ratko freaked out.

Of course, I was exaggerating. No one would slit our throats in North Mitrovica. It wasn't *that* bad. But I didn't know how else to say "danger" in improvised sign language. Ratko and I shared at most two dozen words of vocabulary.

"No, no, no, no, no," Ratko said.

"Yes, yes, yes," I said.

I couldn't convince him, in part because he thought I was trying to convince him the situation was more dire than it actually was.

Ratko pointed outside. "Kosovo," he said.

"No," I said. "We are not in Kosovo. We're in *Serbia*." I pointed outside. "Serbia."

He had no idea where we were.

I pointed behind us. "Serb police," I said.

"International police," he said.

"No!" I said.

"He wore a Serbian uniform," Sean said. "The sign said *Welcome to Serbia*. They're flying the Serbian flag. International soldiers wouldn't do any of that."

"If he were an international police officer," I said to Sean, "he would have spoken English to us, not Serbian to Ratko."

"Of course," Sean said. "Doesn't he get that?"

Ratko had an idea. He punched a number into his cell phone, spoke briefly to the person on the other end of the line, and handed the phone over to me. "Serbian friend," he said. "English."

Perfect.

I took the phone from Ratko.

"Hi," I said to the Serb stranger on the other end of the line.

"Hello, Mister Michael," the man said.

"Do you know what's going on?" I said. "Ratko is trying to drive us to Prishtina from North Mitrovica. Do you know about the Bridge Watchers?"

"Yes," he said. "I know."

"Can you explain the situation to him for me please?" I said.

"Listen, Mister Michael," he said. "I follow the news, I know what you are talking about. There was a problem with some extremists, yes, but the situation has been resolved."

"Are you *sure*?" I said.

"Yes," he said. "I am sure. I follow the situation very closely from Belgrade."

It was certainly possible. Reporters often let the world know when violence and mayhem break out and rarely bother to fill the rest of us in when the trouble quiets down. *If it bleeds, it leads.* If there are no more riots, beatings, or body counts in North Mitrovica, word doesn't get out. Serb reporters, though, are more likely to cover the situation than Western reporters because Serbs are directly involved. So I crossed my fingers and hoped Ratko's friend in Belgrade was right.

I handed the phone back to Ratko. "Okay," I said. "Let's go."

"What did he say?" Sean said.

"He said it's resolved," I said. "He's sure of it. I don't know, but somebody is about to be proven right or wrong by reality."

We reached the entry point into Kosovo. It was manned by German soldiers. Ratko rolled down the window.

"Hi!" I said to the soldier who spoke perfect English. "We're trying to get to Prishtina. Can we get through this way?"

"Yes, of course," the soldier said. "You can pass."

"There's no more trouble on the bridge?" I said.

"Not today," he said and handed back our passports. "The way is clear now. Enjoy your stay in Kosovo."

Ratko slowly drove past a long line of tanks, armored personnel carriers, and other NATO military vehicles.

"Montenegro good!" he said loudly after we cleared what briefly looked like a war zone.

Sean and I laughed. There are no tanks on the streets of Montenegro.

I felt relieved after talking to the German soldier. If the road was safe up ahead, he should know. But we still hadn't cleared the Mitrovica bridge into the Albanian region of Kosovo, and I couldn't fully relax until we did.

Serbian national flags were flown from houses even though we were no longer in Serbia. Serbs on both sides of the border insist Kosovo is Serbia even though it is not, at least not anymore.

We drove past a mosque with the top of its minaret blown off. It looked like a gigantic pencil that had been snapped in two.

KFOR (NATO's Kosovo Force) billboards showing two NATO soldiers and a helicopter had been erected in this Serb enclave of Kosovo. I thought it highly unlikely that Serbs in North Mitrovica appreciated seeing those every day.

"You know we're banned from going to Serbia now, right?" I said to Sean.

"*What*?" he said.

"We just got entry stamps into Serbia," I said, "but no corresponding exit stamps. If we leave through the Kosovo airport and don't go back out through Serbia, they will know we visited Kosovo. And they won't let us back in."

"Are you sure?" he said.

"Yep," I said. "We'll have to do a stamp run to conceal our visit to

Kosovo or we'll be no more welcome in Serbia than we would be in Syria with Israeli stamps."

Sean groaned. "I wanted to show my wife Belgrade," he said.

"Then you have to get a new passport."

He needed a new one anyway. His current passport was stamped when he visited the Turkish Republic of Northern Cyprus, so he's banned from visiting Greece. Serbia and Greece are the only Balkan countries that act like Arab countries by trying to control the international travel habits of foreign tourists, businessmen, and journalists.

Ratko had no idea how to find the bridge in North Mitrovica to the south side of town, so he asked a random stranger, a young Serb man, in the middle of the night for directions. The young man told Ratko to follow him in his car, and we were taken to another bridge, a smaller one—*not* the infamous crossing guarded by the thuggish Bridge Watchers—and we crossed into the Albanian region of Kosovo.

"We made it," I said when I saw a sign that said *Kosova*—the Albanian spelling.

A little more than an hour later, the brightly lit skyline of Prishtina loomed ahead just over a hill.

"At last," I said. It was two o'clock in the morning.

Ratko didn't know how to find our hotel. I showed him my printed map, but it didn't help because none of us knew where we were. So he pulled into a gas station and asked the attendant for help. The attendant shrugged. A young Albanian man who looked like a Seattle-area hipster stepped out of his car and came over.

"Hi," I said. "We're trying to find the Hotel Afa. Do you know where it is?"

"Let me see," he said and looked at the map. "Yes, I know where that is."

Ratko spoke to the young man in Serbian.

"Um," the Albanian said. He understood Serbian, as do all Albanians in Kosovo who were schooled there before the 1999 war. But they do not like to speak the language of their former oppressors. He looked at me with a pained expression on his face. "Does he speak..." he said. Then he sighed. "Never mind." He then spoke to Ratko in fluent Serbian.

"He's Montenegrin," I tried to add helpfully, referring to Ratko.

"It's okay," the Albanian man said and laughed, "it's okay." He got back in his car and escorted us all the way to our hotel.

"Thank you," Sean and I said when we arrived. "Thank you so much."

"Of course," the man said and shook hands with all three of us. "Welcome to Kosova."

Two days later, Sean and I met two American police officers on a training mission in the charming Ottoman-era city of Prizren. He and I still hadn't figured out the real story in North Mitrovica, and thought these men might know. One was from Texas and spoke in a very slow drawl. The other was from Southern California.

"Was it dangerous for us in North Mitrovica?" Sean said.

"Yes," the officer from California said. "There are some real extremists up there and it only takes one to ruin your night."

"The road is open now, though," Sean said. "So the situation has been resolved?"

"No," the officer said. "This is by *no* means resolved. Nothing in Kosovo has been resolved. We're at the very beginning of a new stage here."

Five

An Abominable Blood-Logged Plain

"The war in Bosnia will look like a tea party if Serbian nationalism runs wild in Kosovo." - U.S. Representative Eliot Engel

"The whole world is a vast Kosovo, an abominable blood-logged plain." - Rebecca West

Strange country, Kosovo. It's European, but it isn't Christian. It has a Muslim majority, but it's one of the most pro-American countries on earth. Foreign soldiers are hailed as liberators and defenders rather than occupiers. Most Western countries recognize its independence from Serbia, but hardly any Arab countries have done so—partly, perhaps, because Israelis as well as Americans are thought of as friends and allies. The United Nations is widely perceived by locals as incompetent, offensive, corrupt, and deserving of banishment.

The capital, Prishtina, is a hard place to love at first sight. Never before had I seen a European city so thoroughly disfigured and degraded by communist architecture. Very little of old Prishtina remains. Nearly every structure left standing was built after World War II when aesthetic standards precipitously plunged all over the world and in no place more than in the communist bloc. Brutal monstrosities are commonplace in Eastern Europe, but in Prishtina you will find them even throughout the city center where more attractive traditional buildings should be.

Newer construction is a bit softer on the eyes, as it is most places in the world, but there is no urban planning and no formal or informal design code. Houses, apartment buildings, and office towers are often built illegally, without permits, higgledy-piggledy and very half-assedly wherever they happen to fit. I've not seen anywhere else in Europe that looks as outlandishly goofish as this place.

Property taxes don't kick in until construction is completed, so unfinished houses are literally everywhere. Prishtina at first glance is a jarring assault on the senses and a devastating rebuke to both communism and modernism. My heart yearned for the ornamentation, tiles, and cobblestones that have been lost.

It wouldn't be fair, though, to judge Kosovars on their built environment. The average person who lives in Prishtina is no more responsible for its botched urban design than people who live anywhere else—and that was doubly true when Kosovo was ruled by a communist dictatorship that was foreign in all but name. The only other European country I've seen with so much physical evidence of decades of oppression and misrule is Albania.

The smaller Kosovar city of Prizren, though, still looks more or less like it did before the arrival of totalitarian bureaucrats with their bulldozers, their clipboards, and their Plans. Prizren looks, as Prishtina once did, like the Eastern-Western hybrid that it is. It looks vaguely Turkish, specifically Kosovar, and thoroughly European with its red tiled roofs, its balconies, its wedding cake ornamentation on the facades, its framed vertical windows, its pedestrian-friendly streets without cars, its outdoor cafés, and its soaring churches and mosques. This is a city you'll want to visit if you ever go there on holiday.

Hardly any tourists visit Kosovo, even though parts of it really are charming and the prices are some of the lowest in Europe. Two short years before the ill-fated date of September 11, 2001, Kosovo still resembled the "blood-logged plain" Rebecca West famously described in *Black Lamb and Grey Falcon*. So it's off almost everyone's radar. Most who think of Kosovo at all still assume it's hostile or dangerous even though it is neither.

It does, however, remind me of other countries that were blood-logged until recently. In 2003, *New York Times* columnist Thomas Friedman belatedly discovered Poland. "After two years of traveling almost exclusively to Western Europe and the Middle East," he wrote, "Poland feels like a geopolitical spa. I visited here for just three days and got two years of anti-American bruises massaged out of me." That's exactly how I felt when I traveled to Iraqi Kurdistan, and how I felt upon my arrival in Kosovo.

American flags fly in front of private homes, private businesses, and public buildings. They are sold at sidewalk kiosks all over the country, along with T-shirts thanking the United States in English. I saw spray-painted graffiti on a wall in a village that said, "Thanks USA and Bush."

President George W. Bush is deeply admired in both Kosovo and Albania, but no U.S. president tops Bill Clinton in the public affection department. A main street leading into Prishtina's downtown was renamed Bill Clinton Boulevard. Vizier Mustafa sculpted an 11-foot a statue of Clinton, which has since been erected there. "He is our savior," Mustafa told a Reuters reporter. "He saved us from extermination." Small businesses are named after him, too.

The Hotel Victory sports the world's second largest replica of the Statue of Liberty on its roof. A taxi company named Victory put the statue on its doors. I found another replica on someone's private property in the small ethnically mixed town of Vitina.

"We are more pro-American than you are," one young Kosovar told me.

"We really like Americans here," a waiter said when he learned where I hail from. "Americans are our best friends in the world. UK is second."

"We appreciate that," I said. "Some people don't like us."

"Bad people," he said.

Restaurants abound with American names: Memphis, Hemingway, Route 66. I even found a patisserie and disco bar named Hillary, after Hillary Clinton.

I stood in front of "Hillary" and snapped a couple of pictures. A man rose from an outdoor table and said something to me in Albanian.

"Do you speak English?" I said.

"I asked you why you are taking pictures of my café," he said. He sounded slightly annoyed and suspicious, but only slightly.

"I'm American," I said. "And I like your sign."

"You are from USA?" he said. "Please come in!"

I walked up the stairs and stepped inside.

"Look," he said. "This is even better." And he showed me enormous pictures of both Bill and Hillary Clinton on the wall.

"What is your name?" he said.

"Michael," I said.

"I am Ilir," he said. "Ilir Durmishi. It is Christian name."

"Ah," I said. "So you're Christian."

"No," he said. "I am Muslim. My father just wanted me to have a Christian name."

He gave me two shots of espresso and a cigarette while we talked American politics.

"Do you think Hillary will win?" he said. This was shortly before she lost the Democratic Party's primary nomination to Barack Obama in 2008.

"It's possible," I said, though I doubted she would.

"I think she will win," he said. "I like Hillary, but I love Bill. He is my guy. You understand why?"

"Of course," I said. And I did. His country wouldn't exist if it were not for Bill Clinton.

"Kosova good?" he said.

"Kosova good," I said.

"Serbia?" he said.

What was I supposed to say? I didn't want to say "Serbia good" and offend him, nor did I want to condemn an entire country just to appease him. I split the difference and made a so-so motion with my hand while bracing myself for what he might say.

"There are good people and bad people in Serbia," he said. I relaxed. He was reasonable. "Maybe the leadership is bad, but some Serbs are good. I have Serb friends here. They like to come and have coffee in my café."

After we chatted a few more minutes, I fished into my pocket for some money to pay for the coffee.

"No," he said. "It is from house. God bless you."

Later I had coffee with a young Albanian man just around the corner from Ilir's Hillary Clinton café.

"Kosovo is a success because we wanted a change," he said. "We are not like Iraqis or Palestinians who don't want change and seem to enjoy living in poverty. Here everyone is thinking about progress and the future."

The past, though, is always present in Kosovo. Events leading up to the bitter separation from Serbia aren't discussed all that often, but it's impossible to think about Kosovo's independence without recalling the blood-logged events leading up to it.

When the future of Yugoslavia looked dim and precarious, Slobodan Milosevic looked for a way to rise in power and keep it. He found one when he transformed himself from a communist apparatchik to a Serbian nationalist at the expense of Christian and Muslim Albanians, atheists as well as Muslims in Bosnia, cosmopolitan Serbs who hated his fire and bigotry, and Catholic Croats.

He summarily revoked Kosovo's political autonomy and purged thousands of Albanians from their jobs in Kosovo's government sector— which was an enormous sector since the system was communist—for no other reason than because they were not Serbs. He replaced their police officers with his own. As Yugoslavia came apart in Bosnia, Slovenia, and Croatia, Albanians formed their own parallel institutions and civil society entirely apart from Milosevic's oppressive regime. Ibrahim Rugova, the literary academic and pacifist, became the widely respected leader of this parallel state and presided over a movement committed to non-violent civil resistance.

Milosevic ramped up the oppression, though, and crushed Kosovo beneath the treads of his tanks. Massacres and brutality predictably followed. Rugova's steadfast insistence on a pacifist response led to his temporary marginalization and the rise of the Kosovo Liberation Army (KLA) guerrilla movement.

Thousands were murdered, raped, ethnically cleansed, tortured, and "disappeared." Neither side was angelic. There are no innocents in the Balkans. Milosevic, though, had the Yugoslav Army at his disposal, and well-trained and well-armed Serb paramilitary fighters who called themselves Chetniks. The KLA, by contrast, had a relatively small number of angry and poorly-trained men with meager equipment.

Pictures of the missing were still on display in central Prishtina when I arrived. I swallowed hard while remembering scenes just like it in New York City after Al Qaeda's violent assault on Lower Manhattan. It is extremely unlikely that any of these people are still alive.

Full-blown war broke out in 1999 between NATO and the largely ineffective KLA on one side, and the remnants of the Yugoslav Army and Serb paramilitaries on the other. Milosevic's forces were eventually driven from Kosovo. NATO and Russian forces moved in on the ground, and the KLA was disbanded. Rugova, the pacifist, was elected the first president of a de-facto independent Kosovo once non-violence was a safe and viable option again. This was one of the few times in history when a pacifist was elected in the wake of a popular guerrilla war.

Sean and I met with entrepreneur Luan Berisha who experienced all this as a civilian. Before we had a chance to cover the war, though, he wanted to get a few things out of the way.

"Listen," he said. "All Albanians, all Kosovars, feel more close in all ways to the West than to the Arab world. Why? Because none of the Arab League countries have recognized Kosovo's independence. The reason why is because Libya and many other countries are linked with Serbia. Israel would have recognized us by now, but politically they can't. If they do, we are automatically doomed for another fifty-nine Muslim countries not to recognize us. I think very highly of Israel. I like Jewish people a lot."

I knew before I traveled to Kosovo that Albanians think highly of Jews and of Israel, but I was surprised by how often it came up in conversation when I wasn't even thinking about it. Albanians differ radically from Arabs in almost every cultural and political respect you can think of, but no difference, I think, is more salient than this one.

"We have very much in common with Israel," he said. "I would never side with the Muslim side to wipe Israel off the face of the world. Ninety percent of Kosovo feels this way. We sympathize a lot with the people who have suffered the same fate as us. We were Muslims even in the Second World War—stronger Muslims than we are now—but even then we protected them with our lives. Our grandfathers protected the Jews wherever they were in the region."

A large percentage of Kosovars are atheists and agnostics, but Berisha described himself as a Muslim—not as a nominal Muslim by family heritage only, but as a practicing Muslim who prays and visits the mosque. Yet he took Sean and me to one of Prishtina's finest restaurants and ordered bottles of red wine for the three of us to share. He drank more alcohol than Sean or I did.

"What was the war like in 1999?" I said. "We watched it on TV."

"The situation became more dangerous," Berisha said, "because the Serbs became more aggressive. They used more ruthless methods."

They certainly did. Ninety percent of ethnic Albanians in Kosovo were displaced, or "cleansed" by Serb military and paramilitary forces. Almost half were driven out of the country entirely. These people never would have been able to return to their homes if not for the U.S. and NATO. That was the point of driving them out in the first place.

"I sent food support and other needed supplies to the population affected by the war," Berisha said. "That means I had the opportunity to visit the areas directly affected. War zones. In Prishtina, it was normal. Normal in the sense that we had gotten used to being beaten by Serb police and to being offended for the last ten years. The lights were on. It was daily life, nothing new. But in the countryside they were having very bad experiences. I saw dead bodies on the road."

Hardly anyone in Kosovo rode out the war without incident, including Berisha.

"I was with my parents," he said, "my whole family. Fifteen of us were sent to a train station at gunpoint."

"This actually happened to you?" I said. "In 1999?"

"Yes," he said, "in 1999. We were expelled from Prishtina, central Prishtina. Old town. The Serbs came to my house. It was a close neighborhood, and we had to open walls that separated the houses so if the Serbs came we could run through the walls from house to house. Now, after thirteen days, on the fourteenth day, a Serb neighbor came to my house and he said *Luan, call your dad.* I called my dad. My Serb neighbor said *For your well-being, as your neighbor, I am advising you to take minimal belongings and leave. Because tomorrow they will come and kill everybody they find here.*"

It's worth underscoring the fact that Berisha's *Serb* neighbor intervened on his family's behalf. Not everyone who gets caught up in violent conflicts like these behaves badly. Not in the Middle East, and not in the Balkans.

It would be wrong indeed to assume every Serb in the region supported what Milosevic's armed forces did. It would also be wrong to assume Albanians were only passive victims and never aggressors themselves.

Sometimes I have a hard time understanding why I'm drawn to places like Kosovo and Iraq where human beings treat each other despicably. I might not be able to do it if it weren't for the stories of decency and heroism that I also uncover.

Here is one of those stories: An Albanian man I met and casually befriended ran into the burning house of his Serb neighbors and saved the lives of two people, at great risk to his own, during retaliatory attacks by an enraged Albanian mob.

"Did you see your Serb neighbors again after you saved them?" I said.

"Yes," he said.

"What did they say?" I said.

"They said, *thank you.*"

At times I remember something Philip Gourevitch wrote in his book about Rwanda that bears one of the most disturbing titles I have ever read: *We Wish to Inform You That Tomorrow We Will be Killed With Our Families.*

"Like Leontius," he wrote in the book's *Introduction*, "the young Athenian in Plato, I presume that you are reading this because you desire a closer look, and that you, too, are properly disturbed by your curiosity. Perhaps, in examining this extremity with me, you hope for some understanding, some insight, some flicker of self-knowledge—a moral, or a lesson, or a clue about how to behave in this world."

Perhaps it's just a conceit on my part—or maybe projection—but I like to believe books like his help prevent societies from becoming future subjects of books with titles like that one. Maybe, though, that isn't right. Berisha himself gave me evidence to the contrary just a few moments later.

"We took only the clothes we had on," he said. "My father could only walk a few meters at a time because of his heart problem. He had an operation in Belgrade the year before. I had my cousin suffering from drug withdrawal. It was a mess. We had to leave. About 200 of us went to the end of our neighborhood, and there stood seven Serb soldiers with their rifles cocked. With just a click they could shoot us. They took everything of value from us. Jewelry, money, anything of worth. Then they said *Get the fuck out to the train station.* We had seen *Schindler's List.* Everything comes into your mind, you know? Then we got into the train. Getting on the train was hell. It was a fight for survival. We had elderly, we had sick, we had kids. You don't know if your sister is going to be left, if your father is going to make it. You don't know what is going to happen.

"The train started, it stopped. We got out of the train. The last wagon, they take everybody out. They said whoever they take out they are going to kill. And it was our wagon. When I stood out, I found Serbian paramilitary forces. Chetniks. Not with beards, but Chetniks, with Serbian flags and God knows what, like idiots. Criminals. In between them was an Albanian guy talking with the Serbs and telling them who is good and who is bad. That guy is choosing who they are going to kill. And they take people out.

"I was scared they were going to take a member of my family. My sister. If they had taken my sister it would have been good to kill her. But they wouldn't kill her, they would rape her, they would...God knows. We went out, they took us to another wagon. They stopped again in another city and, again, the military police entered the train wagon and took people out. I don't even want to tell you what happened to them. When we reached the border with Macedonia, we got out of the train. The Serb police and paramilitaries were saying to people, *don't go off the fucking tracks because everything is mined.* Now you have kids, elderly, they were fucked up, they were not hearing it."

"Why Macedonia?" Sean said.

"They didn't care where," Berisha said. "They expelled 800,000 Albanians in three months. When we reached no man's land, there were about 100,000 people living in the open in cold weather. Pregnant women were delivering. People were dying. The refugees were very ill-treated by the Macedonians. I was there three days. And now I think it is not human to screw up this bad. Believe me, at that time, when you watched *Schindler's List*, you sympathize with the Jews. But without going through that situation yourself, it is impossible. Now when I watch *Schindler's List*, goose bumps go all over my body. That never happened before because we had never suffered like the Jewish people, thank God. But it was the same process. Mentally, it destroyed us. We suffered a lot. If we had the chance then, we would have killed them. But after that.... Are we killing Serbs anymore? No, Serbs are living here. We are not slaughtering anybody. We are not on a witch hunt anymore."

He mentioned *Schindler's List*. He and his family saw the movie *before* they were loaded onto trains during an ethnic-cleansing campaign in Europe. What Milosevic did to Albanians was less severe than Hitler's industrial-scale extermination of human beings at death camps like Auschwitz, but I recall seeing the movie myself and feeling relieved that nothing remotely like that happens in Europe anymore. It seemed appropriate, at the time, that Steven Spielberg shot the film mostly in black and white. The dramatized events took place long ago, after all. Mass ethnic warfare was supposed to be a thing of the past, at least in Europe. But it wasn't, and maybe it still isn't.

"In one city," Berisha continued, "they took a family and put them in the basement. The soldiers went and pissed on them. When they left they threw grenades on them. It killed them all except for one kid who survived. This is what I can never explain to myself, and I cannot justify, what human beings can do. Even beaten, on drugs, you cannot do that. I don't know how it is to experience killing children. For nothing. Why? Because they are Bosnians, because they are Albanians, because they are Serbs. Because they are bloody Croatians! As I said, it is difficult to forget about it. The more you think about it, the more you get different thoughts in your head. So it is best, right now, we ignore that, and try to move forward, and hopefully, in a better life, we will really forgive 100 percent. We forgave them for what they have done in a sense, but not truly from our hearts because they have never accepted what they have done. To this day they say that we are the villains, that we are the monkeys with tails. Today."

He visits Belgrade once in a while. One night, he said, he went out drinking with Serbs who didn't know he was Albanian. He kept his identity secret for hours. Eventually, he said, a well-known writer dredged up the hoary old notion that Albanians live in trees and have tails. Berisha could no longer resist, so he told them.

"I stood up from my chair," he said, "and said, *I am sorry, I cannot sit in this chair any longer.* They said, *Why?* I said, *There is no hole for my tail!* Then they started laughing. As much as I was offended by this, I was very happy for them to see that, for fuck's sake, you guys, you have been burned with propaganda. You live 400 kilometers away, and you know nothing about us. You jackholes."

I spoke to several Albanians who traveled to Serbia recently, and the worst they encountered was rudeness. According to Albanians, it's the same for Serbs who travel to Kosovo.

"Let Serbs come to Prishtina from Belgrade," Berisha said, "with BG license plates on their cars. Let them come. Nothing will happen. People may not like them, but nothing will happen to them because 2004 cost us a lot. It cost Kosovo our earlier independence and recognition by the U.N. We had to wait another four years."

He is referring to the explosion of violence in 2004 following rumors that Serbs chased two Albanian children into the Ibar River where they drowned. Serb and Albanian gunmen fired shots at each other from their respective sides of the river. Mobs of enraged Albanians burned Serb churches and houses for three days. It was a pogrom, basically. According to United Nations spokeswoman Isabella Karlowitz, sixteen churches and 110 houses were destroyed. Dozens were killed. Hundreds were wounded. Kosovo was hardly in a position to declare independence after all that.

"Was the international community worried you would do something crazy?" I said. "Mistreat Serbs?"

"Indeed," he said. "If you ask anyone about 2004, they will say what a fucking mistake. It screwed us up."

Kosovo has been de-facto independent from Serbia since the war ended, but even now the country is not fully sovereign. The United Nations administers much of the country, and NATO's Kosovo Force (KFOR) provides most of the security and is the closest thing Kosovo has to a real army.

American military officers believe the war will start up again if KFOR were to withdraw its soldiers. I didn't meet a single person there who thinks otherwise. Serbs think so, Albanians think so, and Americans think so. That doesn't mean they're right, but I certainly don't feel confident saying they're wrong. It would be naïve and foolhardy to believe soldiers can be withdrawn from a war zone just because the fighting has stopped. Sometimes that's possible, but that's rarely true shortly after an ethnic war.

"The most important thing is for KFOR to be in Kosovo," Berisha said, as did so many others. "KFOR is the ultimate thing that has to be here."

"What do you think would happen if KFOR left?" I said.

"A big war," he said. "Definitely."

"Not just with the Serbs in Kosovo," I said, "but with Belgrade?"

"With all of Serbia," he said.

When I briefly visited Bosnia I was told by a long-time resident British consultant that the U.N. and NATO have scaled back their presence dramatically during the past couple of years. Bosnia is troubled, politically deadlocked, and has an uncertain future, but I didn't get the sense that international soldiers are required to prevent an apocalyptic disintegration. Kosovo isn't like that. Not yet.

The war in Bosnia was much more destructive and violent than Kosovo's, but that's only because NATO intervened seriously in Kosovo after dithering impotently in Bosnia. Serbian nationalists always wanted Kosovo more than they wanted "cleansed" land in Bosnia. Kosovo is tranquil today for the most part, but that could change if the perfect storm of bad decisions is made. It's hard to imagine Kosovo exploding worse than Bosnia did, but many people who live there or have spent more time there than I have think it could happen, at least theoretically, and are determined to ensure it doesn't.

"If you go to Krusha e Vogel in Kosova," Berisha said, "you will find most of the households without males. You find most of the women, if not old, raped. That means some of them were pregnant. This ill fate, Bosnia suffered even more. Many women in Bosnia were left pregnant. Today, their kids are considered bastards. They don't have a future. They are ill treated by Serbs, they are ill treated by their parents, they are ill treated by the whole bloody country."

"They are ill treated by their parents?" Sean said.

"Yes, definitely," Berisha said, "even the mother. I have watched a lot of documentaries about it, they are having horrible problems. Horrible problems. I went to Belgrade, and I am still trying to say to myself that not all Serbs are bad. And I hope I am right."

"You are right," I said. I met a handful of terrific Serbs in Belgrade who know very well that Albanians don't have tails, did not deserve to be ethnically-cleansed, and should not be shackled to Serbia against their will.

"Because what they have done," Berisha said, "is they have destroyed that woman's life, and they have destroyed the new life that comes to be born. And they have created a mess—in Bosnia, in Croatia, in Kosovo, whatever they have touched. Bosnians and Croatians, they defended themselves. Croatians, when they took action to take the Serbs out, they committed atrocities beyond imagination. But they had to take the bloody Serbs out of the country. They had to fight. When you fight for your own house, your own family, believe me, you don't see black and white. You see only black."

Six

With Their Backs to the Sea

Imagine what would happen to Jewish veterans of the Israel Defense Forces who tried to move from Tel Aviv to an Arab country to open a bistro and bar. Only a few Arab governments would even let them through the airport before deporting or even arresting them. If they could somehow finagle a permit from the bureaucracy, they wouldn't last long. Somebody would almost certainly kill them even if the state left them alone.

Not only are Albanians less anti-Semitic than Arabs, even though most of them are Muslims, they're less anti-Israel on average than Christian Europeans. Israelis *can* open a bistro and bar in Kosovo without someone coming to get them or even harassing them. Shachar Caspi, co-owner of the Odyssea Bistro and the Odyssea Bakery, proves it.

Caspi's bistro is in the hip, bohemian, and stylish Pejton neighborhood in Prishtina's city center. A huge number of café bars that look expensive but aren't make up the core of the area. The hyper-local economy in Pejton is apparently based on fashionably dressed young people selling espresso and alcoholic beverages to each other. If you ever visit Prishtina, you ought to book a room for yourself in that neighborhood.

I wanted to know how Israeli Jews ended up in a Muslim-majority country and how it was going. A young Israeli woman who manages the Odyssea Bakery didn't feel like being interviewed, so she directed me to her boss at the Odyssea Bistro around the corner. "He will be more than happy to talk to you," she said. "He will tell you anything you want to know."

I showed up at the bistro unannounced and introduced myself to Caspi, a young Israeli man who shaved his head in the hip Tel Aviv style.

"Let's sit at the bar," he said.

The bartender served me an espresso with milk on the house.

"So how did you end up in Kosovo?" I said.

"It started in about October of 2005," he said. "I came to work for an Israeli businessman. He had a big company that he wanted me to work for. After a year we thought there was a good potential in the food business, so I contacted a friend in Israel—he is one of my partners—and we started a small coffee place with two local partners. But we didn't get along too well, so we went our separate ways and sold our part. We then acquired another local partner and a partner from Holland who is a silent investor. The four of us established this company. And now we have this bistro and the bakery, and another sandwich bar in the E.U. building. This looks very similar to places in Tel Aviv."

A lot of places in Prishtina, and not just Caspi's, reminded me of hangout spots in Tel Aviv. The aesthetic is remarkably similar, but the building materials in Kosovo are of a slightly lesser quality than what's available in Israel. Restaurants in Prishtina—aside from Caspi's—are not designed to resemble those in Tel Aviv on purpose, but the resemblance is there nevertheless. The aesthetic in Serbian restaurants and bars, meanwhile, reminded me of those in Lebanon. I mean that as a compliment. The Lebanese have more style than just about anyone.

The Israeli contribution to the local food and drink scene isn't a secret. I found Caspi's establishment in the *Bradt Guide*, which lists Odyssea as Israeli-owned. I knew already that Kosovo is friendlier to Israel than most countries in the world—especially compared with other Muslim-majority countries—but I was still slightly surprised to see this. It only takes one Islamist fanatic to blow up a bistro. And it would only take a small amount of the right kind of threatening pressure to drive Caspi, his business partners, and his employees out of town or at least underground. But nothing even remotely like that has happened.

"People know you are Israeli." I said.

"Of course," he said. "Of course. Everybody knows we are Israelis."

"Nobody cares?" I said.

"On the contrary," he said, "people like it. They come to speak to us. They want to be in contact. Here I didn't see anybody that was negative. On the contrary the people are very warm, very nice. They take Islam to a beautiful place, not a violent place. When they hear I am from Israel they react very warmly."

Lots of Kosovar Albanians confirmed what Caspi said.

"Kosovars used to identify with the Palestinians because we Albanians are Muslims and Christians and we saw Serbia and Israel both as usurpers of land," a prominent Kosovar recently told journalist Stephen Schwartz. "Then we looked at a map and woke up. Israelis have a population of six million, their backs to the sea, and 300 million Arab enemies. Albanians have a total population of eight million, our backs to the sea, and 200 million Slav enemies. So why should we identify with the Arabs?"

"Israelis are okay," said a waiter named Afrim Kostrati at a café named Tirana. "The conflict is not our problem. We are Muslims, but not really. We have respect for Israelis because of the U.S. I have good friends from there."

"Albanians everywhere are aware that Jews want to help them in this conflict," said Professor Xhabir Hamiti from the Islamic Studies Department at the University of Prishtina. "And Jews are aware and thankful to Albanians for saving their lives during the Second World War. So we have our sympathy for Israel. I don't think the Muslims here are on the side of the Palestinians."

When working in other countries I sometimes have to wonder if my interview subjects are only telling me what they think I want to hear. It happens sometimes, especially in the Arab world—not so much because Arabs want to be deceitful, though that does sometimes happen when interviewing members of extremist organizations. Most just want to be polite and agreeable. Caspi's ability to work openly as a Jewish Israeli bistro owner in Kosovo, though, is strong evidence that the Kosovars I spoke to were not just telling me what they thought I wanted to hear. Besides, invective against Israel and Jews is not something many Arabs feel they should have to conceal from reporters. I don't believe I've ever met an Arab in the Middle East who pretended to like Israel. It's just not something that happens.

Jews and Israelis in Muslim-majority countries are like canaries in coal mines, as are women in Muslim-majority countries. You can tell a lot about a place by observing how each population is treated. The Taliban impose an oppressive dress code on women at gunpoint, for instance, and the Hamas Charter is explicitly genocidal. It's possible to take the radical Islamist temperature of a Muslim society simply by measuring the misogyny and anti-Semitism at both the government level and among the general population. The only country in the entire Middle East that isn't anti-Semitic at the government level, the popular level, or both, is the state of Israel.

Kosovo is clearly outside the mainstream of the Middle East. At the same time, it is one of the few countries even in *Europe* that isn't at least anti-Israel, if not blatantly anti-Semitic, at the government or popular level.

I even met some Kosovar Albanians who were somewhat philo-semitic. One woman who gave me the rundown on local culture and politics showed me a book that I would never expect to see in any Muslim country other than Bosnia (though Bosnia is only 48 percent Muslim).

It was a copy of the *Sarajevo Haggadah*.

The book has an interesting history. It's the text of the traditional Jewish Passover Haggadah and was written in 14th century Spain. It may have made its way to Sarajevo when Jews fled the Spanish Inquisition and were welcomed as refugees in the Balkans by the Ottomans.

Muslim clerics saved the book from destruction during the Nazi occupation, and it was hidden in a bank vault during the Serbian nationalist siege of Sarajevo. It is one of the most valuable books in the world.

It's hard to describe how startling it is to see any book written in Hebrew in a Muslim-majority country. Perhaps I've spent too much time in the Middle East where something like that just would not happen. What ails that region begins to seem "normal," at least by the standards of the Islamic world, after enough constant exposure. The Kurds are startlingly different. The Albanians are startlingly different. The story behind the *Sarajevo Haggadah* is especially salient considering *where* and by *whom* the original was saved from destruction.

I rented a car in Prishtina so I could meet up with American soldiers at Camp Bondsteel for a brief embed in Eastern Kosovo. I laughed to myself when I found a CD of Israeli music in the car stereo that the previous customer left behind.

I was obviously not in Syria, Gaza, or Lebanon.

"During the Holocaust they used to keep the survivors inside of shelters," Caspi said. "And vice versa. In 1999 the first plane that landed in Prishtina for support was an Israeli plane."

"To support what?" I said.

"The war," he said.

"Was it humanitarian?" I said.

"Yes," he said. "The plane had medical support and doctors and some security, and they took refugees to Israel. I know some Albanians who live to this day in Israel."

"Muslims?" I said.

"Yes," he said. "They took them. Most of them came back here. I have talked to more than five people already that lived between 1999 and 2001 in Israel until everything was quiet here. Then they came back."

Israel accepted Muslim refugees from Bosnia, too. And I know of at least one Bosnian Muslim woman—whose family has had a close relationship with Israel for many years, but who prefers to tell the details this story herself in a book—who was rescued from Sarajevo during the siege by Israelis and given citizenship.

"Why did Israel get involved?" I said to Caspi.

"It is like when Israel went to India when they had an earthquake." he said. "They went to Africa when there was a disaster in Mombassa. This is what Israel *does*."

He sounded slightly irritated, as though I didn't know that already. I did know it already, I just wanted to hear what he had to say.

"They send medical assistance to places that have disasters," he added.

"Arab countries wouldn't accept help like that," I said. It wasn't a question.

"No," he said. "Actually after the tsunami they wanted to send it to Indonesia and they didn't let them because it was a Muslim country. But Israel and Kosovo have a very good relationship. The prime minister visited Israel a few months ago."

"Why do you suppose it is different in Kosovo?" I said.

"I think that a lot of people in the world think that the war in Israel is a religious war," he said. "I don't think it is a religious war. I think it is totally about land and the occupied territory, and the religion is what leaders try to take advantage of to promote their own interests. Like what Sheikh Yassin did with the suicide bombers, saying they will go to heaven. They try to make it a religious war but it is not. It is about lands. I have a lot of friends here. And my girlfriend, she is Muslim. I am very serious about her. And to tell you honestly, most of the Israeli people are not religious people. The last time I was in Synagogue was when I was 13 years old. I had to do the Bar Mitzvah and since then I haven't gone. If you go to Tel Aviv, 98 percent of the people are super liberal, and they will accept you if are a Palestinian, if you are Chinese, if you are Jewish. If things go well I want to bring my girlfriend back home to Israel."

Caspi's Israeli employee at the Odyssea Bakery around the corner thought I was slightly strange for wanting to interview someone in Prishtina for no reason other than the fact that he is Israeli. Caspi, though, understood.

"I know why it is an interesting story," he said. "An Israeli business in a Muslim country."

"It just wouldn't happen in the Middle East," I said. "I don't even think it would happen in Jordan."

"No," he said. "It wouldn't. And that's the whole point. Religions can co-exist. For example, my girlfriend, you know, I am in love above my head. I want us to be together. I think religions should integrate."

D uring World War II Albanians were well-known by Jews as friend-lies who could be trusted. Christian and Muslim Albanians alike refused to surrender Jews to the Nazi authorities. Jews were safer among Albanians than they were anywhere else in Nazi-controlled Europe.

After concluding my Kosovo trip, I attended a conference in Tirana, Albania's capital, titled: "Albania, the Albanians, and the Holocaust." Among those in attendance were Albania's prime minister and president. Dan Michman, chief historian at Jerusalem's Holocaust museum, Yad Vashem, was one of the speakers. I asked him if it was really true that Jews had a 100 percent survival rate there during the Nazi occupation.

"Yes," he said. "Actually, if you look inside the borders of 'Little Albania'—excluding Kosovo and the Albanian regions of Montenegro and Macedonia—there were three times as many Jews living here at the end of the Holocaust as there were before the war started."

The dark side of the Nazi occupation of Kosovo were the 6,000 or so ethnic Albanian collaborators who joined the so-called Skanderbeg Division of the Waffen-SS. The Germans had serious problems with that division, however. Thousands deserted within the first two months, and the rest were disbanded after a mere eight months of "service."

At the conference, the Albanian prime minister, Sali Berisha, delivered a thundering condemnation of Islamist radicals that you'd be unlikely to hear from a head of state anywhere else in Europe. "Israel will accept an independent Palestinian state," he said. "But Israel cannot accept the fundamentalists amongst Palestinians because their ideology is identical to that of the Nazis."

Seven

The Bin Ladens of the Balkans

Around a thousand *Mujahideen*, veteran Arabic fighters from the anti-Soviet insurgency in Afghanistan, volunteered to fight a jihad against Serbian Orthodox Christians in Bosnia in the mid-1990s. They thought they would be welcomed, and they were right. The European community imposed an arms embargo on all of Yugoslavia during the Bosnian civil war, so the multi-ethnic and multi-confessional Bosnian army—which included Serb and Croat Christians as well as Bosniak Muslims and secularists from all communities—chose to accept help from the so-called "Afghan Arabs" because they were desperate.

The Arab *Mujahideen* later probed the KLA to see if they could lend a hand there, as well. Kosovo, though, isn't Bosnia, and the KLA wasn't keen on throwing open the doors to their country to Middle Eastern religious fanatics. The Kosovars told the Arabs to get lost.

"In the two years that I covered the conflict in Kosovo," journalist Stacy Sullivan wrote, "never once did I see the *Mujahideen* fighters I saw in Bosnia, or hear KLA soldiers even allude to any kind of commitment to Islam. Most said they were offended by such allegations, bragged about how they were Catholic before the Ottomans came and converted them, and said their only religion was Albanianism."

Even so, the likes of Al Qaeda wanted to "help." A Brooklyn man named Florin Krasniqi claims that some of Osama bin Laden's representatives approached him and said they wanted to send men into Kosovo to fight a jihad against Serbs.

Krasniqi is an Albanian-American roofer who ran what he called the Homeland Calling Fund to raise money for the KLA back home. He raised $30 million from Albanian-Americans and sent cargo planes stocked with weapons and uniforms from the United States to Northern Albania where the goods were then smuggled over the border into Kosovo.

"We were approached by fundamentalist Muslims from every direction—Al Qaeda—but most of the leaders of the KLA just didn't feel right about working with them," he said to Dutch filmmaker Klaartje Quirijns in the documentary film *The Brooklyn Connection*. "I would have cooperated with the devil to free my country. I didn't care who they were." Later, however, he said the KLA commanders were right to turn down help from Islamist extremists.

And it's a good thing they did, or Kosovo's Islamist problem might be much more severe than it is.

The KLA may have refused radical groups entry into Kosovo from the Middle East during the war, but dubious characters from the Gulf states have been showing up in Kosovo anyway since the war ended. Saudi-funded NGOs volunteered to help rebuild mosques destroyed by the Yugoslav Army and Serbian nationalist paramilitary forces, which is fine and good as far as it goes, but there's a catch. The same individuals hope to transform Kosovo's liberal Balkan Islam into the much sterner Wahhabi variety practiced in the unforgiving deserts of Saudi Arabia.

"We don't call them Wahhabis here," a prominent Albanian woman told me. "We call them *Binladensa*, the people of bin Laden."

Believe me, in Kosovo that isn't a compliment.

I'm accustomed to spending quality time in moderate Islamic environments. I lived in the most liberal and cosmopolitan Sunni neighborhood in Beirut next to the American University, and I've vacationed with my wife in famously moderate Muslim countries like Tunisia and Turkey. Kosovo still surprised me, though, and forced me to redefine my understanding of what a moderate Muslim even is.

At least 99.5 percent of Kosovo's women dress like women elsewhere in Europe. I saw one or two women wearing Islamic headscarves per day at the most, even in villages. On some days I didn't see any.

Alcohol is widely available. You don't have to find establishments that cater to tourists (there are no tourists in Kosovo) in order to get a drink like you do in false-moderate Muslim countries like Jordan. There are more bars per block in the capital than anywhere I have ever lived. Supposedly the dating scene in Kosovo is still fairly conservative, but the locals could have fooled me. Young women frequently dress in sexy outfits that show off their bodies. They dance, boozed-up, in clubs the way they do in Manhattan—only some of them, amazingly, with glasses of scotch balanced on top of their heads. Pornography is sold on the streets, even outside the capital. What kind of Muslim country is this?

It's European.

In Iraq's Anbar Province, Al Qaeda shot people for smoking. They warned local vegetable vendors not to place cucumbers and tomatoes next to each other in markets because it's "perverse." (Cucumbers are male while tomatoes are female, or so goes the theory.)

Reactionary clerical fascists of that sort would have to machine-gun all but the entire nation of Kosovo into a mass grave to get their way. Their hatred of the place must surpass even that of the worst Serbian nationalists. Its very existence as a culturally liberal Muslim-majority country threatens to destroy their ideology. Their absolute worst nightmare—the thing they are ultimately fighting to stop—is the transformation of the Arab world into something resembling Kosovo.

"Muslims here identify themselves as Muslim-lite," an American told me in the charming city of Prizren, "like Pepsi-lite."

"We are Muslims," one waiter told me, "but not really."

Not even the villages are conservative by Islamic standards. Kosovo is the least Islamicized Muslim-majority country I had ever been to. The only possible exception was Albania proper itself. Islamic civilization is far more varied than it appears from the outside. Prishtina has no more in common culturally with Islamicized cities like Cairo and Riyadh than Cairo and Riyadh have with Seattle.

I had coffee at a locally renowned restaurant called Pishat with

Professor Xhabir Hamiti from the Islamic Studies Department at the University of Prishtina. "This is a famous restaurant," he said. "Madeleine Albright ate here."

He earned degrees in Jordan, Lebanon, and Saudi Arabia.

"When were you in Lebanon?" I said. "Before the war?"

"It was in 2002," he said, "so after. But there were still signs of the civil war. I noticed in Lebanon, Shias and Sunnis, Hezbollah and these kind of parties, they hate each other more than they hate Christians. It's very bad."

"It's true," I said.

"Hezbollah are idiots," he said. "They are not Muslims."

"They say they are," I said. I am not always sure if Muslims who say this kind of thing are in denial about their more sinister co-religionists or if they mean to excommunicate them.

"Their behavior is not Muslim," he said. "Look to the practices. I hate them."

"Why is it that Islam in the Balkans is more open and tolerant than in the Middle East?" I said.

"Because our mentality is different, completely different," he said.

"Is it because you're European?" I said.

"Yes," he said. "Another reason is because we have cultivated tolerance between different religions."

Neither Catholic citizens nor Catholic churches were touched in either of the two spasms of violence launched by Albanian mobs against Serbs after the war. The fact that the violence was ethnic rather than religious doesn't mean it was *better*, but it does mean it was different from how it is sometimes perceived from abroad and that religious tolerance is more deeply ingrained than ethnic tolerance.

The reason for Kosovo's relaxed attitude toward religion lies in its history. Albanians, including those in Kosovo, are the descendants of ancient pagan Greeks and Illyrians; more recently, they were Christian before the majority converted to Islam under Ottoman rule. Their religion may be Eastern, but Albanians have been culturally European for all of recorded history.

"The Greeks hardly regard them as Christians, or the Turks as Muslims, and in fact they are a mixture of both, and sometimes neither," Lord Byron wrote of them almost 200 years ago.

"We Albanians," writes Catholic priest Dom Lush Gjergji, "descendants of the Illyrians, are Christians from the time of the Apostles....Without Christianity there would be no Albanian people, language, culture, or traditions....Albanians consider Christianity their patrimony, their spiritual and cultural inheritance."

Kosovar Muslims talk the same way. In fact, the feeling is reflected in the Albanian national flag, which flies all over Kosovo, despite minimal support for a "greater Albania." Its black double-headed eagle is the seal of Gjergj Kastrioti Skanderbeg, who led the resistance against the Ottoman Empire in the 15th century. This national hero of a Muslim-majority country was Catholic.

Indeed, another sign of Kosovo's complex religious identity involves the "crypto-Catholics," those who just went through the motions of converting to Islam under the Ottomans. Kosovo's cemeteries hold many tombstones engraved with Muslim names yet bearing the Catholic cross. Even now, the crypto-Catholics' descendants are still "christened," so to speak, with Muslim names and then baptized into the church.

Many Kosovars are starting to convert "back" to Christianity. Gazi Berlajolli ascribes the trend partly to American influence: "Most of these people were atheists and agnostics, but they don't want to be seen as atheist Muslims," he said. "So they needed to convert to something else. They want to be able to put 'Christian' on their pages on Facebook."

Tellingly, Kosovo's only Islamist party garnered just 1.7 percent of the vote in the election before I arrived. One reason for Kosovo's antipathy to radical Islamism is, in a word, America, which has been the political North Star for Albanians inside and outside Kosovo since 1999. In 2004, a Gallup survey measured popular opinion of U.S. foreign policy around the world. Only ten countries rated American foreign policy favorably, and among those, Kosovo scored highest, registering

88 percent approval. The only reason that number didn't approach 100 percent is because Kosovo's Serb minority is overwhelmingly anti-American.

"We are Muslims," Hamiti said, "we cannot deny that, but as you see in the street, it is completely different. Here people are Muslims, but they think like Europeans. You should write about this because people don't know it."

"What about the very conservative Muslims coming here from Saudi Arabia and building mosques?" I said. "Do you think this is a problem?"

I think it's a problem. It is even a problem in the United States.

"Yes," he said. "It is a problem in my opinion. But, as you know, during the war we had 250 mosques destroyed and burned. The Serbs wanted to call this war a religious war to get sympathy from Europeans. They still do. After the war many humanitarian organizations came here, in general from the Gulf—Kuwait, Qatar, others. They are from outside, and I am convinced that neither here nor in Albanian churches will Albanians allow them to continue. We are working very hard to stop these kinds of movements. These kinds of movements are dangerous for all nations, for the faiths, for all religions. The traditional Islam that has been cultivated in these areas is the best guarantee for the future. I am a Muslim. I am a scholar. I know how to deal with Islam in my country. There is no need for Arabs to come here. I have no need for their suggestions, no need for their explanations. They are Muslims, we are not against them, but we are against the way they are using Islam in my country. We have our own schools. They have been here for 600 years. We created our Islam ourselves here, and we can continue our Islam with our own minds."

I understood already why the KLA told the Arab *Mujahideen* to stay out during the war, but I wanted to hear a local person explain it from his or her perspective.

"The KLA," I said. "Why did they say no to the *Mujahideen?*"

"In Bosnia," he said, "the *Mujahideen* called the war a holy war, and they wanted to call the war here a holy war. But it was not a holy war, it was a war against the Serbian regime and paramilitary forces. So to prevent this we told them, *No. You can send money to buy guns, but you cannot be with us in the war.* That was a good idea. They destroy everything they touch."

We both said "Chechnya" at the same time.

Albanians wanted help from the West, not the Islamic world. They are well aware that large majorities in most Muslim countries are anti-American. Huge numbers of Muslims outside Kosovo and Albania believe Americans fought wars in Iraq and Afghanistan because they hate Muslims, despite the rescue of Muslims in Kosovo.

"You know we're not against Muslims," I said.

"I know," he said. "I saw it with my own eyes in the U.S. Religion is very free, everybody is free to do whatever he wants, to worship the god he wants. I saw it with my own eyes."

"What do you think about Iraq?" I said. "You and Kosovars in general?"

"The Muslims here are on the side of the Americans," he said. "They had to stop this kind of dictatorship in the Middle East. [Saddam Hussein] killed many innocent people, and he was going to continue his wars against his neighbors. That was a good step, to remove him from his position. But the pictures that we see on the TV are bad pictures for us and I think also for Americans. Who wants to see American soldiers die in Iraq? Or who wants to see innocent people, women, children, old people, die? I think there is going to be a solution. But they cannot leave, they cannot leave. Shias and Sunnis hate each other more than they hate Americans."

Professor Hamiti wasn't the only person I talked to about the so-called *Binladensa.* Two prominent Kosovar Albanian women agreed to talk to me as long as I wouldn't name them. Both work in official and diplomatic circles. Nothing they said is particularly controversial, but their opinions don't necessarily represent the institutions they work for. I'll refer to them here by the female Albanian pseudonyms Fana and Lumnije.

The three of us had coffee at an outdoor restaurant in the wooded countryside near a small river.

"How successful are the Wahhabis here?" I said.

"They are successful in rebuilding mosques," Fana said, "and they pay people to get covered, to shorten the pants."

Conservative Arab women wear headscarves—and sometimes even veils or enveloping abayas—while Wahhabi men wear short pants that ride above their ankles. I saw a handful of women with headscarves, but I never noticed even a single man anywhere in Kosovo wearing Wahhabi pants. There can't be all that many around.

I heard from all sorts of people in Kosovo that Gulf Arabs pay people to dress differently, but I have no way to verify whether it's true or not. In any case, lots of Albanians think it's true. I also heard rumors that Hezbollah once paid women in Shia villages of Lebanon $100 a month to wear headscarves until they gave it up as both expensive and futile. Genuinely conservative women will wear them without needing *baksheesh* from Hezbollah, while liberated women are hard to bribe. Lebanon's relatively modern "dress code" among bourgeois Muslim women was hard won and will not be rolled back so easily.

"I have heard about it," Fana said. "I don't know for sure. Most likely true, they have money. Gulf money, not just from Iran. But Albanians are very traditional, so it is difficult to get them to change. It is difficult for the Wahhabis to get roots here in Kosovo."

"You should see how the general public receives these people," Lumnije said. "They certainly are not liked. I don't think they will succeed."

I wanted to know what Albanians were doing to curtail the influences of these people so Kosovo really doesn't become what its critics fear it is turning into.

"It is a bit tricky, Michael," Lumnije said, "because in the Kosovo constitution all European standards are applicable. And if you look at it from the point of view of European conventions and human rights, they have a right to religion. Yesterday we had a case where a young girl was denied entrance to a school because she was covered. As human rights officers, it is a problem we have to deal with because she has a right to preserve her religion. That is her choice."

"We don't have a law that says she can or can't come to school," Fana said to Lumnije. "It is European law, but we have no law."

"Yes," Lumnije said, "but these are very tricky cases in Europe also. In France it was a big problem. I attended summer school in 2003 in England, in South Wales. We had an international night and I was shocked to find that the representative of the USA was a covered lady, originally from Iraq. And the representative from Canada was another, originally from Afghanistan. The conference was about young people who change the world. It had nothing to do with religion, but they were representing the U.S. and Canada."

"That is surprising," I said, "but very American."

"And Lumnije, coming from a Muslim country, was wearing shorts!" Fana said.

All three of us laughed.

"They were arguing with me all the time," Lumnije said. "*What kind of a Muslim woman are you?*"

I can understand why the women from Iraq and Afghanistan argued with Lumnije, even though, frankly, they were being reactionary. Albanian Islam is so different from Islam in Iraq and especially Afghanistan that it must have been truly shocking when conservative women from those countries met a thoroughly Western-looking and Western-thinking woman in shorts who claimed to adhere to the same religion. Kosovo surprised even me, and I'm accustomed to spending time in relatively secularized Muslim countries.

"How many Wahhabis are here?" I said, meaning the medium-sized city they lived in. We were not in the capital.

"Here?" Fana said. "Maybe 100. Maybe fifty."

"Are they dangerous?" I said.

"No," she said. "They don't do anything."

"I will tell you one thing," Lumnije said. "The problem is that this issue has not been raised, except for when they talk about the mosques. I haven't noticed any journalists tackle this thing. I hope that they will deal with it at some essential level, regulating it by law. In OSCE [the Organization for Security and Cooperation in Europe], for example, there is one girl who is covered, but she is a professional interpreter, very well-educated. At one point the Kosovar delegation went to Germany and they hired an interpreter and she was supposed to go. When they saw that she was covered they refused to take her."

"The Kosovars refused to take a covered woman to Germany as a professional interpreter," Fana said, "and the U.S. sends a covered Iraqi woman to Wales as a representative!" She laughed out loud at the irony.

"They didn't want Kosovo to be perceived as a conservative Muslim country," Lumnije said.

"And I definitely think they were right," Fana said. "We are not European, we are American! We are the 51st state!"

"Kosovo is the most reliable," Lumnije said.

"It is a small country," Fana said, "but you can rely on us completely."

I am not particularly worried that Kosovo will become a state sponsor of terrorism like Iran, or a terrorist statelet like the Taliban-ruled parts of Afghanistan and the Hezbollah-controlled portions of Lebanon. Anything is possible, but it's extraordinarily unlikely. There are too many anti-Islamist antibodies in the society.

"We've been here for so long," United States Army Sergeant Zachary Gore said to me in Eastern Kosovo, "and not seen any evidence of it, that we've reached the assumption that it is not a viable threat." I trust American soldiers when it comes to the assessment of threats. I have seen them at work in Iraq, and they are less complacent about dangerous Islamists than any other people I have ever met.

Kosovo is hardly more religious than anywhere else in Europe, but Albania itself is perhaps the least religious of all. Before Enver Hoxha's thoroughly oppressive communist regime came to power at the start of the Cold War, around 30 percent of Albanians were Christians while 70 percent were Muslims. Now hardly anyone belongs to any religion.

"For fifty years Albania was under a horrible dictatorship," Luan Berisha told me. "For the fifty years they were under Enver Hoxha nobody dared to practice any religion. There was no god for them. There was only Hoxha. For fifty years it was very bad. Bosnia has suffered a lot, but what Albanians have suffered is unbelievable. Nobody can even explain it to themselves, honestly. Really, he brainwashed them away from religion. People don't believe in anything. As soon as you don't believe in anything, you have a problem with everything. You don't even know where to start. And now they are slowly starting to come back into beliefs. It took them eighteen years, but a lot of people are changing, and actually quite a few Muslims are no longer calling themselves Muslim, but are saying: *I am Christian*. Which is fine because they don't know what Islam even is. They never touched it. They never went to a mosque."

Albania and Kosovo aren't the only countries in the Balkan Peninsula where ethnic Albanians live. They also inhabit a portion of southeastern Montenegro near the Albanian border. Their little region on the coast is beautiful, prosperous, and appears to be more thoroughly Europeanized even than Kosovo.

Ethnic Albanians also live in Macedonia near the Albanian border, and *their* region of *that* country is very troubled indeed. For a host of complex reasons, the *Binladensa* of the Balkans in Macedonia are successfully Islamicizing, and even Arabizing, parts of the country.

I drove on winding roads through dense woods and snowy mountains to the ethnic Albanian city of Tetovo in next-door Macedonia. Shpetim Mahmudi met me at a covered outdoor café as black clouds hung low in the sky and fat raindrops pelted the sidewalk and the awning over our heads. I shivered in my light jacket.

"Let's go inside," he said, "where it's warmer and drier."

Mahmudi taught at the University of Tetovo and belonged to the Bektashi order of Sufi mystics. The Bektashis are part of a distinct branch of Shia Islam. Many of its adherents insist it's the most liberal branch. These are the last people in the Islamic world who will join any kind of jihad. They drink alcohol, for instance, and they are not obliged to pray five times a day. Bektashi women don't wear oppressive clothing. Their feelings of openness toward people of other faiths are authentic. They are detested by Wahhabis, Salafists, and other radical Sunnis as much as they would be if they were pagans or Jews.

We found a table and asked for some coffee. He leaned in close to whisper when the waiter stepped out of earshot.

"We are really in trouble here," he said. "We are really in trouble with the Wahhabis."

Almost everyone in Kosovo despises the Gulf Arab immigrants who are doing their worst to make the place more conservative and even fanatical, but things are different in Macedonia. And what I saw there was startling.

Kosovo is a Muslim-majority country. Macedonia isn't. Only a third of Macedonia's people are Muslims. Most Muslims in both countries are ethnic Albanians, but the difference between the two comes like a shock. Kosovo's culture and politics are thoroughly secular. Its believers are not demonstrative about religion. A huge number of people in Tetovo, though, looked like they had been airlifted in from Saudi Arabia.

I saw dozens of women covering their heads in the Middle Eastern style before I even got out of the car. I even saw women wearing all-enveloping black abayas that cover everything but the face, the closest thing the Arab world has to the burkhas worn in Afghanistan and the primitive backwoods of Pakistan.

Headscarves are not strictly Islamic. There are Muslim countries all over the world where hardly anyone wears them. They are cultural imports from the Arab world. There is, of course, nothing wrong with wearing a hijab by choice (they are required by law in Iran), and it would be wrong to assume a woman or her family are Islamist extremists based on head gear alone, but I was still startled to see so many in Macedonia since Albanian women don't traditionally wear them. It was obvious that soft-imperial Arab "missionaries" from the Gulf are having a much more profound effect on the ground in Macedonia than in Kosovo.

"We don't pray five times a day like the Sunnis," Mahmudi said. "We are similar to Ismailis, and we're treated badly in Turkey because we don't go to the mosque. Here in Macedonia, the Sunnis don't treat us as Muslims. They want to be the only ones representing the entire community, and they say we should come under their umbrella."

Bektashi Sufis are no less Islamic than the Wahhabis. They are arguably even more so. Their order is hundreds of years older. But they aren't chauvinists about their religion, and they don't spend billions in petrodollars on a crusade to convert the rest of the planet.

"We have nothing to do with the Arab ways," he said, "but now we're dressing like them. This is not nice for us. We are close to Americans, not the Middle East."

"Is it getting better or worse here?" I said.

"It was worse ten years ago," he said. "But it has always been worse in Macedonia. There have always been more fundamentalists here. Macedonia is poorer and less educated."

It's hard to believe it was worse ten years ago. The difference between the Albanian region of Macedonia and Albanian regions everywhere else in the Balkans is extraordinary. Also, there were no Wahhabis in Macedonia or anywhere else in Yugoslavia during the communist era. The Macedonian Muslim community appears to be fracturing. If a majority of Albanian-Macedonian Muslims are becoming more secular and modern at the same time a minority is becoming more radical— watch out. Extreme polarization rarely ends well, especially in the Islamic parts of the world.

Few outsiders know it, but Macedonia experienced war more recently than any other country in the former Yugoslavia. It erupted in 2001, and it was the only conflict in the former Yugoslavia where Serbian nationalists weren't among the combatants. Albanian separatists fought and lost a struggle for independence against the Macedonian state. At least they didn't face anything like the brutal ethnic-cleansing campaign Albanians suffered in Kosovo and Bosniaks suffered in Bosnia. Casualties were relatively light on both sides and the international community shrugged.

I did not visit the capital, Skopje, but the portion of the country I did see made Macedonia seem like the most backward republic of the former Yugoslavia. I saw many old wheezing Yugos on the roads, for instance, and I didn't notice any, not a single one, anywhere else on my entire trip through seven Balkan countries. Macedonia was not a place I wanted to stick around long.

I later drove through it again with a car full of Kosovars on a trip to Tirana, Albania's capital, and one of my traveling companions said something that didn't surprise me. "There are no young people left in this village," she said as we passed through a small town near the Albanian border. "Most of them moved to America. They will never be back."

"How much power do the Wahhabis have here?" I said to Mahmudi as we sipped our coffee in the café.

"They control seven mosques in Tetovo," he said.

"Out of how many?" I said.

"There are forty mosques here total," he said. "Many people don't like them."

He was obviously afraid of them, or at least very cautious. He spoke so quietly when I asked him about the Wahhabis that using my voice recorder for the interview was impossible. I had to take notes by hand. He spoke at a normal volume when discussing other topics, but this one had him rattled. I felt like I was interviewing a dissident in a total-surveillance police state. No one anywhere else in the former Yugoslavia—not in Serbia, not in Bosnia, and not in Kosovo—ever whispered like this when we talked about religion or politics. It seems the Wahhabis have successfully transformed this portion of Macedonia into what former Soviet dissident Natan Sharansky calls a fear society.

"Why is it so much worse here than in Kosovo?" I said. "It feels oppressive."

"It's different in Kosovo," he said, "thanks to America and NATO. If Kosovo cooperated with Muslim countries instead, it would be different. Americans are bringing their culture to Kosovo and Albania, but not to Macedonia."

Instead it is Arabs who are bringing their culture to Macedonia. And the Macedonian government—astonishingly—is helping them do it.

Mahmudi's place of worship—his tekke—is under assault by radical Sunnis who have seized most of the sprawling ancient Ottoman compound by force. They converted portions of it for their own use and desecrated its graves and its shrines. He took me there in my rented car, but we first paid a visit to the Painted Mosque.

We parked and walked in the rain. I zipped my camera inside my jacket to keep it dry.

"What do ethnic Macedonians think of Americans?" I said. Ethnic Macedonians are Slavic Orthodox Christians who once belonged to Yugoslavia, but they are not Serbs. They speak their own language, which is similar to Bulgarian, and they have their own cultural traditions.

"They burned American flags in Skopje recently," he said. "They feel close to Serbia. But George Bush recognized Macedonia's new name, so they are more pro-American now. The name is important here. I can understand."

Most people from outside Greece and Macedonia couldn't care less about a parochial issue like the name of the country, but locally it's a big deal. Much of ancient Macedonia lies inside the borders of Greece. The Greeks protested its name as though it were a copyright violation, so the country was all but forced to provisionally name itself The Former Yugoslav Republic of Macedonia instead of simply the Republic of Macedonia, or Macedonia. Controversy over whether "The Former Yugoslav Republic of" must remain part of its name still riles nationalists in both countries.

The ancient Painted Mosque, built by the Ottoman Turks in 1459, is the most beautiful small mosque I've ever seen. Arabian doors, Roman-style columns, and the finest Middle Ages style of ornamentation is lovingly painted on every square foot of surface in vivid colors.

"The fundamentalists hate painting," Mahmudi said, "but they have to deal with this."

Though the mosque dates back to the 15th century, Mahmudi told me the colors were touched up again in the 18th. "They say the new colors are not as good as the originals," he said.

It's an architectural wonder no matter how muted its colors may be. I found myself wishing I could visit an entire city built with this amount of aesthetically pleasing detail. The *Binladensa* who despise it are wallowing in an intolerant philistinism that borders on barbarism. They would destroy everything beautiful and civilized in this world if they could.

And they are trying. They've already wrecked parts of Mahmudi's tekke.

We parked inside the compound and proceeded with caution. The Sufis only control parts of it now. Wahhabi-inspired Sunnis have commandeered the rest of it.

"You see that?" he said and gestured toward a building with opaque glass windows. "They took it from us and turned it into a classroom for their propaganda. An Egyptian woman teaches Albanian women in Arabic even though no one speaks Arabic here. Don't let anyone see you take a picture of it."

There weren't many people around. We both made sure no one was looking. Then I snapped a quick photo and covered my camera again with my jacket.

"They attacked us again on the fifth of May," he said. "They ripped down our Bektashi flag. They broke the spindles on the shrine here and stole the donation box. And they threatened the dervish."

Dervish Abdulmytalib Beqiri is in charge of the tekke—or at least the parts that haven't been forcibly taken over. Mahmudi introduced me to him inside one of the few remaining buildings the Sufis control. The three of us sat down to talk over coffee.

"Welcome to our tekke," Dervish Beqiri said in Albanian. Mahmudi translated. "Thank you very much for your time."

"Thank you for letting me visit," I said.

"Americans are most welcome here," he said.

"I see you have an American flag," I said and glanced toward a flag next to a candle in what looked like an ancient gun slot cut into the wall. I don't believe I had ever seen an American flag inside an Islamic holy site anywhere in the world, not even in Kurdistan.

"Yes," Dervish Beqiri said. "We light up the flag with a candle at night. Do you know what those slots are for?"

I had an idea.

"What are they for?" I said.

"They are for protecting the tekke," he said. "We used to fire guns through those slots."

The Bektashi Sufis participated in various resistance movements against the Ottomans.

"Bektashis here always fought for the Albanian cause," said Dervish Beqiri. "Some clerics were at one tekke fighting the Turks, and the Turks came and occupied it. Inside were some Orthodox Christians. The baba was very well-known and he took these Christians, put dervish clothes on them, and introduced them to the Turks as Dervish Mark and Dervish Michael, the same names, just with Dervish added. So this baba covered them and saved the lives of Christian people. Both the Christians and Muslims were fighting for the Albanian cause. The Bektashis will fight against occupation. For freedom. For schools. For educating people. Equality and tolerance are our values.

"When Osama bin Laden attacked the two towers," he continued, "the first clerical leader in the world who judged this crucial attack as non-human was the world Bektashi father at the headquarters in Tirana. He publicly denounced this attack. He even went to the embassy of the

U.S. to present his judgment."

"How long have you had problems with the Wahhabis here?" I said.

"Serious trouble started three years ago when they broke gravestones," he said. Just outside the door was also a Jewish gravestone with Hebrew letters chiseled into it. "They didn't respect our saints. They also broke pictures of Imam Ali on the walls, and of the world head of the Bektashis. They cut the pictures with knives. They think we are too close to Christianity, in part because of the pictures and candles. Then the Sunnis came in and occupied the tekke. They said, *This is Muslim territory.*"

Of course, the tekke was "Muslim territory" already. Bektashis are Muslims. But Sufis are often thought of as heretics and non-Muslim infidels by reactionaries.

"Look how they are manipulating people," he said. "They want to convert the tekke into a woman's madrassa. They want to move their administration here."

"They are influenced by Arabs?" I said. It wasn't really a question.

"Yes," he said. "They are. And our government is weak. Arabs can manipulate us because our government is neglectful."

The Macedonian government is worse than neglectful, actually. The state has formed an alliance of sorts with the Wahhabis, which is an extraordinary thing for a Christian-dominated government to do in a country where a third of the population are Muslims.

"Why would the government do this?" I said.

"It is convenient for the government because they can point at Albanians and call us terrorists," he said.

Some of the tekke's buildings were damaged during the fighting in 2001, but the dervish said the Bektashi community wasn't involved, at least not at the institutional level. I photographed a number of bullet holes.

"Individually," he said, "there may have been some involved. We are always against fighting. We are for finding peaceful solutions. In the past, Bektashis were involved in making wars, but it was for the Albanian cause, mainly against the Ottomans, and for making an independent Albania. We were very deeply involved in this. As Bektashis we are not against the state, and the state rules wherever we are. For example, Bektashis are in 31countries. Greek Bektashis are fighting for the cause of Greece, Albanian Bektashis for the Albanian cause. We respect the rule of the state no matter where we are. Bektashis in America will fight if America is involved in a war to protect America and American rules."

"Before the election," Mahmudi said, "at night you could hear weapons shooting. Just two days ago someone was shooting near here. Someone was shooting from here, inside the tekke. Many times we have reported to the police that people are shooting from inside this part of the tekke at night."

"They are intimidating you," I said.

"The Sunnis are looking at the people coming here with an unfriendly eye," he said. "Even the guests that used to come here often are no longer coming because they are scared. They are always provoked. The only people coming to the tekke are the people who must come, who have something important to do."

"So they are trying to take the whole thing?" I said.

"They are trying to make us not come here at all," Dervish Beqiri said. "They are trying to take over everything. It is a cycle of aggression. I was alone when the crucial attack happened. I saw some people speaking Albanian when I went out behind to feed the chickens. They attacked the grave of a saint, they broke the shrine, and they stole the donation box. They also broke the Bektashi flag, the green one that was just next to the Albanian flag. They didn't touch that one, the national flag, the Albanian flag, they just broke the Bektashi flag. This means the attack was done by Muslim people. If it was Macedonians they would have broken both flags. So Muslims did this, for sure. Also there was a verbal attack after this from the people praying in our place that has been transformed into a kind of mosque."

"What did they say to you?" I said.

"Some are trying to accuse us of doing this to ourselves," he said.

"But Bektashis never do things against their properties. All Bektashis believe in the same graves. We keep them and pray to them. We believe that if we damage a grave God will punish us, so we are very afraid to do this, we would never do this. We keep the saint graves. The Muslims know this. They are trying to provoke us and claim that we have done it to ourselves. But no, really they did it. Plus, I see these Wahhabis around. Usually at night the Wahhabis are coming, sometimes in trousers, sometimes in their clothes, sometimes with the things on their heads and with beards."

The next building over in the compound had been forcibly converted into a Sunni mosque. Speakers for the muezzin's call to prayer were bolted to the side of the chimney. During our interview the call to prayer screeched from above. "Allahu Akbar…" the muezzin called. My Sufi hosts groaned.

"Ugh," Mahmudi said and made a face. "You see what we have to listen to five times a day? This is supposed to be a quiet place for meditation."

"In the beginning, at night," Dervish Beqiri said, "when they had full control of the city because of the war, they were coming, preaching to the local people, preaching Wahhabism. When they came here, the Wahhabis, with the intent to take full control of the Muslim community, they used these people who had been studying in Saudi Arabia and other Arab countries. They couldn't succeed in taking full control of the Muslim community because the Muslim community is not only Macedonian, but it is Kosovar, and from other Balkan countries, and their religion is influenced by the Hanafi Turkish school. It is Hanafism. They are now trying to at least change this tradition from Hanafism to their tradition. They are mainly Wahhabis, Salafi Wahhabis. They are using the fact that the local people are poor and unemployed, they are paying them to convert to Wahhabism. Also they are making people pray five times a day."

"How much are they being paid?" I said.

"We are not sure," he said, "maybe 200 or 300 dollars or Euros per month. They are paying more to convert women."

I am only aware of small violent incidents in Macedonia since the civil war in 2001, but that isn't for lack of trying on the part of some people. Seventeen suspected terrorists were rounded up in this city the previous year, and shortly after I arrived they were given a combined total of 192 years in prison. One is from Serbia, one is from Kosovo, one is from Albania, and the other 14 are apparently from Macedonia. Lirim Jakupi, the Albanian from Serbia, is nicknamed the "Nazi Commander." They are allegedly Wahhabis linked to local foundations from Saudi Arabia. They were caught with modern sophisticated weaponry, including laser-guided anti-aircraft missiles.

When Mahmudi escorted me back to my car, a woman entered the tekke wearing a tent-like abaya. She looked like a Saudi. I was in Europe with liberal Sufis, but this woman, who had helped religious totalitarians take over the tekke, looked like a Saudi.

"Look at that," Mahmudi said. "We never had that. Take a picture, take a picture."

I took several and I don't think she saw me.

"Please publish these pictures," he said. "Please show the world what is happening here."

Post-script: On June 13, 2010, journalist and author Stephen Schwartz informed me that Shpetim Mahmudi killed himself on June 3. He was 31 years old.

PART THREE

THE CAUCASUS

Eight

From Baku to Tbilisi

"Russia can have at its borders only enemies or vassals." - George F. Kennan, United States Ambassador to the Soviet Union

"You must draw a white-hot iron over this Georgian land!... You will have to break the wings of this Georgia! Let the blood of the petit bourgeois flow until they give up all their resistance! Impale them! Tear them apart!" - Vladimir Lenin

Baku, Azerbaijan, is the least communist-looking post-communist capital I've encountered, but when I took the train from there to Russian-occupied Georgia during the hot summer war of 2008, it could not have been more obvious that the South Caucasus region once belonged to the Soviet Empire. Azerbaijan's countryside is much rougher and poorer than the oil-rich capital, and my trip across that landscape to Georgia felt in many ways like a trip backward in time, as if a year were subtracted from the date for each of the eighteen hours I sat on the train. By the time I reached the outskirts of Gori in central Georgia and ran into Russian soldiers carrying equipment marked with the Soviet Union's insignia, the trip back in time to the days of Moscow's totalitarian empire felt all but complete.

First, though, the journey:

At least I wasn't in any danger the first time I encountered a communist relic in the South Caucasus. I was merely annoyed. But I was also intrigued. The train linking the two countries has been preserved like a living museum piece.

At the train station in Baku I bought a sandwich, orange juice, muffins, and large bottles of water for the long slog by ground to the Georgian capital Tbilisi. I set down my bag of provisions in front of car number one, which was to be mine as soon as boarding began. Two feral cats crept up to my bag and I gently shooed them with my foot. They returned when I wasn't looking and in an instant managed to rip open my package of muffins and tear pieces off. I shooed them again, but felt slightly bad. I have cats of my own at home and these two were hungry. I had six muffins and could spare one. So I broke one into pieces and fed them.

A young Azeri boy leaned over and watched the cats eat, but his father told him to stay away from the animals. He turned then to me.

"Where are you from?" he said.

"I'm from the United States," I said.

I was an obvious stranger even in a city of millions. I've been told I walk and even *stand* like an American. Humans are exceptionally skilled at noticing these subtle differences even if they can't quite identify what it is they're detecting. Once in a while I try to mimic the body language used by people in the countries I visit so I can blend in, but I had no reason to do so in Azerbaijan. I expected to feel slightly nerve-wracked when I reached war-torn Georgia, but I could relax in Baku.

"You are going to Tbilisi?" the Azeri man said.

"Yes," I said. "You?"

"Yes," he said. "I am from Azerbaijan, but I live in Georgia. Now there are no flights."

Georgia shut down its airport when Russia invaded. The country was accessible only by ground.

"It is stupid," he said, "but this is Georgia. Comfort is only zero."

So far he was right. The train had sat all afternoon on the platform in the sun. It was broiling hot when I climbed aboard and even hotter inside my assigned compartment. The climate control is turned off when the train isn't moving. The air was so humid it practically *tasted* of water. My clothes stuck to my skin. The window in my compartment was sealed and wouldn't open, so I stepped into the hall next to one that did. A Georgian man introduced himself as Levan and joined me by the window and lit up a cigarette. He beamed when he learned of my profession.

"We love you," he said. "You are doing such a good job showing the truth of what is really happening. They are animals, imperialists. They can't admit the Soviet era is over. We really appreciate the international media."

"Thank you," I said, although I hadn't yet written a word about Georgia and didn't deserve credit for anything he had read.

"Are you going to the region?" he said. I knew which region he meant. He meant the north-central part of the country in and around South Ossetia—including the Georgian city of Gori, the birthplace of Stalin—that was occupied by the Russians.

"I don't know," I said, which was true at the time. I wanted to go as far as Gori, but hardly anyone was allowed past the checkpoints.

"The Russians are shooting at journalists," he said. "They are shooting at everybody. They don't care who you are."

Levan was the only person on the train who smiled at me even once. The rest of the passengers, Georgian and Azeri alike, wore a flat emotionless poker face and seemed suspicious not only of me, but also of everyone else. I adapted and only let myself stare at other people without saying hello or even nodding or smiling.

"Five years ago we had a much better train," Levan said. "I don't know what happened to it."

This train was not good. Most windows didn't open, the doors didn't always stay closed, the carpets were stained, the beds were narrow and hard, and the toilet defied obscenity-free description.

"This looks like a Soviet train," I said.

"It is," he said. "It was built in East Germany in the 70s."

I didn't know it at the time, but the train I took from Baku to

Tbilisi is identical to the train viewers can see in the nail-biting thriller *Transsiberia* starring Woody Harrelson and Ben Kingsley. The film takes place almost entirely on a Russian train from Beijing to Moscow. Someone who worked on the movie is very familiar indeed with the train system in the former Soviet Union and took pains to get even the smallest details right. The film was even shot on one of these trains. I instantly recognized the dingy curtains, the chipped Formica tray tables, the broken light switches, the sealed and smudged glass, and most of all the bullying women who ran the thing like a jail on a track.

None of the attendants on my train were men and none were younger than fifty. They were all bulldogs in the shape of middle-aged women and were obvious products of a communist system. They barked orders at every passenger and seemed beaten down themselves as if their superiors treated them the same way. They glowered at me as though my very existence was a grave offense against the universe and would get me hurled off the back of the fast-moving train at the first opportunity.

Half the compartments in my car were empty, yet I had to share one with an elderly Georgian woman. She could not understand what it meant that we had no language in common. She kept speaking to me in Georgian. I kept telling her that I don't speak Georgian, but she insisted on talking to me anyway as though I might learn her language if she raised her voice and kept at it. I leaned back and cracked open a book, but that didn't help. She just kept talking. "I'm sorry, but I don't speak Georgian," I said again and shrugged.

I stepped out of our shared compartment and into the hall as the train left the station. Levan, the English-speaking Georgian, joined me there. He stuck his head and arms outside an open window and lit up another cigarette.

"Levan," I said. "Can I get you to ask one of the attendants if I can move to an empty compartment?"

"You can move in with me if you want," he said.

"Thanks," I said. "I appreciate that. But I'd rather have my own space. I need peace and quiet so I can write."

"Of course," he said and did not seem offended that I did not want to share space with him.

He summoned an angry attendant and spoke to her in Russian.

"She wants to know if you have ten manats," he said. Ten Azeri manats is about twelve American dollars. I sighed, pulled a ten manat note out of my pocket, and handed it over. Then she nodded as if to say I could move wherever I wanted without being beaten.

I walled myself off in a private compartment and edited a long essay about Kosovo that would soon appear in a British quarterly magazine. The air conditioning had kicked in and the train was finally comfortable. When the sun went down I let myself be rocked to sleep by the wide swaying of the old communist train as we slowly made our way to the border with Georgia.

A train attendant shook me awake and hollered at me in the morning.

"*What?*" I said, momentarily forgetting where I was and wondering who on earth was screaming at me in a language I did not understand. I squinted. Behind her loomed a uniformed man with a rifle. *Oh,* I thought. This was the border.

The man with the rifle was an Azeri soldier. He asked to see my passport. I handed it over. Then he asked me to open my luggage. I did so. He rummaged through it briefly, then left me alone. Another soldier stepped into my compartment with a bomb-detection kit. The attendant glared at me through all this as though I was a saboteur or a terrorist who was about to be summarily shot.

After they finally left me alone I stepped bleary-eyed into the hall. Levan was there in his usual place smoking a cigarette near the window. He saw me cast an irritated glance at the nasty attendant.

"Is this your first time on this train?" he said.

I nodded.

"I can read your thoughts," he said.

"These women act like they had the same job in the Soviet days," I said. Not much in Azerbaijan made me think of the communist era, but the train experience from beginning to end made me wonder how much had changed.

"I'm sure they did," he said and laughed. "I've taken this train all over the Soviet Union, from Tbilisi to Moscow to Siberia. It's always the same women."

I was on my way to Georgia to cover the Russian invasion, but Azerbaijan had a so-called "frozen conflict" of its own in the South Caucasus that few have even heard of and fewer know much about. This war, the forgotten war of Nagorno (or "Mountainous") Karabakh, has so far racked up a much higher body count—tens of thousands—than any lately inside the borders of Georgia. More than a million people have been displaced from their homes. Their displacement is most likely permanent. An uneasy ceasefire holds most of the time, but the conflict itself is not even close to being resolved. It's a Mideast- and Balkan-style ethnic bomb that could easily blow up the region again and tempt Russia with another imperialist adventure in its "near abroad."

Armenians say their ancient region of Nagorno Karabakh was given to the Azerbaijan Soviet Socialist Republic by Moscow in 1923 shortly after Vladimir Lenin's Bolshevik regime reconquered the briefly independent South Caucasus nations. Azeris insist the region did not belong to any Armenian state and that Moscow merely rejected Armenia's petition to *acquire* the disputed territory and kept Karabakh within Azerbaijan.

After the Berlin Wall came down and the Soviet Union began unraveling, Armenia wanted Karabakh. Bloody communal warfare broke out between ethnic Azeris and ethnic Armenians in both countries and, most viciously, in ethnically mixed Karabakh itself. Armenian soldiers managed to expel the ethnic Azeris and seize almost all Karabakh territory. The Armenian military now occupies the area. It's an island, though, surrounded on all sides by other parts of Azerbaijan. So Armenia, in order to create a land bridge, is also occupying every inch of Azerbaijan to the south and west of it. The whole southwestern corner of the country—most of which is outside the disputed region of Karabakh—has been de facto annexed to Armenia.

Though it is entirely dependent on Armenia for support, Nagorno Karabakh calls itself an independent republic. No other country recognizes its existence.

Even if you visit Armenia, you still have to get an additional visa in the capital Yerevan (the only place in the world where you can obtain one) to visit Karabakh. If you go there, Azerbaijan will put you on a blacklist.

Armenia and Azerbaijan—including the Karabakh region— were both ethnically mixed before the war started. Now, aside from individuals in mixed marriages, neither are. Ethnic cleansing in both countries was thorough.

This conflict, like many of its kind, is morally ambiguous. It is also of little particular interest to most who live outside the region as long as it's frozen. As Caucasus expert and author Thomas Goltz put it in his book, *Azerbaijan Diary*, "The Azeris...did not know how to suffer in a way that could readily find its way into the print or broadcast media."

This conflict would have felt entirely like a sideshow during my Caucasus trip except that it damn near got me arrested at the border on my way back to Azerbaijan. The authoritarian women running the train weren't the worst people I ran into on my journeys between the two nations. That dubious honor goes to the Azeri border authorities who inspected the train on my way back.

My luggage was searched by hand just as before, but this time the customs agent—he wasn't a soldier—lost his mind when he found my *Lonely Planet* guidebook to Armenia, Georgia, and Azerbaijan.

"Armenia!" he bellowed and stabbed his index finger at the title. Then he turned to me and narrowed his lizard-like eyes.

"Armenia," I said and made a thumbs-down gesture to signal my disapproval in sign language.

I have nothing against Armenia or Armenians. Their close alliance with Russia is a bit dubious, but it's also understandable in its historical and regional context. Armenians, like everyone else in the geopolitically volcanic Caucasus region, feel threatened. Unlike the others, though, they turn to Russia for protection. My thumbs-down verdict was manufactured for my own good to appease the Azeri official who was understandably furious at Armenia but absurdly paranoid about me and my *Lonely Planet*.

My thumbs-down gesture did me no good at all.

He summoned a half dozen colleagues on his radio, waved the book in their faces when they showed up, and said God-knows what about me and what he thought I might be up to. They jabbered amongst themselves, all quivering mustaches and frowns.

"Do any of you speak English?" I said and sighed.

None apparently did.

"Can you help me?" I said to a nearby Azeri civilian whom I hoped might be able to translate.

"I speak little English," he said. That was enough.

"That book," I said, "is for tourists." I tried to keep it simple. "Hotels. Restaurants."

"Ah," he said and nodded. Then he translated for the officials.

The man who discovered the book screamed at him to shut up.

"For *tourists*," I said to the officials, hoping they might get a clue. "Hotels. *Restaurants*." I threw my hands toward the ceiling to show I was frustrated with them instead of afraid. I had nothing to hide and they needed to know that.

They passed the book around, thumbed through it, and stared intently when they flipped to some pages with maps. Then they deliberated for several minutes before finally handing the book back.

"Welcome," said the chief officer as he firmly shook my hand. They departed and left me alone.

"So much trouble," said the Azeri civilian who witnessed all this, "over that little book."

Getting into Georgia on the train was easier than getting out. As soon as the Georgian customs officials stamped my passport and finished hand-searching my luggage, I stepped off and into a taxi. A friend warned me in advance that the train sits at the border for hours, yet an inexpensive taxi ride would get me to the capital in less than forty-five minutes. So I took his advice and arrived in Tbilisi long before any of my fellow passengers.

The taxi ride was my introduction to Georgia and it wasn't pretty. Azerbaijan's countryside beyond the booming capital Baku reminded me of Iraq in some ways with its bad roads, walled off houses, general poverty, and its vaguely Middle Eastern characteristics. But this part of the Georgian country was considerably rougher and poorer. It looked brutally Stalinist.

Hideous smokestacks made up the skyline. Nothing new had been built in decades. Homes were falling apart. Monstrous public housing blocks desperately needed paint, new windows, and general repairs. Many of the factories were shuttered. Very little economic activity was evident. It was as though the area was still operating under a command economy even though it is not.

More than half the cars on the road were banged up Russian-built Ladas. Nearly all had cracked windshields, including the taxi I rode in. These Ladas are tiny. They have tiny doors, tiny steering wheels, tiny dashboards, tiny seats, and no seat belts. A Lada is the *last* car you'd want to crash in.

A thick film of gray ash from the skyline of smokestacks covered everything, including the leaves on the trees. This blighted region looked like an apocalyptic dystopia where absolutely everything modern was broken. My heart ached for Georgia.

I really did feel like my eighteen hours on the train set me back eighteen years as well as sending me sideways a few hundred miles. This portion of Georgia might look even *worse* now than it did when it was part of the Soviet Union. The buildings and cars had more time to deteriorate and nothing had been fixed up or repaired.

"In the Caucasus," Robert D. Kaplan wrote in *Eastward to Tartary*, "one could be optimistic in the capital cities, but in the provinces one confronted the hardest truths....Compared to [South Ossetia], rural Georgia was like Tuscany."

He wasn't exaggerating. And if South Ossetia was in even worse shape than this part of Georgia, then God help the Ossetes.

The Stalinist apartment blocks were uglier and more dilapidated than any I've seen in post-communist Europe, including Albania. This unreconstructed corner of the Soviet Union gave me an idea just how nasty and oppressive that system was. You can't always learn much about a country's past political system by looking at its current physical infrastructure, but in this part of Georgia you can.

Most Eastern European countries were in no better shape immediately after the communist era ended, but they've been able to pull themselves up in the meantime with help from the European Union. Georgia, though, is an outpost of Europe so remote that it is in Asia, too far away to be rescued by the E.U. or NATO.

"I remember how some of the Eastern bloc countries looked just after the fall of the wall," independent journalist Michael Yon said to me in an email shortly after I arrived in Georgia and told him what I had seen. "East Germany was like zombie land but quickly emerged because of West Germany; Poland was, too, but quickly emerged; Czechoslovakia (or now Czech Republic and Slovakia) was nothing like what you see today and was nothing but gray and shortages; Romania was like *Hell*. Hungary was okay, but it had started to emerge ahead of the rest. Any of these countries that you have seen in the last fifteen years were *nothing* like that eighteen years ago."

Tbilisi itself, though, is better.

Aside from its geographic location, Tbilisi could be any European Mediterranean capital—though with an Eastern twist.

Aesthetically exquisite in some places, and at least average in most of the others, Tbilisi is a pleasant city to visit despite the fact that it's loud and smells of exhaust. The post-communist recovery in Georgia's largest city is far more advanced than in the border area I saw when I first arrived. It's Asian, but it looks and feels European. It's in at least adequate physical shape even if it isn't exactly what I would call prosperous. Seeing it was a relief.

But Tbilisi felt tense, as though the air was electrified. The Russian invasion unleashed a refugee crisis all over the country and especially in its capital. Every school in Tbilisi was jammed with civilians who fled aerial bombardment and shootings by the Russian military—or massacres, looting, and arson by irregular Cossack-like paramilitary units swarming across the border.

Russia seized and effectively annexed two breakaway Georgian provinces, South Ossetia and Abkhazia, ostensibly to protect civilians from Georgian government fire. It also invaded the region of Gori, which unlike them had been under Georgia's control. Gori is in the center of the country, just an hour's drive from Tbilisi. Ninety percent of its citizens fled, and the tiny remainder lived amid a violent mayhem overseen by Russian occupation forces that, despite Moscow's claims to the contrary, were not yet withdrawing.

I visited one of the schools transformed into refugee housing in the center of Tbilisi and spoke to four women—Lia, Nana, Diana, and Maya—who had fled with their children from a cluster of small villages just outside Gori.

"We left the cattle," Lia said. "We left the house. We left everything and came on foot because to stay there was impossible."

Diana's account: "They are burning the houses. From most of the houses they are taking everything. They are stealing everything, even such things as toothbrushes and toilets. They are taking the toilets. Imagine. They are taking broken refrigerators."

And Nana: "We are so heartbroken. I don't know what to say or even think. Our whole lives we were working to save something, and one day we lost everything. Now I have to start everything from the very beginning."

Seven families lived cheek by jowl inside a single classroom, sleeping on makeshift beds made of desks pushed together. Small children played with donated toys; at times, their infant siblings cried. Everyone looked haggard and beaten down, but food was available and the smell wasn't bad. They could wash, and the air conditioning worked.

"There was a bomb in the garden and all the apples on the trees fell down," Lia remembered. "The wall fell down. All the windows were destroyed. And now there is nothing left because of the fire."

"Did you actually see any Russians," I said, "or did you leave before they got there?"

"They came and asked us for wine, but first we had to drink it ourselves to show that it was not poisoned. Then they drank the wine themselves. And then they said to leave this place as soon as possible; otherwise they would kill us. The Russians were looking for anyone who had soldiers in their home. If anyone had a Georgian soldier at home they burned the houses immediately."

Her husband had remained behind and arrived in Tbilisi shortly before I did. "He was trying to keep the house and the fields," she said. "Afterward, he wanted to leave, but he was circled by soldiers. It was impossible. He was in the orchards hiding from the Russians in case they lit the house. He was walking and met the Russian soldiers and he made up his mind that he couldn't stay any more. The Russian soldiers called him and asked where he was going, if he was going to the American side."

"The Russians said this to him?" I said.

"My husband said he was going to see his family," she said. "And the Russians said again, 'Are you going to the American side?'"

"So the Russians view you as the American side, even though there are no Americans here."

"Yes," she said. "Because our way is for democracy."

Senator John McCain may have overstated things a bit when, shortly after the war started, he said, "We are all Georgians now." But apparently even rank-and-file Russian soldiers view the Georgians and Americans as one. Likewise, these simple Georgian country women seemed to understand who their friends are.

"I am very thankful to the West," Maya said as her eyes welled up with tears. "They support us so much. We thought we were alone. I am so thankful for the support we have from the United States and from the West. The support is very important for us." She tried hard to maintain her dignity and not cry in front of me, a foreign reporter in fresh clothes and carrying an expensive camera. "The West saved the capital. They were moving to Tbilisi. There was one night that was very dangerous. The Russian tanks were very close to the capital. I don't know what happened, but they moved the tanks back."

My translator, whose husband worked for Georgia's ministry of foreign affairs, made a similar guess that the West helped save the capital. "The night they came close to Tbilisi," she said, "Bush and McCain made their strongest speeches yet. The Russians seemed to back down. Bush and McCain have been very good for us."

Likewise, the women seemed to understand what Russian imperialism has always been about—and not just during the Soviet era. "Why do you think the Russians are doing this in your village?" I said.

"They want our territories," Nana said. "Some of them are Ossetians, too, not only Russians, and not only soldiers. Some are there just to steal things, from Ossetia and Chechnya."

Russia didn't want to annex Gori permanently, in all likelihood, but it did want, as it always has, a buffer zone between itself and its enemies. It was George F. Kennan, America's ambassador to the Soviet Union, who said, "Russia can have at its borders only enemies or vassals." Now Georgia has been all but dismembered.

"We will never forget this," Lia said. "Never. Ever."

T he Georgian government denied all foreign journalists access to the army, but I met a local man who came up with a workaround for me.

"I can take you to the hospital," he said, "and you can talk to soldiers who have been wounded. The government won't be able to stop you."

I felt apprehensive about meeting wounded soldiers. Would they really want to talk to someone from the media or would they rather spend their time healing in peace? I didn't know, but I had a job to do, so I decided to go. If they didn't want to talk, I'd leave them alone.

A doctor led me past broken windows down dark and filthy hallways to a room full of Georgian soldiers and a civilian who were wounded in South Ossetia. They said they felt okay enough to speak to a foreign reporter. Four men shared the hot room. They lay on their beds, shirtless, wrapped in bandages and sheets and smoking cigarettes. The place smelled like a tavern.

"Every day and every hour the Russian side lied," said Georgian soldier Kaha Bragadze, whose leg had been pierced by shrapnel from a Russian air strike. "It must be stopped. If not today, then maybe tomorrow. My troops were in our village, Avnevi. On the 6th of August they blew up our four-wheel-drives and our pickups. Also in this village—it was August 5th or 6th, I can't remember—they started bombing us with shells. Two soldiers died that day, our peacekeepers. The Ossetians had a good position on the hill. They could see all our positions and our villages. We couldn't see who was shooting at us."

"Were they just bombing peacekeepers," I said, "or also civilians and villages?"

"Before they started bombing us they took all the civilians out of their villages," he said. "Then they started damaging our villages—houses, a gas pipe, roads, yards. They killed our animals. They evacuated their villages, then bombed ours."

Another Georgian soldier, Giorgi Khosiashvili, concurred. He lay on his back with his broken arm in a sling.

"I was a peace keeper, as well," he said, "but in another village. I was fired upon on August 6th. On the 5th of August they started shooting. They blew up our peacekeeping trucks. They also mined the roads used by civilians. On the 6th of August they started bombing Avnevi. And at this time they took the civilians out of Tskhinvali and sent them to North Ossetia [inside Russia]."

A tattooed civilian man, Koba Mindiashvili, shared the hospital room with the soldiers. He, too, was in South Ossetia where he lived outside Tskhinvali, its de-facto capital. His left knee was propped up and wrapped in white bandages.

"When they started bombing my village," he said, "I ran away. The soldiers wounded me. They robbed me and shot me in the leg with a Kalashnikov. I don't know if it was Russians or Ossetians. They took my car, took my gold chain, and shot me."

"They didn't care if it was a house or a military camp," Giorgi Khosiashvili said. "They bombed everything."

"You actually saw this for yourself?" I said.

"Yes," he said. "I saw it. It was the Russian military airplanes. If they knew it was a Georgian village, they bombed all the houses. Many civilians were killed from this bombing."

"It was Russians or Ossetians who did this?" I said.

"It was Russians," he said. "The Ossetians don't have any jets."

In the lobby of the Marriott Hotel downtown I ran into Dr. Mátyás Eörsi, the deputy floor leader of the Hungarian Liberal Party and president of the Liberal Group in the Parliamentary Assembly of the Council of Europe. He had been concerned with Georgia's troubles for some time and he flew from Budapest to Tbilisi as soon as the fighting broke out.

His view of Russia's great game is a dark one, informed as it is by having lived much of his own life under the boot heel of Moscow in Eastern Europe.

"The Council of Europe is a pan-European organization," he said. "Its most important mission is to protect human rights, the rule of law, and democracy in its member countries. This is the first time since the Turkish-Greek war, which was quite long ago, that two member countries were at war. All of our principles are breached when one of our member countries occupies another one."

But what could the Council of Europe *do* about something like this?

"The weakness of the Council of Europe compared with NATO is that we have no military. The weakness compared with the European Union is that we have no money. But those weaknesses, in my opinion, can be our strength because then we can speak up honestly. We can be more straightforward in our messages and keep a more united European standpoint on what is right and what is wrong. So what we can do is say very clearly that what is happening here in Georgia is fully unacceptable. And Russia should be aware that though they have certain tools to divide Europe, when it comes to war, Europe cannot be divided. Our goal is to work on this to maintain or create a united European position on this war."

The Council of Europe had no leverage over Russia to speak of. Russian ruler Vladimir Putin couldn't care less about passive objections from Europeans or anyone else.

"I hesitate to draw a parallel with 1939 and 2008," he said, "but this is a lesson for Europe."

"You're referring to Nazi Germany's invasion of Czechoslovakia?" I said.

"Yes," he said. "And, by the way, if you look at the arguments they are very similar. Germany was calling for protection of the Germans in Sudetenland. It is very similar. It's not an exact parallel, but I see some similarities. Protection of minorities is a legitimate goal, but a country must be very careful in choosing the proper tools. I think there are many more Russians living in Brooklyn than in South Ossetia. If something is wrong, if there is a pogrom, an ethnic conflict, Russia will, what, attack the United States? You know what I mean. They should be more careful."

"Can you tell me about the mood in Europe right now," I said, "or at least in Hungary?"

"The European public mood," he said, "in general, is to avoid any conflict and try to reconcile. It could be different in countries that were earlier under control of the Soviet Union. When I hear, for example, that [Georgian President Mikheil] Saakashvili was provoking Russia, immediately it occurs to me that Soviet troops came to Budapest in 1956 and it was claimed that Hungarians were provoking Russia. The same thing happened in 1968 with Czechoslovakia. So, again, I see this parallel. Russia lost the Baltic countries that were part of the Soviet Union. There was a huge fight in Ukraine and in Georgia whether the leaders of these countries will remain under the umbrella of Russia. Russia punished them for their decision not to remain under their sphere of influence."

"Russia has behaved this way toward its neighbors for a very long time," I said.

"During the first NATO enlargement," he said, "when lots of European leaders were running to Moscow and saying *we don't want to harass you or provoke you*, [President Jimmy Carter's national security advisor Zbigniew] Brzezinski said there is some democratic progress in Russia in terms of internal politics, but Russia's external politics are not democratic at all. You can see that Russia is opposing the Baltic countries, Central European countries like Hungary, the Czech Republic, and Poland. This is not a democratic foreign policy. Brzezinski concluded that, because of this resistance by Russia, if NATO is not enlarged it will not calm down Russia. It would be the other way around. It would feed the radicals in Russia who say, *this is the language we have to use toward the West* because then they will shut up and stand back."

NATO expansion is not part of some Western plot to eventually conquer Russia, but it's not hard to understand why it looks like one from Moscow. If the Soviet Union won the Cold War and the Warsaw Pact expanded to include Belgium and France, Americans and especially the British would surely worry that they might be "next." Russia assumes that NATO expansion means the exact same thing in reverse that the expansion of the Warsaw Pact would have meant. The analysis is wrong, but Russians are just as prone to cognitive egocentrism—the projection of ones own psychology onto others—as everyone else.

"They used to be a world power," Dr. Eörsi said. "Countries they used to control can't be controlled anymore. There are millions of Russians who lived in poverty in the Soviet Union who said, *yeah, but we are a superpower*. They lost this feeling. And Vladimir Putin is delivering this feeling to them that Russia is again becoming a superpower."

"We're all going to be thinking about Ukraine differently after this," I said.

"Absolutely," he said.

The Ukrainian government at the time hoped to join the European Union and NATO. Relations between Moscow and Kiev could hardly get any worse without leading to war. If Russia was still willing to invade neighboring countries, bringing a nation from its sphere of influence into the Western sphere could be dangerous.

"What do you suppose Europe can do to shore up the defense of Ukraine in advance?" I said.

"I think a Membership Action Plan for NATO should be given to them immediately," he said. "I also think it's time to say that the 2014 Winter Olympic Games should not be held in [the Southern Russian city of] Sochi."

"Let's say for the sake of discussion that a Membership Action Plan were given to Ukraine tomorrow," I said. "How long would it take for Ukraine to be formally inside NATO and under its military protection?"

"Any short amount of time," he said.

"Two days?" I said. "One day?"

"One day," he said.

"So Ukraine could," I said, "theoretically, be in NATO by the end of the week."

"You remember how Turkey became a member of NATO?" he said. "It took one day. Greece? One day. It was a different geopolitical situation, with a big Soviet Union and Greece having gotten rid of the [military dictatorship]. It was just like letting them into the European Union. Greece never met the criteria of the European Union. It can be done at any time."

"Do you suspect that if Russia actually gets what it wants here," I said, "that Azerbaijan would be next or Ukraine would be next?"

"My very sad conclusion," he said, "is that there would be no need for a second war. Because everything will fall automatically. If Russia wins, then the pro-Russian faction in Ukraine will win because of the fear that it could be done to them at any time."

He was right. That's exactly what happened. The stridently pro-Western Ukrainian government of Viktor Yushchenko was soon replaced by the moderately pro-Russian government of Viktor Yanukovych.

I asked Eörsi if I could take his picture.

"Sure," he said "Do you want me to smile or be serious?"

"Look serious," I said.

"Yes," he said. "This is serious." He looked grimly into my camera as I pressed the shutter button.

"I've noticed that not many Georgians are smiling," I said. "Is that normal?" Unlike him, I had never been to Georgia before and didn't know how people acted and felt under normal conditions.

"Why would they?" he said. "They have no reason to smile."

"You mean because of the war," I said.

"Well," he said, "it's also a national trait. In America when someone says *how are you*, you say, *I am fine*. In Hungary, in Eastern Europe, the best you can say is *I am surviving*. That's the most optimistic response possible."

Nine

Behind Russian Lines

Thomas Goltz showed up in town a few days before I did. He's the author of *Georgia Diary*, as well as *Chechnya Diary* and *Azerbaijan Diary*—three classic works of hard-boiled reportage from the Caucasus region—and I hoped to arrange a time to meet up with him for an interview.

"I'll be at the Marriott at 6pm," I wrote to him in an email, "and if you're there at the same time we can do this." He hadn't answered by a quarter to six, but I took a taxi from my cheap hotel to the expensive Marriott anyway just in case he got my message at the last minute and felt like having a drink.

My taxi driver pulled up in front of the main entrance at exactly the same moment as Goltz's. I recognized his bald head and his whisk-broom mustache at once. *Good*, I thought. *He showed up.* I stepped out of the car and waved hello.

"Let's go to Gori," he said.

Surely, I thought, he had to be joking. Gori was closed. Gori was occupied by the Russians.

"Stay there," he said before I could shut my taxi door. He came over, motioned for me to get in, and sat next to me in the back. He wasn't joking. And it's a good thing I had my camera with me because we were off.

Georgia appeared much more prosperous, or at least much less blighted, on the western side of Tbilisi than it did on the eastern side near the border with Azerbaijan. It's natural that economic development and post-communist repair wouldn't be geographically even, but for a while there I was worried economic development barely even existed outside the capital's city center.

"How does it feel to be in Free Georgia?" Goltz said.

"Good," I said, although I was feeling less good by the minute as traffic thinned. Gori is only an hour's drive from Tbilisi. The Russian occupation began well short of that distance. Free Georgia wasn't going to last much longer.

We approached a checkpoint manned by Georgian police. Our driver spoke to them for a few moments and said we were journalists from America. They waved us through without checking our passports or any other pieces of identification.

"What was that about?" I said.

Our driver didn't speak English, so Goltz asked him in Georgian and translated.

"It's the idiot's checkpoint," he said. "They asked where we're going. If we said we're going to Gori as though we have no idea what's going on, forget it. If we say we're going to get as far as the Russians will let us, okay. As long as we know what we're doing."

We drove a few minutes in silence. This portion of the highway hadn't been cut by the Russians, but we were the only ones on it, as if Godzilla was rampaging just up ahead.

I hadn't seen a country so depopulated since I drove with my buddy Noah Pollak in Northern Israel under Hezbollah rocket fire in 2006 when more than a million refugees fled south toward Tel Aviv. This was the second time in two years I found myself in a landscape that looked like the end of the world.

"That hill to the right is the edge of South Ossetia," Goltz said. I snapped a photo. "That's how close to Tbilisi the Russians will be permanently based."

We had only left Tbilisi fifteen minutes before. It would take almost no time at all for the Russian military to reach the capital if the order was given.

"There are probably Russian positions on top of that ridge," he said.

My camera was equipped with a serious zoom lens, which doubled as a telescope when I needed one. I studied the top of the ridge through the lens but didn't see any Russian positions—yet.

After another fifteen minutes of driving I knew we were near the end of Free Georgia, as Goltz had earlier put it. The first Russian checkpoint had to be just up ahead.

Someone planted an American flag on the side of the road.

"Look at that," Goltz said.

According to Gallup International's 2004 survey of global opinion, the world's most pro-American countries, in order, were Kosovo, Afghanistan, Israel, and Georgia. And that was *before* the Russians invaded.

Okay, I thought after we passed the American flag. The Russians should be right up ahead.

Instead, a gaggle of journalists and local civilians congregated on each side of the road around the next corner.

We weren't interested in joining the herd. We wanted to get as far as we could, so we kept driving. Nobody paid us much mind, but at the same time nobody wanted to follow us up the hill and around the corner where we were about to face the Russians.

A roadblock appeared up ahead. Someone had placed a line of tires across the road. A half dozen armed and uniformed men stood on each side of it.

"Are they Russians or Georgians?" I said.

"Russians," Goltz said.

It was too late to back out. Whatever would happen would happen.

Our driver slowed and pulled over the car a hundred or so meters before the roadblock. He braced himself as if he expected to have rifles pointed at him or at least to be shouted at.

I stepped out of the taxi and slung my camera around my back instead of over my chest, opened my hands, and slowly turned around so the soldiers could see what I was carrying. The last thing I wanted to do was make them nervous. I wasn't armed and I wasn't going to suddenly point my camera at them.

Goltz and I slowly but confidently approached them as though we had already done this dozens of times and had nothing to worry about. He spoke to them in Russian. I flipped open a pack of cigarettes and offered them to whoever wanted one. A young brown-eyed soldier nodded and helped himself.

I produced a lighter and lit his cigarette for him. Our hands touched as we shielded the flame from the wind. He softly nodded thanks and seemed less threatening than he did from a distance. He was relaxed, didn't seem to mind that we had shown up, and seemed unlikely to point his weapon at me.

Goltz spoke jovially to the soldiers in their own language as I slowly paced back and forth. The Russians joked and laughed with him. They were among the few people I saw in the entire country who laughed or smiled. The Georgians certainly had little to smile about. Honestly, though, the Russian soldiers didn't have much to smile about either, and I was slightly surprised to see it.

Whether it's true or not, I have no idea, but I heard from many Georgians that some Russian soldiers were furious when they came upon Georgian military bases and saw that their Georgian counterparts had superior food, clothing, and living conditions. I might be tempted to dismiss this as self-serving propaganda that makes the Georgians feel better, but Russian soldiers really are notoriously underpaid and underfed even inside their own country.

My sometimes traveling companion Sean LaFreniere had visited Russia a few years before, and he saw uniformed Russian soldiers begging for money and food on the streets in both Moscow and St. Petersburg. And he met a Russian woman who told him about the ordeal her younger brother endured in the army.

"She told me that her little brother had recently returned from his first few months of 'boot camp' in the Russian army," he wrote on his blog. "When he arrived home for a holiday dinner, his family found him a broken shell. He had been physically, psychologically, and even sexually abused as part of his 'training.' His parents and siblings refused to let him return. They have been hiding him for months while trying to acquire papers to get him out of the country. Many Western newspapers have documented similar suffering by Russian soldiers. The *BBC* and the *Guardian* recently ran stories on one Private Sychev. He lost his legs and genitals to gangrene after ritualized abuse by the comrades in his unit. Other recruits are forced into pornography and prostitution to enrich their superior officers."

I never heard any expression of hatred toward the people of Russia by Georgians. I didn't even hear any complaints about, let alone hatred for, the Abkhaz or the Ossetians in the breakaway regions. Georgians are, of course, unhappy with the Russian invasion, but they didn't seem to be making it personal. I heard much more serious denunciations of Armenians from Azeris every day in Azerbaijan than I heard from anybody in Georgia toward anyone. Azerbaijan's anger toward Armenia for its occupation of Nagorno Karabakh is understandable, though a bit unhinged and over the top in some quarters, so the muted reaction toward Russians among Georgians surprised me.

I even heard that some Georgian civilians took pity on the underfed Russian soldiers and cooked meals for them in their kitchens. I don't know if it's true. What I do know is that many Georgians believe it is true and think it a plausible thing for Georgians to do. And I didn't detect anything in the Georgian character that made me believe the rumors to be false.

"Go ahead and take pictures of whatever you want," Goltz said.

"They don't mind?" I said.

"No," he said, "it's fine."

So I took a few pictures and carefully studied the faces of the soldiers as I pointed my camera at them. None seemed to mind even when I zoomed in, but I got a serious creep vibe from one soldier with a shaved head and a scorpion tattooed on his hand.

"Want to go to Gori?" Goltz said.

"They'll let us?" I said.

"Let's go."

He summoned our driver who gingerly drove up to meet us from his parking space at a distance.

"I guess they're going to escort us?" I said.

"I don't think so," Goltz said. "Let's just go."

"We can just drive there by ourselves?" I said.

We got back in the car. Our taxi driver slowly drove past the road block as though he expected to be stopped again at any moment. But nobody stopped us.

After we rounded a corner we had the road to ourselves again as we headed straight toward the occupied city of Gori.

"What's going on, Thomas?" I said. Whatever he said to those men in Russian apparently worked, but were we *really* supposed to be driving toward Gori? Just about everyone else was being turned back.

I do know of at least one journalist who was allowed to "embed" with Russian soldiers for twenty-four hours in Gori. They drove him around and let him sleep at their base. I would have pounced on the opportunity if it were offered, but almost no journalists from any country were allowed inside the occupied city without a visa from Moscow, as though Gori was now part of Russia.

"This sure feels strange, doesn't it?" Goltz said.

Yes, it felt strange. And totally wrong. And more than a little bit stupid. My internal threat detection system crackled.

"I once walked in the neutral zone between Iraq and Iran," I said, which is true. Goltz laughed.

There's a strange little wooded area along a stream in Biara, Iraq, along the Iranian border where no one is really sure where the line is. Walking there felt powerfully wrong even though I had Iraqi guides with me, and I didn't dare linger in that zone for even a full sixty seconds.

I didn't even know I had crossed into the neutral zone until after it happened. I could have run into an Iranian border patrol at any moment and would have had nothing to say for myself. I quickly retreated back to Iraq.

Driving inside the Russian occupation zone without an escort felt exactly the same. The atmosphere positively sizzled with danger. What would we say if we came upon a Russian patrol who demanded to know what on earth we were doing?

"We're going to keep driving through as many checkpoints as we can," he said.

A Russian military truck approached from the other direction. I dropped my camera into my lap. The driver seemed to pay us no mind. I relaxed slightly when he passed.

The road was otherwise empty until we came upon another Russian checkpoint. Two soldiers stood next to an armored personnel carrier and a Russian flag on a pole. The American flag we had passed earlier was at most only five miles behind us. So an American flag and a Russian flag were planted just a few minutes away from each other inside a third country. The Cold War between the Soviets and the West was over, but at least part of the world was still divided into Russian and American spheres of influence, and Georgia looked and felt like the center of it.

Our driver approached the checkpoint slowly, but the Russians waved us through before he even stopped.

I felt better. Apparently it was sort of okay for us to be on that road since the soldiers at the first checkpoint let us pass.

The countryside still seemed entirely depopulated but for the birds overhead and in the trees. They carried on as though nothing were out of the ordinary. I found that profoundly eerie for reasons I can't quite explain. Some think animals have a better sense of danger than humans, but I have my doubts about that. Everything was wrong in this part of Georgia. I saw scorch marks in some of the farmland. Trees and grass on the side of the road had been burned away.

"There was fighting here recently," Goltz said. "Those burns are from the war."

We approached a third Russian checkpoint clocking in at sixty-five kilometers from Tbilisi, nearly at the gate to the city of Gori. The soldiers manning this one were not at all happy to see us. One stepped into the road and fiercely pointed his finger in the direction we came from. He yelled something in Russian. Our driver quickly turned around and got us out of there.

"I guess we aren't going to Gori," I said.

"We had to try," Goltz said.

I carefully studied the landscape using my zoom lens. A tank perched on a hill in the distance next to some houses kept watch over the road. The Russians were no longer shooting at people, but they could have shot us at any time had they felt like it. No one would have been able to stop them or save us.

I turned my lens back to the road and faintly made out a distant vehicle with a gunner in a turret barreling toward us at top speed.

"That one has a gunner," I said and put down my camera before he got close enough to see with his naked eye that I was pointing something long and narrow at him. Unless he was watching us with binoculars, I could see farther than he could.

"No sense getting ourselves shot if we don't have to," Goltz said.

Off to the left was a small ad hoc Russian base. I snapped a quick photo.

"Did you get that?" Goltz said.

"Got it," I said.

The driver said something to Goltz. Goltz translated.

"He wants to get back," he said. "He said it's especially dangerous out here at night, that the Russians want a provocation so they can take his car."

It would be dark soon and we were almost an hour outside Tbilisi. The sun was just about to go down.

"I need to get back anyway for a radio interview," Goltz said. "If you have any other plans in this area, say something now."

I laughed. "By myself in the dark with no car?" I said. "I don't think so."

We passed the second Russian checkpoint without incident, then approached the first one again where we had stopped earlier. More men manned the checkpoint this time. Two of them were irregulars. Goltz told our driver to stop.

The irregulars were not wearing full uniforms, but they were armed with rifles and had unsheathed hunting knives tucked into their belts. Unlike the uniformed Russians, these two had blonde hair and blue eyes. They didn't look remotely Asian like some of the others, nor did they quite look like Slavs. I couldn't place them ethnically. They obviously weren't indigenous to the Russian Far East. Were they from Moscow? From Central Russia? One had shaved his head over his ears and wore what looked like a wide mohawk. He was built like a heavyweight wrestler.

Both militiamen triggered every one of my danger signals. "Bad vibe" doesn't quite say it.

Goltz started blabbing at them in Russian. He sounded strangely foolish to me, as though he, unlike me, did not sense we might be in danger. In hindsight, though, I think he did. He just didn't show it. The only words I understood were "Dagestan" and "Montana."

He kept repeating "Dagestan" and "Montana" and sounded like an oblivious American tourist. I wondered what on earth he was doing. I wanted to get out of there. The uniformed Russian soldiers laughed at whatever Goltz said and seemed perfectly relaxed and non-threatening, but the out-of-uniform irregulars looked distinctly unimpressed and barely able to tamp down coils of instinctive aggression.

I did not even think about taking their pictures. These men emitted the odor of psychopaths, as if the only reason they hadn't killed us yet was because they were told to wait a few minutes before plunging their knives in. They said nothing and kept back a bit from some of the uniformed Russians, as though they weren't the ones in charge, but I knew it was time to leave when one of them slowly wrapped his fingers around the hilt of his blade.

Goltz saw it, too, and he told our driver to go. And so we drove off.

"I was making stupid jokes," Goltz said, "about how Dagestan means the same thing as Montana." Dagestan is a troubled Muslim-majority Russian republic in the North Caucasus across from Azerbaijan and next to Chechnya. Goltz lives in Montana. "Both mean *country of the mountains.* What I was saying was stupid, but I did it so we could stall and get a good long look at those Chechen militiamen. It's one of my tricks."

"They're from *Chechnya*?" I said. "How do you know?"

"I don't," he said. "But they probably are. They're *definitely* not Russians. I have a bit of a sixth sense about ethnicity in an ethnic-conscious place like the former Soviet Union," he said. "I *know* the Chechens. I hung with the Chechens."

That explained why I couldn't place them. I could tell they weren't Russian Slavs, but I've never visited Chechnya.

"If I could have stalled us just ten more seconds," he continued, "I would have said *I'm a Chechen who lives in the United States* in Chechen to see if I could get one of those toughs to fucking smile."

I had noticed something while stalled at that checkpoint that didn't even register until after we left. The letters *CCCP*—the Russian abbreviation for the Union of Soviet Socialist Republics—were written in black ink on the rifle slings the militiamen carried. Of course it didn't mean much aside from the fact that their weapons and gear were old, but it hadn't even occurred to me while I was looking at them and their communist era equipment. It seemed perfectly appropriate at the time. Communism, of course, is over. Yet during our day trip in Central Georgia—and even a bit on my train ride to Georgia—I felt distinctly like the Soviet Empire was back or had never left.

"I can't imagine a more serious geopolitical situation anywhere in the world than where we are right now," Goltz said as we reemerged inside Free Georgia. "Despite the fact that everything looks calm and we can joke with the Russians, this is as big as it gets."

Ten

The Scorching of Georgia

Because Gori was closed I decided to visit Borjomi, a small tourist town next to the Borjomi-Kharagauli National Park, the first of its kind in the Caucasus region, which Russian jets had reportedly lit on fire with air strikes.

I hired a Georgian bear of a man named Alex to drive me in his four-wheel-drive over the mountains. Normally you can get to Borjomi from Tbilisi on the main highway in just a few hours, but the highway passes through Gori, and Gori was occupied and blockaded. The only other route open was over the mountains across a high alpine plateau where trees cannot grow. That road was hardly in better condition than a smuggler's path, and it's only passable during the summer after the snow and ice have temporarily thawed.

Alex and I stocked up on road food—chocolate, cookies, soft drinks, and chips—before we set out. It was going to be a long drive and there were no good places to eat on the way. He did not need a map since guiding tourists around the country is his regular job. He likes to travel abroad, too, when he can.

"Were you able to travel during the communist era?" I said.

"I went to East Germany in the 1980s," he said. "Inside the East German wall was still the Soviet Union. It was the same rubbish."

Georgian President Mikheil Saakashvili's popularity had declined since the Rose Revolution that brought him to power in 2003, and I wondered how the war was affecting public opinion.

"Saakashvili screwed up," Alex said. "In June and July these idiots massed everybody on the border and made a big exercise." He reflexively referred to the Russian soldiers and leadership as "these idiots" and was referring here to the biggest military exercise inside Russia since the Chechnya war. It took place on the Georgian border immediately prior to the invasion. "They were planning war. Saakashvili could have done something, but didn't."

The six hour drive to Borjomi taught me to appreciate pavement. Road conditions were fine for the first thirty miles or so, but as soon as we started heading into the mountains, smooth tar turned to gravel.

"Is the road like this the whole way?" I said.

"Sometimes it's worse," Alex said.

It got worse almost instantly. Gravel gave way to rocks the size of golfballs and fists. Alex's four-wheel-drive handled okay, but I was violently jostled around in my seat. Sleep was impossible. So was taking photographs without stopping. After a while I was nauseated.

"A week ago I took eighteen Israeli tourists on this road," Alex said.

Israelis are unflappable. Hardly any tourists went to Georgia during the Russian invasion, but I wasn't surprised to hear that some Israelis showed up. They know from experience that you can travel to a country at war if you stay out of the conflict areas. That's how it was during Israel's second Lebanon war. The northern part of the country was abandoned and on fire, but the rest of Israel was unscathed. It was the same way in Georgia.

Vaguely Middle Eastern-sounding music from Azerbaijan played on the radio for a while, but static eventually overwhelmed the signal. We were in a remote part of Georgia where hardly anyone aside from nomadic sheep herders live, and even they're only there temporarily. Alex did, however, manage to find a single station broadcasting news from Tbilisi. After a few moments he angrily turned it off.

"The French ambassador was stopped for an hour and a half by Russian soldiers on his way to Gori," he said. "This is killing my nerves."

Russia had effectively cut the country in half. It was possible for civilians in four-wheel-drive vehicles like Alex's to cross Georgia's midsection over the mountains, but rerouting all highway traffic from Tbilisi up there would not have been possible. Large trucks weren't able to haul goods over that road, especially not while fully weighted down. Low-clearance passenger vehicles like my own car at home were doomed to high-center or break an axle.

At one point we came upon a van stalled on the side of the road. Alex pulled up next to it and asked the driver if he needed help. The driver said his engine didn't have enough power to get him to the top of the rise, but that he had a tow chain. So Alex attached the van to his truck and pulled the van a few hundred meters up the steepest part of the incline.

The road was even worse up ahead. One stretch was so steep I worried his truck would succumb to gravity and actually flip over backwards. I felt like I was in an SUV commercial.

The top of the pass above Borjomi consisted of nothing but alpine tundra and rock. It was too high for anything else to grow. Georgia has a subtropical climate, but cold wind lashed my ears when I stepped out to take a picture of the valley below.

"I was up here in June," Alex said, "and it was snowing."

If Russia ever decides to close the main road during winter, Georgia will truly be cut into pieces.

The Borjomi area looks a lot like my native Pacific Northwest in the United States with its rugged mountains, cold streams, and evergreen forests. It was still burning. Columns of smoke rose from scorched hillsides.

"Can we stop?" I said to Alex. "I need some pictures."

The air smelled strongly of wood smoke and the fires were in a strange state. I've seen plenty of forest fires in Oregon. We get them every year. These were different. Forest fires, whether started by negligence, lightning, or arson, tend to be large single infernos. Individual fires burned all over the place near Borjomi.

Theoretically they could have been the remnants of a single large fire that had been mostly doused, but these were spaced far enough apart that I could tell several had been started at once in different locations. I couldn't even see the bulk of the damage because it was well away from the main highway and deeper into the forest.

I didn't notice anything unusual when we reached the town of Borjomi, but Alex did.

"This place is usually full this time of year," he said. "But now everything is empty."

That wasn't surprising. Aside from Alex's Israeli clients from the previous week, and a handful of Americans I would soon meet, few tourists thought it wise to visit Georgia during Russia's invasion and occupation. Even Georgians who wanted a break from the stress of conflict had a hard time getting there. Taxi drivers were charging $500 for a one-way trip from the capital because the rocks on the road banged up their vehicles. Alex charged me far less than that, but even his four-wheel-drive took a hit when a deep gouge in the road knocked out his front shocks.

I made arrangements to meet Mako Zulmatashvili before Alex and I left Tbilisi. She agreed to show me around town, introduce me to some local officials, translate for me, and put me up for the night in her mother's guest house. She waited for us at a park across the street from the train station.

"I have some bad news," she said. "We no longer have a room for you."

Her brother Giga's American in-laws had long ago scheduled a visit from the United States. They arrived a day early and needed the room that would have been mine. Giga had recently married a young American woman who spent a few years in Georgia with the Peace Corps, and her parents were visiting from Connecticut for the first time. They picked a heck of a time to see Georgia, but they were committed and refused to be deterred, even by war.

Alex and I ended up marooned in a Soviet-era hotel so the American family members could have the room.

The rack rate was cheap—a mere twenty dollars per night—but it was worth even less. That was obvious long before I got to my room. There was no front desk in the cavernous lobby. The woman who ran the place greeted guests on the front steps. She fished room keys out of her pocket and led Alex, Mako, and me to an elevator that promptly went dark as soon as the doors closed behind us.

The hotel manager sighed, fumbled for a button on the panel in the dark, and pressed something—I don't know what—that made the lights come back on.

"This is Georgia," Mako said and laughed.

Only a single window with drawn curtains lit the passage to my room. If I hadn't used the flash on my camera, I'm not sure I would ever know what the corridor looked like. Perhaps that would have been best. Filth covered the carpet, the walls, and even the ceiling. A horrendous stench of mildew, mold, and decay had built up over decades.

"I'm sorry there's no room at the house for you," Mako said. "I hope this is okay."

"It's fine," I said.

"It is just for one night," Alex said and shrugged.

The hotel would not have been fine if we were staying for more than one night, but it was worth sleeping there once for educational purposes. The place was something to see. I will never really know what Georgia was like when it was part of the Soviet Union, but this hotel gave me an idea.

The usual building materials you expect to see in a Western hotel, or in one of Georgia's more recently built or refurbished hotels, were not available during the communist period. The architects and designers had to make do with what little they had. The skeleton was made with poured concrete. Thin sheets of wood were slapped on the walls inside the rooms to soften things up. Cheap red fabric was stapled to these thin sheets of wood and used as a sort of wallpaper. The room made me think of a high-end tree fort made of cement.

The mattress on my bed was at most one inch thick. There was no tub in the bathroom. The "shower" was a faucet sticking out of the wall two feet off the ground. I had to sit on the floor next to the sink to wash my hair the next morning.

Mako felt bad that I ended up relegated to a communist dump of a place, but I honestly didn't mind because my two-star hotel in Tbilisi felt splendidly luxurious when I got back.

She invited me to her house to meet her family. Marina, her mother, wore an "I (Heart) New York" T-shirt and served cookies and tea.

"This town survives on tourism and not much else," she said. "I don't know what we're going to do."

Another American named Charles joined us. He had booked the other spare room in the guest house and was visiting Georgia as an actual tourist on holiday. He lived in Damascus, Syria, where he studied Arabic, and he came to Borjomi by ground through Turkey and Iraq.

"You're the craziest person in the room," I said.

He shrugged and seemed to think nothing of backpacking around some of the world's most frightening countries for fun.

"On the night the tanks came toward Borjomi," Mako said, "I couldn't sleep at all. I thought it was the last days of Georgia's existence as an independent country. Then smoke and ashes and pieces of burning wood covered the town. We could hardly breathe."

"There isn't much food left in the grocery stores here," her mother Marina said. "We can't bring food in from the Poti port or from Tbilisi."

Meanwhile, despite everything, many Georgians insisted they were showing hospitality to their invaders.

"We're cooking meals for them," Mako said, "and letting them use our showers. They have nothing. We have always liked Russians here in Georgia. Do people in Russia even *know* we're letting them use our showers?"

"If Russians invade America," I said, "they aren't using my shower."

Everyone laughed. Hardly any American would let an enemy soldier use his or her shower. But of course that hardly meant Georgian civilians were happy with the Russian invasion.

"They're playing *Braveheart* over and over again on TV," Giga's American wife said and smiled.

The next morning Mako took me to meet Valerian Lomidze, editor-in-chief of Borjomi's weekly newspaper. He gave me a few photographs of the fires taken by his reporters before I arrived.

"The fire started in five places at the same time," he said. "Obviously it was not started by natural causes. The fires started all along a straight line, as though they were under a flight path."

"Why do you suppose the Russians would do this?" I said. "To destroy the tourism industry in this part of Georgia?"

"They did different things in different places to destroy our various industries," he said. "We have nothing else to survive on in this part of Georgia except tourism. Russians said they came here for peace. But what peace? They bombed the port, the forests, the cities, and blocked the highway. These regions had nothing to do with the conflict areas."

The only contested portions of Georgia were Abkhazia and South Ossetia, which Russia has now de-facto annexed. Gori, Borjomi, and Poti were, like Lomidze said, well outside those areas.

"Russia is part of the conflict," he said, "not bringing peace."

He has worked at the same newspaper since 1974.

"What was it like during the Soviet era?" I said.

"We had more support from the government," he said. "We could publish three times a week, but now only once a week. But we had no freedom to write. We had to work for the government and the party. Now we can write whatever we want."

The Borjomi municipality's Governor Vakhtang Maisuradze said he could speak with me for a few minutes, and two women from his government—Eka Londaridze, head of the local environmental protection agency, and Keti Mandjavidze, who worked with refugees in Borjomi displaced by the Russia invasion—sat down with me briefly while I waited near his office.

"We have been getting help from Turkey," Londaridze said, "but they're out right now and we're expecting help to arrive from Ukraine."

"What were the Turks doing to help you?" I said.

"They had two planes that they sent to Georgia," she said. "They brought water to put the fire out."

The Turkish pilots filled their tanks with lake water in nearby Turkish Kurdistan, dropped the water on the fires, and returned to Turkey to load up on more.

"Are the fires actually inside the park?" I said.

"It's not the park exactly," she said, "it's the wildlife safe area, not where the trails for hiking are. It's where our ancient trees are."

The ecological destruction near Borjomi was significantly less severe than what Saddam Hussein unleashed in the Persian Gulf region when his soldiers ignited Kuwait's oil wells in 1991. Burning trees are much easier to extinguish than blazing geysers of fuel, but it seemed to me just as militarily pointless.

"There was panic," Mandjavidze said. "People thought the Russians were coming into our area. Lots of smoke came into Borjomi. People were helping each other and standing together."

"It was ridiculous," Mako said. "For two days it was hard to even breathe in Borjomi."

Russia's occupation and de-facto annexation of Abkhazia and South Ossetia are almost certainly permanent, but it seemed unlikely even at the time that the Russian military would maintain its blockade of Gori and the highways for much longer. Still, I wanted to know: how effective *was* the blockade? Russian soldiers can implement one again at any time, for any reason at all, and no one can do much to stop them.

Where does an 800-pound gorilla sit? Wherever it wants. Russian troops are now permanently based so close to Georgia's transportation arteries that the country could be bisected again just a few hours or even minutes after an order is given. That threat will hang over the country for a long time.

"How are the supplies in town?" I said. "Do you have enough food and fuel?"

"We have food and fuel, but there is almost no children's food or diapers," Mandjavidze said. "So we're in a hard situation with our children."

"There is enough food in the stores?" I said.

"There is enough," she said. "People are coming from the other side and from Armenia bringing food to the town."

"If the Russians stay where they are for a few more weeks," I said, "keep the roads closed, and the port blockaded, will there still be enough food?"

"*That* would be a big problem," Londaridze said. "After a month people would be starving. We have some ways to get food here, but not enough. The main way is from Tbilisi and it's blocked. We would need to find some other way. From Tbilisi it's impossible to get to the Borjomi area."

"If you watch the Russian TV channels," Mandjavidze said, "they say Georgia is a fascist country, it's run by a Nazi party." She laughed. "They say everything that happened here we did to ourselves."

Mako and I were summoned to Governor Maisuradze's office.

"Tell me in your words what happened here," I said.

"Not until the real answer is out can I specify whether it was Russians," he said. "But nevertheless, for sure, somebody started this fire. It wasn't caused by the weather. Many people saw planes flying over and some heard bombing. On the first day the fires started in a straight line at regular intervals in places that people cannot get to by cars."

He drew five evenly spaced dots connected by a straight line on his notepad. Then he made a plane-in-flight motion with his hand over that line.

"It had to be from a plane," he continued. "And this is also where witnesses said they saw a plane flying over. But until the experts go into the forest and find out biochemically what happened, I can't say anything more."

"Can you guess—and I realize you would be guessing—why the Russians might theoretically want to bomb this area?" I said.

"What did they want to do in Gori or in Poti or anywhere else in Georgia?" he said. "They wanted to cause panic. They wanted to damage the economy. It's pretty obvious that this was their plan. Of course. People can't get food in here. This is what they wanted. The main goal for this area is to become ecologically developed for tourism. The most effective way for them to damage us was to burn our forests. The only other thing they could have done was bomb our mineral water plant, but they didn't, thank God."

Borjomi is famous in the former Soviet Union for its naturally flavored mineral water. It tastes slightly sour, but only slightly, mostly like club soda, but with a slight twist that is impossible to identify. Supposedly it's a love-it-or-hate-it beverage, but I tried a bottle and didn't have a strong reaction one way or the other.

"Russians love our mineral water," Mako said. "They wouldn't want to bomb the plant because then we couldn't make more."

Londaridze and Mandjavidze didn't think the blockade was hurting Borjomi *too* badly so far, but it was still only a few weeks old, and it was during the summer. What if the blockade lasted for months? What if it lasted for years?

"We survived twenty one centuries," the governor said. "We will survive twenty one more even though we don't have anything now. We can't get food and supplies, but we will survive another twenty one centuries." He slapped the desk with the palm of his hand. "That is my answer."

PART FOUR

THE BLACK SEA

Eleven

Twenty Years After the Fall of the Tyrant

"You shoot them and throw them in the basement. Not a single one should come out alive." - Elena Ceausescu

Romania's tyrant Nicolae Ceausescu ran one of Europe's most ruthlessly repressive dictatorships until 1989 when he and his wife Elena were overthrown by their captive subjects and executed on television. "I don't remember even a fingernail being lost by way of casualties," Christopher Hitchens wrote of the anti-communist revolutions that swept Europe in the late 1980s, "except in Romania, where a real Caligula had to be dealt with."

Unlike some formerly Eastern bloc countries, its reputation still hasn't recovered entirely even though it belongs to the European Union and NATO. The country was so thoroughly brutalized by its own government that it remained an emergency room case even a decade after its communist rulers were dispatched.

"The featureless plain filled with cardboard and scrap-metal squatters' settlements as awful as many I had seen in Africa, Asia, and Latin America," Robert D. Kaplan wrote about Romania in his book, *Eastward to Tartary*. Despite its location in Europe, Romania was a Third World country. "The train [from Hungary] began to move," he wrote. "My face was glued to the window. An elevated hot water pipe caught my eye. Where the pipe's shiny new metal and fiberglass insulation ended and rusted metal and rags began—the same point where mounds of trash and corrugated shacks began to appear, where cratered roads suddenly replaced paved ones—marked Romania."

The country doesn't look anything like the Third World anymore. It would not be in the European Union if it did. I was slightly surprised, though, by how many scars from the communist era, both physical and emotional, were still visible when the Ministry of Foreign Affairs invited me and three of my colleagues to visit near the end of 2009.

Roughly 25 percent of Romania's work force left the country during the transition to the market economy. Even now, while Romania looks reasonably prosperous on the surface, people are struggling in a high-expenses low-wage economy.

"We wanted to have some social protection," said Dan Lazar, an economic advisor to the president. "We had to choose between high unemployment with high salaries, or low unemployment with low salaries. We chose the model with the lower unemployment."

Catalin Baba, another economic advisor to the president, said the unemployment rate was still only around six percent even during the steep global downturn that began in 2008.

Low wages or not, there is a lot of money in Bucharest, the capital, especially compared with the Romanian countryside. That's how it is in every country I've visited, and that's most likely how it is everywhere in the world. Romania is strange because some of the smaller cities look like they're richer.

Ceausescu's communist urban planners chopped up Bucharest with a meat axe. They pulled down most of the classical buildings that once made the city aesthetically pleasing and put up hideous concrete crap in their place. The streets are too wide. Buildings often don't match and at times there is far too much space between them. There isn't much coherent fabric or feel to the place even in most of the old city center. It is the antithesis of Paris.

The brilliant Anthony Daniels, who often writes under the pen name Theodore Dalrymple, loathes ghastly brutalist architecture as much as I do. He properly blames the Swiss architect Le Corbusier and his baleful influence for wrecking so many once beautiful cities like Bucharest and even marring cities like London.

"Le Corbusier was to architecture what Pol Pot was to social reform," he wrote in *City Journal*. "In one sense, he had less excuse for his activities than Pol Pot: for unlike the Cambodian, he possessed great talent, even genius. Unfortunately, he turned his gifts to destructive ends, and it is no coincidence that he willingly served both Stalin and Vichy." Le Corbusier, he says, "was the enemy of mankind" and "does not belong so much to the history of architecture as to that of totalitarianism."

The grotesque modern architect once described a house as "a machine for living in" and is still scandalously lionized by many professionals in the field even today. (Do such people stay in the asteroid belt of tower blocks in the suburbs of Paris when they visit on holiday, or do they prefer the beautiful "outdated" parts of the city such as the Latin Quarter like normal human beings do?)

Corbu's work and that of his disciples is hard on the eyes in Western cities, but it's positively savage in some of the formerly communist capitals. There you can see what all of Europe might have looked like if the man were able to convince Western leaders—and he tried—to raze their cities and let him start over.

No sector in Bucharest survived communism intact. Only a handful of streets look like the Europe most of us know, if not from visiting then at least from photographs. The vast majority of the traditional buildings left standing are wedged now between shoddy modernist blocks. Some neighborhoods beyond the city center consist almost entirely of dreary public housing units that don't even meet Corbu's dismal standards. On a blank gray wall in the parking lot across from my hotel, an artist painted cogs in a machine the size of Godzilla chewing the city to pieces.

I felt a tremendous sense of relief when Olivia Horvath from the foreign ministry brought me to the tiny section of the old city that hadn't been bulldozed.

"*This* is fantastic," I said, marveling at the cobblestones, the pitched roofs, the balconies, the vertical windows, and the classical ornamentation. "It's too bad the whole city doesn't look like this."

"I love this place," she said. "It's amazing. You should have seen it a year ago. It was terrible. For so many years I dreamed that the old city would look like this someday and mow it does."

A few blocks away is Romania's parliament, the second largest building in the world after the Pentagon.

When it was still under construction before he died, Ceausescu called it the "Palace of the People," though of course ordinary people never would have been allowed to set foot in it. The apartments lining the main boulevard in front belonged to high-level officers of the repressive Securitate, the agency of total surveillance that turned the country into a vast open-air Panopticon. Even today that boulevard looks like the intimidating *Champs-Elysees* of a totalitarian state. It's so monstrous in scale that it can only be properly photographed from the air.

Back then, fake stores that pretended to sell goods not even the elite could afford were at ground level. According to Ion Pacepa— Ceausescu's chief national security advisor and a general in the Securitate who defected to the United States in 1978—Ceausescu once visited Macy's on a trip to New York and thought it, too, was a fake. He wondered aloud in the car how long it took the Americans to "set it up."

Some of my official meetings took place inside that hulking mothership of a parliament building, and I took photographs inside and out whenever I had a chance.

"What do you think of this building?" Olivia asked me. She seemed to think I loved it since I took so many pictures.

"It's impressive in some ways," I said, "but it's also—well, it's big."

"We hate it," she said. "So much of the city was destroyed to make room for it. And it constantly reminds us of *him*."

Western Europe lost a bit of confidence in itself and its civilization after the near-apocalyptic traumas of the two world wars, but Romanians, like others in Eastern Europe, have emerged from a third and much more recent trauma in a very different psychological state.

Bogdan Aurescu, Romania's Secretary of State for Strategic Affairs, spoke for most of his countrymen when he explained it.

"The level of affection," he said to me in his office, "or preference for a partnership relation with the United States is high, one of the highest in Europe. The French have a preference for the Obama Administration, but Romanians don't make distinctions between a Republican administration and a Democratic administration. It's irrespective of ideological affiliation."

His assistant served hot cups of black Turkish coffee and bottles of water.

"During the communist years," he continued, "there was a sense of disappointment that the U.S. was not here. We felt separated from the Western culture we feel we belong to. Western culture, including American culture, was and still is a part of our identity. That was very much reflected after the Romanian Revolution twenty years ago in strong support for both E.U. and NATO accession. We are culturally oriented, without any possibility of doubt or shift, towards Western democratic culture."

Romanians are acutely aware that they're Westerners, and they want everyone who visits to know it. More than once I was told they are "Latins in a sea of Slavs" who look to Italy as a model, though the former is obvious to anyone who speaks or is even familiar with a Latin-based language. Italian is as similar to Romanian as it is to Spanish. I could easily understand fragments of spoken Romanian and a substantial amount of written Romanian even though I never studied the language.

Romanians seem more conscious of themselves as children of the Roman Empire than anyone aside from Italians. In every city I visited I saw a statue of Romulus and Remus, the mythical founders of the city of Rome. Even the way they pronounce the name of their country makes it sound Italian. (Americans pronounce it Ro-MAY-nia while they say Roman-EE-ah.) The old maxim that absence makes the heart grow fonder would appear to apply to nations and cultures as well as to individuals.

"How are your relations with Russia right now?" I asked Aurescu.

"It is not an easy relationship," he said. "We are at the *Ostmark*, the eastern border, of European and NATO space. We assume certain risks from the instability of the Black Sea region. It is important for us to extend as much as possible this space of prosperity and stability and of shared democratic values within the region."

"Does it make you nervous that Romania is the easternmost country in the European Union?" I said.

"It doesn't make me particularly nervous," he said, "but it is a reality we cannot ignore. We are next to a region that is sometimes unstable. Look at the evolution of political life in Ukraine and Moldova. And take into account the fact that very close to the Romanian border there is a frozen or protracted conflict in Transnistria, which is not yet solved. Each and every winter there are problems with the gas supply via Ukraine from Russia and other sources. Across the Black Sea there are problems in Georgia."

Members of Parliament Borbely Laszlo and Sever Voinescu made many of the same points, but Voinescu's party—the Democratic Liberal Party—was on its way out. Would a change in government have any affect on Romania's foreign policy?

"No," Laszlo said. "The foreign policy in Romania does not depend much on the changing of the government. We have very clear targets. We have very clear goals."

"I agree," Voinescu said. "I don't think anything will fundamentally change in our foreign policy. One of our main tasks is to increase our influence inside the European Union. We are also very much dedicated to our trans-Atlantic relationship. We are the most pro-Atlanticist nation in Europe right now. According to a German Marshall Fund survey, Romanians are even more pro-Atlantic than the British. We have troops in Afghanistan. We have 1,100 soldiers, as you know, and they are in a very, very difficult area."

"Which area are they in?" I said.

"Helmand," Voinescu said.

"Oh," I said. "That's the most difficult area."

"It is very difficult," he said. "It's tough. I mean, that's where the war is."

"Regarding our presence in Iraq," Laszlo said, "we didn't have a tough debate like in other countries in Europe."

"Why do you suppose that is?" I said.

"I don't know," he said ponderously as he leaned back in his chair. "In Romania there wasn't a debate in the parliament. And the population here accepts that we have to help with soldiers in Iraq and in Afghanistan."

"It's controversial in the U.S.," I said.

"Yes," he said and laughed. "We know."

"Almost everywhere," I said.

What about Russia? Romania was never a constituent part of the Soviet Union, but its citizens were yoked to Moscow's world despite Ceausescu's dubious presentation of himself to the West as independent.

"Russia is a passionate issue in Romania," Voinescu said. "The past is a shadow upon our relationship. There are people in Romania saying we should do business with these guys. Don't talk about history, about politics, just make money. There are others saying we cannot forget what happened, that we should be careful, that Russia's foreign policy always has a seed of aggressiveness inside. We blame the president or the minister of foreign affairs when our relationship with Russia is not as good as we want, but sometimes I have a feeling we forget this is a two-way street. When you have a relation with a huge country, a global power, one should understand that the tone of this relationship is decided by the big power. Romania took a path towards the West. Russia still has not come to terms with this."

Romania—like Poland, Iraqi Kurdistan, Kosovo, and Albania—feels a lot like a "geopolitical spa," to use Thomas Friedman's formulation, to American visitors.

"People here liked President Bush more than people in other places," Voinescu said, "but they now love President Obama. Romanians are ready to embrace any U.S. president. There is a certain kind of emotional attachment to whatever the Americans decide about their own country. I think people liked President Bush because they liked his toughness on certain issues. You know that in this part of Europe, after the whole communist era, you need sometimes a stronger approach when you talk about various issues. On the other hand, they like Obama because, you know, his charm is seductive everywhere."

I don't know if President Barack Obama reciprocates that feeling of affection, but Vice President Joe Biden almost certainly does. He visited Bucharest at the same time I did to discuss a missile shield the administration hoped to install there instead of in Poland. He and the Romanian president addressed local journalists at a press conference, which I also attended. What he said might read like diplomatic boilerplate, but I was barely twenty feet from him when he spoke, and judging by his body language and the tone of his voice, he's either an exceptionally skilled political actor or he's absolutely sincere.

"We serve together in Afghanistan," he said, "in the western Balkans, and in Iraq. And I feel obliged to tell the Romanian people how grateful President Obama and I and the American people are for the Romanian troops that are in Afghanistan. Our troops—and I mean this sincerely, my son just got back from Iraq after a year as a captain in the United States Army—our troops are *proud* to serve next to Romanian troops because you are incredibly competent. Your kids—I wish you could all see, as I got to see, just how incredibly competent they are. You should be proud. And to all the mothers and fathers, sons and daughters, husbands and wives of those 1,100 Romanians that are stationed in Afghanistan, I mean this sincerely, as a parent, thank you. Thank you. Thank you."

Communism changed our mentality," said Daniel Apostol, editor in chief of Romania's *Money Channel*. "We are still fighting now to come back to what we were. We lost the culture of private property. We lost this sense of privacy and respecting each other's time and respecting people as individuals, as human beings. That was the worst thing that happened to us. This is why we are struggling so much now to get back to the capitalist society, to the free market, which can run only if there is respect for private property."

"You had to learn these concepts as an adult?" I said.

"Yeah," he said. "We didn't have it before. And we are still learning it. We cannot just one day say, 'Okay, we get it.'"

I couldn't see or feel what he was talking about exactly, but I did hear things that struck me as odd.

"You should take the bus in this city," said Alina, my translator. "Every time there is an argument between two people, everyone on the bus gets involved. Everybody takes sides. A husband will yell at his wife, and half the bus takes his side while the other half takes hers."

Maybe this sort of thing would have happened in Bucharest even if communism never existed, but it certainly wouldn't happen in the U.S. where we're taught from childhood to mind our own business and leave other people alone.

Apostol is my age. He was a teenager when Ceausescu's regime was overthrown, so he remembers it vividly. It began during one of the president's outdoor speeches when thousands of people suddenly stopped applauding and cheering and started booing and jeering at him instead.

"I went home," he said, "and my mother said there is something on the TV, Ceausescu is speaking on TV. I switched on the TV set and saw that huge gathering in Bucharest. People started screaming at him. I thought it was a joke. I didn't realize what was actually happening."

Ceausescu initially didn't realize what was happening either. In hindsight it's obvious that the audience only applauded because people feared terrible consequences if they did not, and it's entirely possible that each person who privately loathed the man while pretending to love him thought few others felt the same way. At the very least they dared not to be the only one yelling at the government in public.

It's nearly impossible for individuals to resist totalitarian states.

The first people who say anything are hauled off to prison or worse. It's hard for Westerners to truly appreciate just how much nerve it takes to say no to that kind of tyrant even in private let alone outside while the boss is giving a speech. As Jay Nordlinger recently wrote, Ceausescu and his wife "had the entire country wired. Citizens were spied on, day and night. And they were defenseless. Privacy was virtually nonexistent. Every single telephone came equipped with a microphone—not merely to record phone conversations, but everything that went on in the room."

No regime, though, can arrest everyone in a crowd of thousands. There is safety in numbers even if it is not absolute. As soon as a few brave souls in the back of the audience dared to boo and hiss at Ceausescu, everyone realized they *weren't* the only ones who hated his guts. The tipping point came at once, and the Ceausescus would be tried and executed on camera in a matter of days.

Still, Daniel Apostol couldn't believe what he was seeing on television when citizens in that crowd let the dictator have it.

"But you knew other communist governments had already fallen, didn't you?" I said.

"Yeah," he said.

"So," I said, "it wasn't unthinkable, was it?"

"We knew what was happening in Poland, in Hungary, and the Czech Republic," he said. "We knew that."

"So didn't you feel like Romania might be next?" I said.

"We were frustrated because all over the world things were changing," he said, "but nothing changed inside Romania. What was wrong with us? I had to ask, is this really happening? Or, no, it's impossible, these people did a stupid thing and will be in jail in a few hours. In the evening I went out in the center of town. Everything was in turmoil. The political leaders were out of their offices. There was a revolution in every city on the 21st of December and on the 22nd everything was burning in Bucharest."

What did he think about the world's remaining communist governments?

"I don't have any good feelings about them," Apostol said. "I can't say anything positive. I just can't. Nothing good came to me from the communists. Okay, I'm alive. I was born. I am still here and now no one bothers me. But I would have a much better life if they never came."

B ucharest is an interesting place for students of totalitarianism. I can still feel that it was once communist. While walking around near Ceausescu's monster palace and the Borg hive neighborhood of the old Securitate, that feeling was overwhelming, even crushing.

The Transylvanian countryside is another world. The region north of the capital would make an outstanding European vacation destination, especially for travelers on a budget. You can soak in the atmosphere and charms of old Mitteleuropa while spending less than a third of what it costs in the nations immediately to Romania's west.

It's hard to believe the city center of Brashov, just a little more than an hour's drive north of Bucharest, is even in the same country. The communists more or less left it alone architecturally, and the city leaders—or whoever is in charge of such things—seem to have made aesthetic restoration a higher priority than the local officials in Bucharest who are still only half-finished restoring what's left of the old city.

Some of Romania's smaller towns and villages seem to have recovered so nicely, even though they don't have very much money, that I could almost believe Ceausescu neglected them and focused all his attention morbid on Bucharest. The Institute for the Investigation of Communist Crimes in Romania, however, dispelled that illusion.

The institute files criminal charges against individuals who tortured and murdered their fellow citizens for the old regime.

"We have launched complaints against more than 300 persons accused of killing people during the communist era," said Raluca Grosescu, head of the Research and Documentation Department. "The institute is also building a politics of memory by developing educational projects."

"What have you learned and uncovered in your investigations," I said, "that wasn't known before you started working?"

"At the macro level," she said, "it was known that in Romania people were killed, but there are personal stories which were completely unknown. When we move to the micro level, the human level, we help the families find the bodies and learn what happened to each person."

She said most were killed for opposing the collectivization of agriculture, so there went my theory that Ceausescu messed with the countryside less than the capital.

"They were peasants," she continued, "who didn't want to give their properties to the state. They were people who formed resistance groups in the mountains."

The killers worked for the dreaded Securitate.

"Some admitted it and even apologized to the families," she said, "but these are rare cases. Let me give you an example of the general behavior. We lodged a complaint against a former communist general of the Securitate. He admitted on a TV show that he was involved in political torture, but he said it was legal at the time, that he was defending the communist state from its enemies. He said he was not sorry. In fact, he was proud of it because he defended his country. Most of the perpetrators have this kind of attitude."

I asked her what on earth the average Romanian must think while listening to these people on television.

"The first ten years of transition," she said, "were characterized by the politics of forgetting."

The same thing happened in Lebanon after the civil war there. So many people had done terrible things to their neighbors that a general forgiveness may not have been possible, at least not for a while. Amnesia helped them live with each other in the meantime. I asked one Maronite Christian why he still hated Israelis for the siege of Beirut in 1982 but was able to forgive his old Lebanese enemies. His answer might not be what you'd expect.

"I don't have any choice," he said as he hardened the muscles in his jaw line. "Because…they live here." His voice sounded anguished as though he were remembering horrors I can only imagine, horrors that he tried hard not to think about but could never truly forget. "The Israelis don't live here. The Israelis live *over there*, so I don't have to forgive them!"

I couldn't help but think of the Middle East since I've spent so much time there. My colleague and occasional travel companion Larry Luxner from the *Washington Diplomat* couldn't help but think of Cuba since it's part of his regular beat. Raluca Grosescu had recently returned from Havana herself, and he wanted to know what she thought of it.

"Cuba is still a country with a communist regime," she said. "Fighting against communists in a post-communist period is easy, but when you fight against communists during a communist period, it is not so easy. When I was in Cuba last year, it reminded me of what was happening in the 1980s in Romania."

"Would you say it is more repressive there than under Ceausescu," Larry said, "or not quite as much?"

"From an economic point of view," she said, "it is worse in Cuba than it was in Romania. They are transitioning to a market economy, but the economy is still controlled by the state. Cuban people try to work in tourism in order to get some convertible pesos because you cannot buy anything in Cuba with pesos. You cannot buy anything. So what's happening—and this is sad—is you have people abandoning their work. Architects are working in bars. Students are making tourist guides."

"What's the younger generation in Romania like?" Larry said. "Do you have to pull them in to be interested in what you are doing? Do they care? The ones who never saw communism?"

"Most of them don't care," she said. "I think this is normal. They care about their own lives, the present. But at the same time there is new interest in the past. This is something that happens in many countries after transitions of around twenty years. It happened in post-Nazi Germany. The politics of memory started in the 1970's. In Israel also. During the first twenty years it was a problem to talk about what happened. Only in the 1960s did they begin a politics of memory. It also happened in other countries like Greece where they had dictatorships."

"Why do you suppose this happens after twenty years?" I said. "Is it because there is a whole generation of people who don't know much about it?"

"I believe," she said, "it's because there is a whole generation that wasn't involved. In Romania, for example, more than ten percent of the population were informers of the Securitate. Another twenty-five percent of Romanians were members of the Communist Party. Ten percent were part of the nomenclatura. In this moment we have a generation willing to talk about the past because it is not their personal history. It is painful to talk about your own involvement."

I've always wondered what democrats who grew up in communist countries thought of communists who grew up in democratic countries. Hardly anyone in the West ever voted with their feet, so to speak, by moving to a communist country, but communist dictatorships created millions of refugees all over the world who fled their homelands for Western democracies. East Germans were willing to risk being shot to make a run over the wall and Cubans still risk drowning to reach Florida, yet once in a while I still meet Westerners who have warm spots in their hearts for tyrannical regimes like Fidel Castro's.

"What do you think," I asked her, "of people in the West who think communism is a good idea but haven't actually experienced it? You know the types I mean. The people who wear Che Guevara T-shirts."

"Ah, yes," she said. "They are ridiculous. But somehow I can understand them. Let's take the example of France. In France they were all socialists when they were young. Sartre was a close friend of Castro's. Gerard Depardieu was a close friend of Castro's. They believed in this ideal, but after they saw what Stalin did they couldn't look to the Soviet Union. So they turned their hopes to Cuba. Then they saw what Castro did. The only one who still seemed to live up to the ideal was Che Guevara. So they turned to Che Guevara. I understand them. They were wrong their entire lives and it's difficult to admit it."

Twelve

Where the West Ends

"The forced collectivization of agriculture decreed by the Soviet master and his party likely cost the lives of more people than perished in all countries as a result of the First World War." - Michael Marrus

"They had gone over the country like a swarm of locusts and taken away everything edible; they had shot or exiled thousands of peasants, sometimes whole villages; they had reduced some of the most fertile land in the world to a melancholy desert." - Malcolm Muggeridge

I bought a map of Eastern Europe in an old Oregon bookstore that's as big as a couch when unfolded. The most heavily trafficked roads appear as fat red lines on the paper. Almost all lead directly to Moscow. Even as late as the year 2012, the nerve center of the former Soviet Empire looks on my map like a world-devouring octopus capturing less important capitals in its tentacles.

On a cold night in late October I pointed at a thin red line on that map leading across the former Soviet frontier into Ukraine from a remote corner of Poland.

"Hardly anyone will be on this road," I said to my old friend Sean LaFreniere. He had just met up with me in Romania so we could hit the road again. "We shouldn't have to wait long at the border."

That logic seemed sound at the time, but I'm here to tell you: never, ever, choose less-traveled roads in countries that used to be part of Russia. Driving from even the most backward country in the European

Union into the remote provinces of Ukraine is like falling off the edge of civilization into a land that was all but destroyed.

Sean and I hadn't learned that yet, though, and we wanted a scenic route. European road trips aren't like road trips in the American West where we live. Outside our major metropolitan areas, huge empty spaces and wide open roads are the norm. Most of Europe is crowded and neither of us wanted to sit in the car for hours in line at the border.

We had no idea what we were in for, but a Polish border guard warned us after stamping our passports.

"It is very *strange* over there," he said. "And nobody speaks English."

Screwing up in the strange parts of the world is never fun and is usually miserable, but you learn things by doing it. You see things that governments and ministries of tourism wished you would not. Ukraine is so strange that you can even see these things in the dark. We actually saw more of Ukraine's strangeness *because* we showed up in the dark.

I don't remember what time we crossed the frontier. Eight o'clock in the evening? Anyway, it was dark. When I say it was dark, I mean it was *dark*. The back roads of Western Ukraine are as black at night as the most remote parts of the American West where no humans live in any direction.

Yet Western Ukraine is not empty.

And, oh God, the roads. I don't care where you've been. You almost certainly have never seen anything like them.

The second worst road I've ever driven on was in Central America in the mid-1990s. It's only a fraction as bad as the road Sean and I took into Ukraine. This one would have been no worse off had it been deliberately shredded to ribbons by air strikes. The damage was so thorough that the surface could not possibly have been repaved or repaired even once since the Stalinist era.

I white-knuckled it behind the wheel while Sean cringed in the passenger seat. I did not dare drive faster than five miles an hour. Even at that speed I had to weave all over the place to avoid the worst of the gaping holes, some of which were as wide as mattresses and deep enough to swallow TV sets.

I saw no cars, no street lights, not even a single light from a house. Ukraine looked depopulated. My maps said there were villages all over the place, but where were they? Did we just drive into an episode of *Life After People*?

"This is exactly like Russia," Sean said. "Exactly."

He had visited Russia two years earlier and will never forget the vast darkness at night on the train between Moscow and St. Petersburg. "We're in Russia!" he said

Then the ghost figures appeared.

They walked on the side of the road in wine-darkness. They did not carry flashlights. They seemed, like us, to be out in the middle of nowhere. It was then that I realized we had entered a town. In the periphery of my headlight beams I could faintly make out a few unlit houses shrouded in shadow away from the road, which was as broken and crumbling as ever. I still hadn't seen any other cars on the road, nor did I see any parked on the side. I don't know if the roads were so bad because nobody drove or if nobody drove because the roads were so bad.

"They should put up a sign on the border," Sean said, "saying *That was Europe. You like that? Now prepare for something completely different.*"

We were on our way to Chernobyl, or at least we thought we were. *City Journal* assigned me to go there and write about the spooky ghost city of Pripyat that, along with the surrounding area in the so-called Exclusion Zone, was struck by a local apocalypse in 1986. The Soviet Union's Chernobyl nuclear reactor number four exploded and showered Pripyat, where 50,000 people lived, and the countryside around it with a storm of deadly radiation. Only thirty-one people were dead in the immediate aftermath, but the World Health Organization thinks the long-term effects of radiation poisoning will eventually kill another 4,000. More than 350,000 people in Ukraine and nearby Belarus have been permanently displaced. The fire still burns today beneath the crumbling concrete sarcophagus that caps the reactor.

No one should wander around there alone. The Ukrainian military won't let you in anyway if you don't have a guide and a permit. Some of Pripyat's buildings are still lethally radioactive, and there's no way to tell them apart from the relatively "safe" ones without sophisticated instruments. The scrap yard, where fire-fighting equipment was abandoned long ago, is spectacularly dangerous. Even mutant animals are rumored to be running around.

Sean and I didn't yet know it, but the Chernobyl administration was about to cancel our permit and refuse to allow anyone entry. They didn't say why, but I assume it was because the zone suddenly became more dangerous than usual. We would not get to go, but going there was our plan and we didn't yet know we would be re-routed. For a while there, we weren't sure we'd get *anywhere* in Ukraine, let alone hundreds of miles away to Chernobyl.

First we had to get to Lviv, the "capital" of Western Ukraine and the heartland of Ukrainian nationalism. That first stop alone was almost a hundred miles away. The road was so shattered I was barely able to drive any faster than I could walk. And we were lost. We couldn't even figure out how to get to Sambir, a small town that was hardly even inside Ukraine at all.

Sambir was spelled Самбір in Ukrainian and only one sign pointed the way. The Cyrillic letters in that particular name resembled the Latin letters well enough that I could figure it out. Then we came to a four-way junction. Road signs pointed to various towns in every direction, but none said Самбір. And none of the towns the signs *did* point to appeared on my map—or, if they were on my map, I didn't know how to transliterate their names into Cyrillic. Which way we were supposed to be going?

"Let's go back," Sean said, "and ask one of those people on the side of the road."

I drove back the way we came until I saw two ghostly figures shambling along in the headlights. I pulled over and rolled down the window.

"Excuse me," I said. "Do you speak English?" I doubted they did, but this was a way of preparing them for the fact that they weren't going to hear any Ukrainian or Russian from me.

The two stopped walking and stared. A young man, perhaps 20 years old, held his young girlfriend's hand. He stared at me with wide eyes and slowly stepped between me and his girl as if I were a threat.

"We're trying to get to Sambir," I said and paused. "Sambir," I said it again in case he understood nothing else but might at least know I needed directions and that he could point the way there. He looked at me and didn't say anything.

"Sean," I said. "Hand me that map."

Sean handed over the map. I pointed at it. "Sambir." I said. "Which way to Sambir?"

The young man took several of cautious steps back. His girlfriend, terrified, moved behind him and peaked over his shoulder. They backed up another five feet or so, then walked away without saying anything.

"Well, that's just great," I said. We were the first foreigners they'd ever seen? Just a few miles from the Polish frontier?

"Go back and take the road that goes to the left," Sean said. "I'm pretty sure it's that one."

"How can you be pretty sure that it's that one?" I said. I had no idea where we were and wanted someone who lived there to tell us.

"It just feels right," he said. "If we see any more people, we can stop and ask."

I was in no mood to argue, and his guess was as good as mine, so we drove back to the four-way intersection and took a left. And we found ourselves in a forest.

"This doesn't look right at all," I said.

"How do you know what it's supposed to look like?" he said.

"I don't," I said. "It just looks like we're going into the middle of nowhere."

"Everywhere we've been is in the middle of nowhere," he said.

Perhaps he was right. Suddenly the road improved slightly. I could increase our speed, so I did, but then BANG. I ran us into a sink-sized hole in the ground at twenty miles an hour. The car shuddered as though a land mine had blown off a wheel.

Sean had rented this car on his credit card. "Oh my God," he said. "Oh my God, oh my God, oh my God."

"It's okay," I said, though I didn't for one second believe it. "There's still air in the tire."

"Not for long," he said and put his face in his hands.

I drove onward again, slower this time. We passed a dark house. Somebody lived out there in the forest.

"There are some people up ahead," Sean said. "Pull over and ask them where the hell we are."

I pulled the car over next to the two figures. Like the others, they looked ghost-like in the headlights. Like the others, they shuffled along as though they were wandering toward no place in particular for lack of anything better to do in a village at night without light.

This time we encountered not two scared teenagers, but an elderly man and his wife.

They looked startled as though they couldn't believe someone was out and about in a car.

"Excuse me," I said. "Do you speak English?" I was certain they didn't.

The woman flinched and the man said, "eh?"

"We're trying to get to Lviv," I said. Then I pointed at the map. "Lviv."

Not knowing better, I pronounced it "Luh-*viv*."

They had no idea what I was talking about.

"Luh-*viv*," I said again, and pointed at the map.

"Eh?" the woman said. "El-*veev*?"

"Da," I said, Russian for *yes*. Many ethnic Russians live in Eastern Ukraine and even ethnic Ukrainians in the west can speak Russian though they'd rather not. The bits of Russian that Sean and I knew were useful wherever we happened to be.

"Da," I said. "El-*veev*."

She pointed in the direction we were heading. "Poland," she said.

"Unbelievable," I said. We were on our way back to Poland?

"Argh!" Sean said.

"We've been driving around for hours," I said, "and we haven't gone *anywhere*."

So we turned back. I drove five miles an hour. I weaved around giant holes in the road, but still ran into five or six small ones per second. I had no idea where we were or where we were going. The night was almost half over and we had made zero progress. All we had done so far was damage the car and burn half the gas in the tank.

We eventually came to another small town even though we saw no more signs to even Sambir, let alone Lviv or Kiev. This time a few buildings were lit. One was a gas station. Incredibly, it was open.

I pulled in. Sean and I got out. We both inspected the banged-up wheel. It looked okay and apparently was not leaking air. We were lucky.

A man emerged from the office and asked us—I assume—if we needed gas.

"Do you speak English?" I said and chuckled. I knew he wouldn't.

Of course he didn't. A gas station attendant in rural Ukraine is no more likely to speak English than a gas station attendant in rural Kansas is likely to be fluent in Russian. Unlike the others we'd spoken to, though, he didn't seem surprised or alarmed that the wrong language came out of our mouths.

He filled the tank. I pointed at the map and said "Sambir." He gave us complicated directions that neither Sean nor I could make sense of. All we could really glean from him was which direction to start with.

I heard children giggling behind the gas station office. A young boy and a young girl, each no older than five, peeked their heads around the corner. They pointed at us and laughed as though we wore clown suits and squeaky shoes. Sean and I were the evening's entertainment. We spoke an alien language and that made us freaks.

"Good grief," I said. "Are we going to have to put up with this all week?"

I can only imagine how the locals would have reacted if we were black.

We drove in the dark on hideous roads for another hour. The gas station attendant told us we were supposed to turn left at some point, but we had no idea where.

"I hope it's not like this everywhere," Sean said.

"If it's like this everywhere," I said, "we won't even get to Lviv, let alone Kiev and Chernobyl."

"Turn left here," Sean said when we came to a road that looked promising for no apparent reason.

"Sure," I said. "Why not?"

I turned left. After a few minutes we came to a rusting dinosaur of a factory. It was dark and abandoned and clearly had been for decades. After we passed it, the road somehow managed to get worse. I had to slow down to three miles an hour to prevent the car from breaking apart. We'd need an off-road vehicle to keep going.

"This can't be the way to Lviv," I said. "No one can drive on this road."

So we turned back. And eventually we found the town of Sambir. We found it by sheer chance, but we found it. There were a few cars here and there, and some street lights, too. There wasn't much to it, but it was the closest thing we had yet seen to civilization in Ukraine. And we finally knew where we were on the map.

We had been in Ukraine for four hours and had barely made twenty miles of progress. Lviv was sixty more miles away.

I saw a sign on the side of the road pointing to Львів.

"That must be Lviv," I said. "I guess their в is our *v*. And the letter *i* is the same. I can tell by the way they spelled *Sambir* on the other signs." Over the next couple of days, Sean and I would eventually figure out and memorize the entire Cyrillic alphabet this way.

The road *did* improve after we left Sambir and headed toward Lviv.

"We need food," I said, though I wondered if that would be possible in a countryside that hardly even had light.

"Look for a sign that says pectopah," Sean said.

"A sign that says what?" I said.

"Pectopah," he said. "That's Russian for *restaurant*. That's not how they say it, but that's what it looks like when they spell it."

A few moments later we saw a well-lit building on the side of the road that looked like a restaurant. A sign read "Ресторан."

"There we go," Sean said.

"It even looks open," I said.

And it was.

We stepped inside. The place was half full and a few people were still grimly eating.

"Do we wait to be seated or just grab a table?" I said. I had no idea how to behave in this country. Rural Ukraine doesn't have any handles. We were on the European continent, but we sure weren't in the West any more.

"Let's just sit," Sean said.

So we sat. A waitress stormed over and rudely slapped menus on the table without even looking at us. She couldn't have made it more clear that she was offended by our existence than if she had thrown them.

The menus were incomprehensible. They were thick as pamphlets and had no English translations or Latin letters. I couldn't even differentiate between the main course section and the beer list.

"How are we supposed to order?" I said. I wouldn't mind randomly pointing and just eating whatever she brought, but I might end up pointing at a dessert or even "water" for all I knew.

A large group of people sat at a long table in the back.

"Maybe someone over there speaks English," Sean said. There were about ten of them. The odds weren't too bad.

He walked over.

"Excuse me," he said. "Do any of you speak English?"

"Yes?" a young woman said a bit carefully.

"Thank God" Sean said. "I hate to bother you, but can you help us order some food?"

"I'm from Poland," she said, "and don't speak Ukrainian or Russian. We're all from Poland."

Great.

"But," she added and gestured toward an older man at the head of the table, "he speaks some Ukrainian."

"Yes," the man said. "I can help you."

I stood up and walked to the table.

"Thank you so much," Sean said.

"Hello," I said. "Thank you."

"Of course," the man said. "Should I translate the menu for you?"

I chuckled. That would take at least twenty minutes. The menu was *huge*. "No, no," I said. "Just please tell the waitress we want some chicken or something. We're not picky, we just can't tell her anything."

So he ordered us chicken.

"Do you want vodka?" he said.

"Yes!" Sean said.

"It's after midnight," I said, "and we still have to drive. But damn do I need a drink. So I'll have a shot."

"What brings you to Ukraine?" the Polish woman said.

"We're on our way to Chernobyl," I said.

She gasped and took a step back.

"Are you crazy?" she said. "I'm not sure I want to know you guys."

She must have been half-kidding, but I could tell she wasn't entirely. What was the big deal? Tourists go to Chernobyl now all the time. And I've been to far more dangerous places.

"He's a journalist," Sean said. "And we're both photographers."

I was annoyed that she found our mission repulsive, but tried my best to keep that to myself.

"Thanks for your help," I said. "We really appreciate it."

"Well," she said. "Enjoy your trip to…Chernobyl."

Back on the road to Lviv, Ukraine still looked depopulated. The road was vaguely okay now, but the small towns and villages in the countryside could hardly have been darker had they been hit by an EMP.

The country clearly hadn't recovered from the ravages of the 20th century. Communism was bad in Yugoslavia and even worse in Romania, but the poor souls ruled directly by the Soviet government *really* got hammered, and few so terribly as the Ukrainians.

The Stalinist-imposed Holodomor—Ukrainian for "hunger plague"—lasted from 1932 to 1933 and killed more people than the Nazi Holocaust. It was a deliberately induced famine meant to put down once and for all the weak yet nevertheless extant Ukrainian nationalism.

"In the actions here recorded," Robert Conquest wrote in his gut-wrenching book, *Harvest of Sorrow: Soviet Collectivization and the Terror-Famine*, "about 20 human lives were lost for, not every word, but every letter, in this book." It was, as Wasyl Hryshko wrote, "the first instance of a peacetime genocide in history."

The great Arthur Koestler witnessed it. He describes, in *The God That Failed*, "hordes of families in rags begging at the railway stations, the women lifting up to the compartment windows their starving brats, which, with drumstick limbs, big cadaverous heads and puffed bellies, looked like embryos out of alcohol bottles."

"In one hut there would be something like a war," Ukrainian-born Soviet dissident Vasily Grossman wrote in his novel, *Forever Flowing*. "Everyone would keep close watch over everyone else. People would take crumbs from each other. The wife turned against the husband and the husband against the wife. The mother hated the children. And in some other hut love would be inviolable to the very last. I knew one woman with four children. She would tell them fairy stories and legends so that they would forget their hunger. Her own tongue could hardly move, but she would take them into her arms even though she had hardly any strength to lift her arms when they were empty. Love lived on within her. And people noticed that where there was hate people died off more swiftly. Yet love, for that matter, saved no one. The whole village perished, one and all. No life remained in it."

Ukrainian-born Soviet trade official Victor Kravchenko could finally stand it no more, and so he defected. "Anger lashed my mind as I drove back to the village," he wrote in his memoir, *I Chose Freedom*. "Butter sent abroad in the midst of the famine! In London, Berlin, Paris I could see ... people eating butter stamped with a Soviet trade mark. Driving through the fields, I did not hear the lovely Ukrainian songs so dear to my heart. These people have forgotten how to sing! I could only hear the groans of the dying, and the lip-smacking of the fat foreigners enjoying our butter."

Sean slept in the passenger seat while I drove in a mental fog. I had long been exhausted by the late hour, the stress from being lost on shattered roads, and our near-complete inability to navigate with poor signage in absolute darkness. I drove on autopilot, barely even aware of what was happening, but I snapped back to consciousness when I found myself suddenly bathed in light inside a European-looking city.

I say it was European-looking, but that was really only partially true. The architecture was European, but something was terribly wrong with this place.

The space between each cobblestone on the streets was enormous. Our rental car's tires made a hell of a racket, as though we were driving on washboard or tank treads. The streets had hardly been more maintained than those in the back country. They rolled like roads in Alaska that are forced upward every winter by frost heaves.

"Where are we now?" Sean said as he awoke, motion-sick, from the rolling of the car and the clattering of the tires.

"Somewhere in Lviv, I guess."

Then I realized what else was wrong with the city. It had no economy. We were driving through at three o'clock in the morning, so I didn't expect to see open restaurants or stores, but I hardly saw any that were even closed. Storefronts scarcely existed and I saw no humans at all. There were no cars on the street and hardly any parked. Lviv looked like a European city emptied of people, or like an alternate universe where none of Europe's post-war progress had taken place. It must have looked similar the day World War II ended.

Before crossing into Ukraine, Sean and I drove north and spent a night in the spectacular Polish city of Krakow, which includes the largest still-existing medieval square in the world. Poland seems to have recovered from totalitarianism better than any other post-communist country I had seen. I can't vouch for what Warsaw is like as I have never been there, but much of Krakow looks like it never *had* a communist government or a command economy. Hungary, too, seems to have mostly recovered. At least that's how its capital Budapest looks. So much of Ukraine, though, is still haunted and ruined.

I found a hotel and pulled up in front. Parking was easy. None of the other available spaces were taken.

Sean and I dragged our sorry and exhausted selves up to our room. It wouldn't be too much longer before the sun came up even though the previous day's sun had only just set when we first reached the border. After driving literally all night, we had only covered a hundred miles.

"Whoa," Sean said when he pulled open the curtains. "Look at what's outside our window."

Good grief, I thought. *What now?*

We had hardly seen any human beings, automobiles or signs of life or civilization since entering the country. We hadn't seen a damn thing yet that was normal. I had no idea what to expect out that window. A gigantic bomb crater hardly would have surprised me. What I saw instead were statues of angels at eye level atop the roof across the street. In the sunlight they must have been beautiful, but in the dark they looked like imps with sinister wings.

I woke early despite sheer exhaustion. Kiev was hundreds of miles away and Sean and I still thought we were going to Chernobyl first thing the next morning. We had no time to waste in bed even though we needed sleep.

I was also eager to see what Ukraine looked like in the daylight. It's not really fair to judge a country by what it looks like at midnight.

Traffic outside the window was light, but I was relieved to see Ukraine had vehicles after all. There were, however, as many buses as cars on the street. The overwhelming majority of the city's residents used public transportation rather than private automobiles—and I was damned sure the reason was not because they were saving the planet or because there was no place to park. They took buses because they couldn't afford anything else.

Sean and I stepped out for a walk. We had to leave early for Kiev, but you can't get a good read on a foreign city without walking around. So we walked around.

Most people on the sidewalks wore black. Nobody smiled or seemed in good spirits. The entire city seemed to suffer from seasonal affective disorder or outright depression.

I couldn't get past the dearth of cars.

"It's weird, isn't it?" Sean said. "You and I both like the parts of European cities that don't have any cars, but this street *should* have lots of cars. It feels eerie and wrong. Even Russia has plenty of cars."

Even a country as backward and miserable and poor as Iraq has plenty of cars.

I expected Lviv to look and feel like the Polish city of Krakow. They resemble each other in photographs. They're reasonably close together, they date from the same time period, much of both were built when Western Ukraine was governed by Poland, yet they feel utterly different and distant. Krakow is lively. Krakow has a modern economy. Its people suffered terribly during World War II and the communist era, but they have rebounded. Past and present tragedy doesn't hang over them anymore.

Few stores sold much of anything in Lviv. Few restaurants or places to sit and hang out even existed. It's possible that part of the city we didn't see was economically healthier, but we were in the city center, the part of town that's on all the postcards. Lviv's medieval square looks beautiful in the pictures I took of it, but in person it felt like a dead city waiting for burial.

"Hey," Sean said. "There's a McDonald's. We can order by pointing at pictures."

I wanted Ukrainian food. Who wants to visit the other side of the world and eat at McDonald's? But we didn't know how to order Ukrainian food. No one spoke English and menus weren't even transliterated into our alphabet let alone translated into any language I could half understand. I can figure out at least some of what's on a menu in a language that isn't my own if it uses my letters, but not so much if it doesn't. Sean was right. McDonald's had pictures of food we could point to.

A long line inside moved at an excruciatingly slow pace. We'd have to wait at least twenty minutes before reaching the counter.

An employee replaced the menu showing pictures of egg and sausage sandwiches with pictures of cheeseburgers. Breakfast was over. The crowd in line heaved a collective sigh of disappointment. It was only—what—ten o'clock in the morning? Who wants a cheeseburger at ten o'clock in the morning? Not Ukrainians. No one in line seemed to want one. Neither did I. It was morning and I wanted breakfast. Yet the McDonald's corporate headquarters on the other side of the planet decided Ukrainians want lunch instead of breakfast at ten in the morning. McDonald's was wrong.

So we left and returned to the main square a few streets away. It looked like dreamy, fantastical Europe when I squinted at it, but only if I squinted hard. The buildings weren't decrepit, but they were in a commercial district with hardly any commercial activity, almost as though Ukraine was still communist. Where were the restaurants? The cell phone stores? The clothing shops? The lawyers' offices? Central Lviv hardly could have been any more lifeless.

I didn't see nearly as many young people around as in Western Europe. The elderly folks looked worn down by a lifetime of poverty, oppression, and brutality. Most of Eastern Europe rebounded after the fall of the Soviet Union, but Ukraine had been left behind. Lviv looked like a Western city that had been shot in the head.

It wasn't at all what I expected. Lviv is in the western part of the country both geographically and politically. It's the capital of Ukrainian nationalism. Most ethnic Ukrainians, at least in this region, feel much closer to the West than they do to Russia. They want to join the E.U. and NATO. They vote for politicians who tell Moscow to pound sand. Ukraine might not even exist as an independent country if it weren't for these people. It isn't like Poland or Hungary or the Czech Republic. It didn't just break free from the Warsaw Pact. It broke free from the Soviet Union. It broke free from *Russia*.

At least the city didn't feel sketchy. Russia is famously crime-ridden, but Lviv felt no more dangerous than anywhere else.

"We should go," I said to Sean as he snapped pictures of old buildings for his architectural photography collection. "We have got to get to Kiev. And it's hundreds of miles away."

I hate driving through a place and passing instantaneous judgment, but the shortage of time left me no choice. I may not have correctly understood everything I was looking at, and I'm probably getting some of this wrong, but that doesn't change the fact that driving from the eastern edge of the European Union into Ukraine was a shocking experience. Western Ukraine may be politically oriented toward Europe, but it is an orphan.

The highway out of the city had been recently paved. With the dangerous chassis-busting holes safely behind us, Sean and I could finally drive as if we were in a normal country. But Ukraine is not a normal country. Well past Lviv on a road that looked more or less like an American Interstate, I saw more pedestrians walking God-only-knows where on the shoulder than I saw cars.

Gentle hills and low mountains gave way to the great steppe of far-eastern Europe that encompasses most of Ukraine, all of Belarus and vast portions of Russia. The landscape was flat as Kansas and almost as empty. Most agricultural fields lay fallow. Horses and tillers plowed working farmland by hand. Sagging single-story peasant houses suffered from dry rot and peeling paint jobs. Ukraine in the daylight appeared to be 200 years in the past.

"I can't believe how these people live," Sean said.

"I've seen a lot worse than this," I said. "You should see what the slums of Guatemala and Cairo look like."

"But these people have no electricity," he said. "And the climate is brutal."

"I've seen rural Guatemalan roofs made of sheets of plastic held down by tires," I said.

"At least they won't freeze to death in the winter," he said.

If you saw my photographs of the Ukrainian countryside, you might think it looks pretty. Many parts of it do, but there's a negative x-factor there, too, something dark about the place that's hard to nail down. Sean felt it more than I did because I had to concentrate on driving.

An oncoming truck driver flashed his headlights at me. Then an oncoming passenger car did the same.

"Something is wrong with the car," I said. "That's the second person who flashed his lights at me."

A third oncoming car appeared over the rise. He flashed his lights at me, too.

"*What now?*" Sean said as I pulled onto the shoulder and stopped.

"We're probably just missing a headlight," I said and hoped it wasn't anything worse.

Sean got out and walked around the car. "The lights are working," he said. Then he kicked all the tires. "The air is fine, too. Even that tire you smashed last night still has air in it."

He got back in and shrugged. I pulled back onto the road.

Just over the slight rise in the road some cops had set up a speed trap.

"Is that why they were flashing us?" Sean said. "To warn us there's cops?"

"Could be," I said. I suddenly found something to like about driving in this country.

And, yes, that is exactly what the flashing lights meant. Whenever somebody flashed his lights at me anywhere in the country, I'd pass a cop in a speed trap within a minute or two. There wasn't a damn thing the authorities could do about it, either. I found this contempt for the government, which everyone knew was corrupt to the core, delightfully post-communist.

The freeway was perfectly smooth now and four lanes wide even though there were hardly any cars on it. Brand new gas stations were *everywhere*. I saw at least six times as many gas stations as you'd find off the exit ramps of American freeways, yet this road carried only one percent as much traffic. Somebody assumed a lot more people would have cars in the future, but there's no way so many gas stations will ever be necessary. The United States was suffering the effects of a burst housing bubble, but Ukraine was in the midst of a gas station bubble.

Small plots of farmland ringed a number of medium-sized cities. Sean saw similar plots outside Copenhagen when he lived in Denmark, but urban Danes tendelittle farms on the side because it's fun to grow vegetables. Urban Ukrainians farm on the side so they won't starve.

"I have never been to a country that made me so sad," Sean said. And he's been to Russia.

He and I both snapped out of our gloom and laughed when we saw a tiny Soviet-built car pulling a wee wooden trailer bursting with turnips. Backwardness and poverty are almost never funny, but there was something undeniably comical about a miniature communist Lada being used in the fields. There was also something admirably resourceful and tenacious about it, like Cubans using shoelaces and spit to keep 1950s era American cars going for so many decades after embargoed spare parts were no longer available.

We found a Ресторан, a restaurant, on the side of the road. A kind old Ukrainian man who spoke English helped us order some food. He insisted that we try the borscht, a beetroot soup from Ukraine that's served throughout the Russian-speaking world. "It's good," he said.

It was not good. No, it was not good at all.

"You're brave to come here," he said.

"We *are*?" I said. "Why?"

I didn't feel brave. I've been to Iraq seven times, to the Lebanese-Israeli border while Hezbollah missiles exploded around me, and to Georgia when Russia invaded. I didn't feel particularly brave even then. I certainly didn't feel brave in Ukraine. Were Sean and I there in the midst of an underreported crime wave?

"Well," the man said. "I guess there are bad people everywhere."

The capital, Kiev, is home to a large population of Russians, around 13 percent of the total. Even many ethnic Ukrainians there speak Russian in their day-to-day lives. The central government has been trying for years to teach the entire country to speak the native language fluently, but most Russians and even many ethnic Ukrainians know it only as a second language—if they know it all. In the more heavily Russian east, and in the Crimea, there is passive and even active resistance. The Ukrainian language, like Ukrainian nationalism, is strongest in the west, especially in the rural parts of the west. Kiev, in central Ukraine, faces toward the east and the west at the same time like the twin-headed eagle on the Russian seal.

The ethnic Russian minority doesn't impose itself or its language on the majority. Rather, until the collapse of the Soviet Union, most of Ukraine was just part of Russia. It was part of Russia before the Soviet Union even existed. Ukrainians briefly tasted independence after the Russian Revolution in 1917, but in 1921 the western provinces of Galicia and Volhynia were taken by Poland (again) while the rest was conquered by communist Bolsheviks. When Moscow completed its conquest of Poland near the conclusion of World War II, it reabsorbed all of Ukraine and overwhelmed the latter's language, culture, and identity.

Russians still feel a powerful connection to Ukraine, not only because a large Russian minority lives there, but because Ukraine is the place where Russian civilization and culture were born.

The medieval European state Kievan Rus was founded in the 9th century when the northern Viking-descended Rus Khaganate moved its capital south from Novograd to Kiev, which had previously been ruled by semi-nomadic and pre-Islamic Turkic Khazars. By the 11th century, Kievan Rus was a vast state that made up much of the core of the European parts of modern-day Russia and Belarus as well as northern Ukraine. It fragmented in the 12th century and was shattered in the 13th by the Mongol invasion.

So Kiev marks the birthplace not only of Ukrainian culture, but also the birthplace of Russian and Belorussian culture. They are distinct now, but all three are the children of Kievan Rus. They have things in common with each other that they don't have in common with anyone else. Together they form a coherent sort of civilization unto itself even if it's somewhat unhappy, noncohesive, and fractious.

Ukrainian nationalism is hardly the fiercest around. It's strong enough that Ukraine could break free, but the cultural distance between Ukrainians and Russians isn't enormous. It's nothing like that between the Russians and, say, the Chechens even though Chechnya is still part of Russia. Some Russians still refuse to accept that Ukrainians are distinct at all. No Russian would insist that Poles or Estonians are actually Russians denying their heritage, but many do say that of Ukrainians despite the fact that Ukrainians have their own language, their own folkloric traditions, and a more westward political orientation. Yet these distinct Ukrainian features are weak, especially in the east where many feel a stronger gravitational pull from Moscow than from Europe.

Traffic picked up as Sean and I neared Kiev's outskirts. The four-lane road leading into the city was now as crowded as an American freeway outside a major metropolitan area.

The farther east Sean and I drove, the more Russianized the country became. When we actually arrived in Kiev, though, I was surprised. The capital's outskirts were of course ringed with communist-style apartment towers, but they didn't have the tired, dreary, and relentlessly gray appearance they have almost everywhere else in the post-communist world. Most of the tower blocks had been painted. They looked more like non-descript apartment buildings in Western countries than oppressive communist public housing compounds.

I could hardly believe what I was looking at when Sean and I reached the old part of the city. Kiev today is simply magnificent. Street after street and block after block is densely packed with classical Russian architecture in outstanding condition. Her buildings are beautifully and stylishly lit up at night. The city somehow looks futuristic and classical at the same time. The old part of the city is vast, it is prosperous, and best of all, it was blessedly spared the Soviet urban planning that disfigured so much of Eurasia. If any part of Kiev is truly run-down and decrepit, I didn't see it.

Unlike Lviv, it is thriving. Restaurants, bars, and stores selling anything you might possibly want to buy, including the most expensive and fashionable imported goods, are literally everywhere. The city appears no less prosperous or lively than London or Paris, at least on the surface. Surely many of its residents are struggling, but they don't look like they're struggling, and at the very least they live in a vibrant and beautiful place.

"This city," Sean said, "looks like a cross between Moscow and St. Petersburg, only it's nicer."

Everything we'd seen so far—everything—was the opposite of what I expected.

I knew Ukraine would gradually begin looking more Russianized as Sean and I drove farther east, but I had no idea that meant things would start to look *better*. Russia is painfully backward compared with Europe, so I assumed that as we moved deeper into Russia's orbit and farther from the European Union that the country would keep getting worse. I could not have been more wrong. Driving from the supposedly Westernized part of Ukraine to the Russianized capital was as shocking as crossing the Polish-Ukrainian border, but in the opposite way.

Ukraine is in some ways the anti-Romania. Most of Bucharest looks grotesquely communist. Hardly anything remains from before Nicolae Ceausescu and his Lady Macbeth of a wife Elena botched the place with their hideous plans. The smaller cities, though, the ones in the north away from the metropole, are lovingly preserved artifacts from the past. Bucharest is a dump of a capital surrounded by a beautiful country. The problem with Kiev—according to a local joke that is truer than it is funny—is that it's surrounded by Ukraine.

Navigation, though, was an enormous pain in the ass. I bought a map of the city in the United States before we left, but it proved to be almost entirely useless. The map is in English. Cyrillic letters don't appear anywhere on it, not even in a smaller font or in parentheses. Yet all the letters on all the street signs were in Cyrillic. Where my map says "Alexander Street," the street sign says "Александр улице." I could have navigated just fine if my map included the names of things in both alphabets, but it didn't.

"Apparently," Sean said, "just about everyone who visits Ukraine comes from Russia. They have no more use for our language or alphabet than we have for theirs."

Westerners who think Ukraine might one day join the European Union and NATO (and that Russia would let her go quietly) might want to re-evaluate those assumptions. The Western world doesn't seem to even exist when you're in Kiev, but Moscow feels like it's around every corner.

Kiev, though, is not Moscow. It is much more orderly and prosperous. It appears to have been thoroughly de-Sovietized while Russia has been to only a lesser extent and next-door Belarus hardly at all. Crime isn't out of control. Ukraine is at least sometimes capable of holding elections that are not rigged. Kiev strikes me as the kind of place Moscow and St. Petersburg would be by now if Russia had gone the way of Eastern Europe and democratized after the Cold War, if it hadn't expanded so far to the east and half lost its European identity, if it had never been conquered by the Mongols in the 13th century and corrupted with the habits of medieval era oriental despotism.

Russians and Ukrainians are different people today, but they were once the same people. The fact that Kiev is outside Russia, by far the most powerful of the three Kievan Rus nations, leads to both tension and binding. Ukraine doesn't have much serious tension between the ethnic Ukrainian majority and the large Russian minority, at least not the kind that has convulsed former Soviet republics in the Caucasus and former Yugoslav republics in the Balkans. Civil war seems at worst a remote possibility. A Russian invasion, though, might be possible in a perfect storm. And continued Russian pressure and dominance is almost a certainty.

Kiev is a fantastic city, by nearly all accounts better than any in Russia, but it's also, unfortunately, expensive. Luxury cities everywhere are expensive, and Kiev is no exception. Sean and I had little choice but to stay at one of the lesser hotels to keep from hemorrhaging money.

The problem with lesser hotels, of course, is that they are lesser.

I decided to wait for Sean in the bar while he called his wife, Angie. I brought a book to read while I sipped from a glass of red wine. I chose to sit at a table for two by myself rather than at the bar. Within seconds, every woman within a 25-foot radius leered at me luridly. The hotel didn't *look* like a prostitute den from the outside or even the inside, but it was.

A woman in her late thirties at the next table scooted her chair next to mine. She wore a tight black skirt and way too much makeup. Her surgically enhanced breasts burst from her brassiere. I kept reading and pretended not to notice her as long as possible so she would get the idea that I was not in the market.

"Hi," she finally said.

I did not want to be rude, but I waited a few extra seconds before saying "Hello."

"First time in Kiev?" she said. She spoke English better than 99 percent of Ukrainians.

"Yes," I said. "It's a great city."

Getting straight to the point, she said, "Do you want to have sex?"

"No," I said. "I'm meeting someone."

"Girlfriend?"

"I'm married."

"You're meeting your wife?"

"My wife is at home in the U.S."

"So, what's the problem?"

She really did seem to be baffled. If my wife wasn't with me, why *shouldn't* I have sex with a willing woman whose breasts were already half exposed? Was I uptight? Gay? Did I have no libido? Her surprise, genuine or otherwise, actually made me feel slightly ridiculous when I said, "No, I'm sorry, no," but I wouldn't rent a prostitute for myself even if I was single.

"My friend is going to be here any second now," I said and I hoped it was true. Sean could be on the phone with his wife for another hour for all I knew.

I put my nose back into my book and discreetly flicked my eyes around the bar while pretending to read. I didn't dare make eye contact with any other woman lest I have to say no to sex all over again, but the dynamic in the bar was highly unusual and hard to tune out. Half the people in there were women. Every single one of them looked like a prostitute. They propositioned one man after another and were turned down by all of them. So I wasn't the only one acting prudish. I suddenly realized what it might feel like to be an attractive woman in a meet market who desperately wished she wasn't getting so much attention. Yet not even in the sleaziest bars are women approached as aggressively as were the mostly Russian and Ukrainian men in that bar.

I later asked the bartender out of curiosity how much the prostitutes cost.

"It depends on what you want," he said, "but the price starts at twenty dollars."

The rooms in the hotel cost four times as much. The women, then, were a bargain. Yet they still had a hard time finding clients.

I didn't want to eat at the hotel with all the hookers around. Nor did I want to contend with the agonizing difficulty of trying to order food in a place that did not even include my alphabet, let alone my language, on its menus. So I asked the concierge to direct Sean and me to a restaurant that had English menus. There apparently aren't very many, but there are a few here and there for those who know where to go.

The recommended place was decorated with a forest of fake plastic trees. The wait staff wore traditional red and white folk clothing that looked vaguely Bavarian. Our waiter spoke English almost as well as the hookers back at the bar.

"So," I said to him after ordering, "how many people in Kiev speak Ukrainian?"

"Only around 30 percent speak it fluently," he said. Everyone, though, speaks fluent Russian. And, like Americans, they expect everyone they meet, including foreigners, to speak the local language.

A drunk woman wandered over from the next table. She must have heard Sean and me speaking English and must have known that we were foreigners, but she wanted to come over and say hi in Russian.

On and on she went in Russian saying I've-no-idea-what while holding onto the back of an empty chair to keep her drunk self from falling. Her husband and twenty-something son smiled and waved and seemed slightly embarrassed by her behavior.

Then all of a sudden she hugged me. She hugged me and then leaned into me and her drunk feet slipped on the floor. As I held onto her tightly so she wouldn't fall, she looked up into my face like a teenager on a date. God help me I thought she was going to kiss me, and right in front of her family, but her husband jumped up to save everyone from *that* unpleasantness and led her away.

Back at her own table, she took from her bag a box of chocolate covered cherries she had bought earlier. Then she returned to my table and gave them to me.

"*Spacebo*," I said and smiled, slightly embarrassed. I did not want a gift from someone so drunk, but what was I supposed to do? Rudely give it back? Her husband, good sport that he was, nodded that it was okay. Then she returned to her seat.

The waiter gave Sean and me shots of vodka and toothpicked cubes of lard on our way out. "This is our tradition," he said and looked slightly concerned that we might reject what he offered. The vodka was good. I could have done without the lard square, but I tried to pretend it was bacon and that I liked it.

"They do the same thing in Russia," Sean said when we stepped out into the crisp air of late October. He was relieved we weren't told to drink more often. "In Moscow," he said, "you have to eat *lots* of potatoes for breakfast if you're an American. Russians will pour you so much vodka everywhere you go that you'll otherwise be pickled by noon."

When the Chernobyl administration cancelled our trip to the radio-active wasteland, Sean and I decided to drive south to Odessa on the Black Sea and to Yalta on the Crimean Peninsula. Before leaving for the Black Sea, however, we had to photograph some of Kiev's spectacular monuments.

Without realizing it, I stopped the car in a place where only police cars could park. A cop yelled at me in Russian and waved his arms. I got the point.

"Sorry," I said and rolled down the window. "I'm moving it now."

He then demanded the impossible: "*Speak* to me in *Russian*," he said.

As if I could flip a switch in my head and use a language I never studied. What could I say in Russian off the top of my head? *Vodka, dobre, Gorbachev, da, perestroika, spacebo, dosvidanya,* and *nyet*.

The longer I stayed in Kiev, the more I felt like I was in Russia. I had to try hard sometimes to remember that I was not. I didn't feel that way in Lviv or in the countryside, but Kiev looks and feels so incredibly Russian—and actually *is* partly Russian—that the feeling was inescapable. I was surrounded by Russian architecture, the Russian language, Russian food, businessmen and tourists from Russia, ethnic Russians who lived there, and by policemen who ordered me to speak Russian.

But Kiev seemed to lack Russia's darkness somehow. Aside from the cop, the people Sean and I encountered in the capital were downright chipper compared with those we met in Lviv. They weren't shuffling around, and they did not seem remotely depressed. Kiev is what Moscow and St. Petersburg wish they were. If I had flown into Kiev and didn't see any other part of the country, if Sean and I hadn't made our way there on such awful roads in the remote darkened countryside, I'd think Ukraine was First World and fully developed. But it's not.

The road from Kiev to Odessa is 300 miles of long, flat, and boring. The pavement isn't cratered like the roads near the Polish frontier, so there's that, but I can't think of anything else the journey has going for it except that it ends on the shore of the Black Sea, a relatively warm place with a slightly cooler version of the Mediterranean climate.

On the way down, Sean and I passed one rusted hulk after another, defunct Soviet-era factories abandoned long ago. These things were everywhere. Ukraine experienced a full-blown industrial collapse when Moscow's communist empire burst.

There was no chance Sean and I would find a foreigner-friendly Ресторан between Kiev and Odessa. Three times a day Sean and I had to eat, and most times the very idea filled us with dread. If no one in the restaurant spoke English, and there weren't any recognizable letters, let alone words, on the menu, how could we order? We couldn't even say to the waitress, "just bring us anything."

We were terribly unprepared linguistically for this trip. I felt ridiculous, like we should have studied at least enough Russian that we could order Chicken Kiev and a beer, but we didn't, and I couldn't find a bookstore anywhere that carried an English-Russian or English-

Ukrainian dictionary.

You wouldn't be wrong to say that someone who travels as much as I do should have known better. I *should* have known better. In my defense, though, I've been to countries on every continent but Antarctica and Australia and never had trouble ordering food. Hardly anyone in Turkey speaks English, but the Turks use a slightly modified version of the same alphabet we use, so I could figure out enough of the language to get around without any problem. The Arabic alphabet is much stranger than the Cyrillic, but English and French are commonly spoken in much of the Arab world. Far more Westerners visit Arabic-speaking countries than Russian-speaking countries, so translated menus and street signs are common. Ukraine looks and feels far more "Western" than Egypt, but it gets fewer visitors and is harder—and harder than I expected—for the non-Russian visitors it does get to navigate.

Sean and I selected a random restaurant in a random wasteland of a brutally Sovietized town we had never heard of. That part was easy. All we had to do was look for a sign that said "Ресторан." Only one waitress was working that day. She spoke no English. We were her only customers. No one could help.

After letting us peruse menus we couldn't read for five minutes, she came back to our table and asked what we wanted.

"Um," Sean said.

"We don't speak Russian," I said.

She glowered at us, not quite with hatred, but close. She raised her shoulders and flexed her fingers as if saying, "what the hell am I supposed to do with you two?"

"Chicken?" I said.

She didn't understand what I said. I may as well have said "qwertyplat." She gave me her *what-the-fuck* look again. If only they had pictures of food on their menus.

Suddenly I had an idea. It was extreme, but I knew it would work if we dared.

"Sean," I said. "I know a way out of this."

"What?" he said.

I couldn't help smirking. "How badly," I said and giggled, "do you want chicken?"

He thought for a second, trying to figure out what I had in mind.

"No," he said and laughed. "You can't possibly mean…"

He knew exactly what I was thinking.

"Yep," I said.

He looked up into the face of our pissed-off waitress and, with a little boy glint in his eyes, he clucked like a chicken. He put his thumbs in his armpits, flapped his elbows as if they were wings, and let out a "bock *BOCK*."

Our sullen and humorless waitress, so typical in Ukraine, burst out laughing. Sean's clucking was *the* funniest thing she had seen in a week. And she brought us some chicken.

"When we get to Odessa," I said, "we have *got* to get on the Internet and study some Russian. This is absolutely ridiculous. I can't handle being this stupid."

Sean drove when we got back to the car. I rummaged through my backpack for a notebook.

"We are going to learn this alphabet *now*," I said as we merged back onto the freeway.

I ripped out a sheet of paper and wrote down every letter in the Latin alphabet and, next to it, every letter I knew in the Cyrillic alphabet, which was at most a third. I deciphered the rest one at a time by scrutinizing the spelling of place names on road signs. "Kiev," for instance, was spelled "Київ." That gave me a few extra letters right there.

That's how I learned Cyrillic. One letter and place name at a time. By the time we reached Odessa, I had the entire alphabet memorized.

But Odessa wasn't as difficult, at least not at first. We found an Irish pub catering to visitors next to a tourist hotel. And they had menus in English.

Odessa has long been more international and cosmopolitan than the rest of the country. Once an ancient Greek colony with links to the

Mediterranean, and more recently a settlement of Muslim Crimean Tatars, the modern city was founded by a decree from Catherine the Great in 1794 and declared a free port. Many of those who built it and lived there in its early days were neither Russian nor Ukrainian, but Albanian, Armenian, Azeri, Bulgarian, Tatar, French, German, Greek, Italian, Jewish, Polish, Romanian, and Turkish. More than a third of the population was Jewish by 1897. It was a world apart even during the worst of the Soviet era. The terror-famine barely grazed Odessa at all.

Today it's a mostly Russian-speaking city, though the old city looks and feels nothing like Russia. It looks and feels remarkably like a gorgeous, atmospheric, and joyous—albeit somewhat generic—city on the Mediterranean. The sprawling suburbs, however, are clotted with ghastly and brutalist communist towers. Outer Kiev must have looked like that before being refurbished.

After the Irish pub, though, Sean and I had a hard time finding another restaurant that could handle our needs in English. Menus weren't as widely translated in Odessa as we had originally thought. I spent hours in the car decoding the alphabet, but that didn't teach me the words for "beer," "chicken," or "steak." I kicked myself for not asking our English-speaking waiter at the pub when I had the chance. Ordering food was still hard. Sean and I yearned for McDonald's, not because we're fans of fast food, but because we could order by pointing.

We felt like the biggest idiots in the entire country. Being functionally illiterate and incapable of communicating knocked forty points off our IQs. And no world traveler worth half a damn seeks out a McDonald's on the other side of the world.

"What kind of person," Sean said, "flies ten time zones from home and says, *excuse me, we have just arrived in your country, can you please direct me to the nearest McDonald's?* Am I that guy?"

He was that guy. At least he was that guy in Ukraine. And so was I.

It was arrogant and even a little imperial of me to expect people to speak my language wherever I went. Native English speakers are the only people in the entire world who can get away with it. Hungarians,

Vietnamese, Israelis, and Somalis *know* no one else speaks their language. If they want to travel abroad, they have no choice but to learn at least one additional language.

The second language most people learn, though, tends to be English. They don't only learn English so they can talk to people from the U.S., Britain, Ireland, Canada, and Australia. They also learn English so they can talk to bilingual Hungarians, Vietnamese, Israelis, Somalis, and so on. A person can get by just fine with English in places as diverse as India, Sweden, Lebanon, Mexico, and Zimbabwe.

It's not much easier for an American to get around in Russia and its sphere of influence speaking English than it would be for a Russian to get around the United States speaking his native tongue. English is not the *lingua franca* in Ukraine, Kazakhstan, or Tajikistan. Russian is.

I knew that long before I left for Ukraine, but I didn't appreciate its significance until after I got there. It was a humbling experience, one that had been a long time coming for me. It was also instructive. What are the odds, really, that Ukraine will ever join the European Union or NATO when it's still so firmly part of the Russian-speaking world?

We hardly had enough time in Odessa to take a quick look around. Yalta was still a long way to the south at the bottom of the Crimean Peninsula. So we got back in the car, wishing we could have stayed longer in Odessa, but happy to know that Yalta, too, was on the shore of the Black Sea and even farther to the south where it was warmer.

I could understand why Russians wished they had not lost Ukraine. Ukraine is the beach. Ukraine has warm water. Imagine how New Englanders would feel in the winter if South Carolina and Florida seceded.

"If you see a McDonald's," Sean said as I drove us south in the car, "you come to a *screeching* halt."

Night fell before we reached the Crimea. Sean and I were both too tired to drive, so we pulled into a gas station to buy cans of Red

Bull. CDs were on sale for five bucks apiece next to the soda and chips. Sean grabbed a couple at random, plus Carl Orff's *Carmina Burana*. The dramatic intro, *O Fortuna*, seemed like the appropriate thing to listen to when arriving in the one part of Ukraine everyone knew might one day, through either war or secession, be reunited with Russia.

Crimea is in Ukraine, but it isn't Ukrainian. This part of the country really is Russian. By this point I had learned the alphabet well enough that I could read, so I knew the gigantic words "Автономной Республики Крым" announced to all visitors at the border that Crimea is an autonomous republic.

Crimea has its own flag. It hosts the Russian navy's Black Sea fleet. It defiantly refuses to place itself within the Ukrainian time zone. Though it's dead south of Kiev, it uses the more easterly Moscow time zone instead. It doesn't have its own national anthem, but I heard the Russian national anthem playing loudly on the boardwalk of Yalta.

This is a town that is long past its prime. It's undoubtedly a nicer place now than it was during the communist era, but, unlike Odessa, it's provincial and tacky. Only a Russian could travel thousands of miles to vacation there without feeling a little let down and that's only because Yalta is Russian and warm. Ukrainians go there because it's nearby and warm.

Only a fourth of its citizens are ethnic Ukrainians. Less than a sixth are Crimean Tatars. Most of the rest are Russians. The government in Kiev has been trying for years to teach everyone in the country the Ukrainian language, but in Crimea it's meeting the stiffest resistance.

One thing the peninsula has going for it, however, aside from an agreeable climate, is its spectacular scenery. While most of Ukraine is flatter than Iowa, the steep craggy Crimean Mountains shoot straight up out of the Black Sea, which shimmers in sun-drenched glory year-round. Even though Yalta is significantly north of the Mediterranean, the climate, at least for a narrow little band near the beach, is startlingly subtropical. It's one of the only places in the world where a native Russian-speaking population can grow palm trees. It's not only the language, but the political autonomy and the general Russian-ness that set Crimea apart from Ukraine. It's also those mountains and the trees and the moderate sea breeze.

Sean and I hadn't booked a hotel, so we checked out a few places at random. The first was prohibitively expensive. The second, a chopped up former apartment building that must have been beautiful in its heyday, reeked of piss.

A third place was cheap, adequately clean, and had a large room with two beds, so we took it.

A Russian communist-era movie played on the TV. I couldn't understand the dialogue, but it was at least passively propagandistic. The main characters, scientists in white lab coats, worked in a sparkling clean high-tech facility, the kind of place science fiction writers of the 1950s imagined was in our future. The movie portrayed an entirely staged idealized version of an advanced communist utopia without gulags, without long lines for potatoes, and without the NKVD. Ukrainians don't need communist-produced re-runs. They, like the rest of us, need a serious film about Stalinism for a mass audience, a *Schindler's List* of the Soviet Union.

In the morning we strolled the boardwalk. The weather was unseasonably cold, almost freezing even though it was only early November, but the sunshine and the palm trees gave the illusion of warmth. Yalta isn't exactly Miami, but Crimeans really do enjoy a charmed climate, especially compared with the climate Russians suffer through everywhere else.

At the north end of the boardwalk stood an angry-looking statue of Vladimir Lenin. I had the feeling he was still up there not because he was a communist, but because he was Russian. Communism is as dead in Yalta these days as it is in Warsaw. Just a few hundred feet away, and comically in the direct line of sight of Lenin's sculpted furious face, was a McDonald's.

Sean and I had breakfast there and it was disgusting. The sausage McMuffins had two sausage patties instead of just one, and not only were they too salty, they were *off*. But at least I could order one without any serious hassle.

For dinner we found a place with translated menus. Yalta just barely gets enough Western tourists once in a while that it occurred to a few restaurant managers to have a handful of menus laying around in the back in other languages.

Two young college-age women a few tables away heard us speaking in English. They laughed. They giggled. They tittered. This went on for at least a half-hour. And they couldn't stop staring. Sean and I were like zoo animals. An Arab, a black African, or an East Asian would have a hellish time visiting this place.

Yalta was nice in a basic sort of way, but it lacked the polish and vibrancy of Kiev and the relative cosmopolitanism of Odessa. No one should ever fly from the other side of the world just to go there. It reminded me of what Samuel Johnson once said about a bizarre volcanic basalt formation in Northern Ireland called the Giant's Causeway. "Worth seeing? Yes; but not worth going to see."

Crimea is a de-facto independent Russian-speaking republic, but if it weren't for Soviet premier Nikita Khrushchev it would still be part of Russia. In 1954 he moved an internal Russian border around and placed Crimea in Ukraine. It didn't seem like a fateful decision at the time, one no more significant than giving Idaho a slice of Montana. He had no idea any part of Ukraine, let alone all of it, would ever break loose from Moscow. He should have known it was possible since it had happened before, but he did not see it coming, or at any rate didn't care, so this Russian-majority region is marooned outside of Russia.

Perhaps the only reason Russian leader Vladimir Putin hasn't moved to "correct" Khrushchev's mistake is because there isn't much point. Ukraine's current government headed up by Viktor Yanukovych was friendlier than the previous government of Viktor Yushchenko, which Putin did everything in his power (short of invasion) to smash.

Ukraine's 2004 election was rigged. Yanukovych was declared the winner when the majority wanted the pro-Western Yushchenko instead, whom somebody almost fatally poisoned with dioxin. His face was hideously disfigured by the toxin for a while, but he slowly recovered. The results of that rigged election were reversed by the Orange Revolution, when general strikes broke out and thousands took to the streets and said, *no*.

In 2009, Russia turned off its supply of natural gas and let Ukrainians freeze in the winter, purportedly because of a financial dispute over prices and debt. The punishment was preferable, of course, to Stalin confiscating Ukrainian *food* in 1921 and 1922, but the message was a familiar one: if you don't follow dictates from Moscow, you will be punished.

The crisis likely wouldn't have been triggered at all if Ukrainians had elected a pro-Russian government. Moscow was already cheesed off by Yushchenko's noises about Ukrainian ascension to the European Union and NATO. The Russian media portrayed Ukraine as a traitor state over it. There wasn't much Moscow could do to stop the likes of Lithuania and Poland from joining NATO, but it won't likely ever let its Kievan Rus cousins leave without resistance.

These kinds of problems don't exist between Russia and Crimea. It might mean war if they did, or if a stridently pro-Western government in Kiev expanded its writ a little too enthusiastically, but that hasn't happened.

Moscow doesn't actually care very much about Yalta. The city made history when Stalin, Franklin Delano Roosevelt, and Winston Churchill met there at the end of World War II to agree about which parts of post-fascist Europe would be in the Western camp and which would be in the communist bloc, but it has been a backwater ever since even if it's a slightly pleasant one nowadays.

What Moscow cares about in Crimea very much is Sevastopol. That's where Russia's Black Sea fleet makes its home. Neither Sean nor I dared take any photographs of it, not even discreetly from the car as we drove past. It's not a good idea to take pictures of military installations anywhere in the world, especially not Russian military installations.

In Sevastopol, once again, I found myself forgetting I wasn't in Russia. The overwhelming majority of people who live there are Russians. The language they speak is Russian. Actual Russian soldiers and sailors were all over the place.

When the Soviet Union cracked up and Ukraine declared independence, Russia initially refused to cede Sevastopol and Crimea at all and only later relented when it signed the Peace and Friendship treaty with Kiev. Moscow need not worry overly much. Its fleet's lease won't run out until 2042. And if Ukraine tries to revoke it, Russia will almost certainly seize it by force, most likely to cheers and applause by locals who would feel liberated. Ukraine barely holds onto the Crimea oblast as it is, and on even numbered days I couldn't help but wonder how long even that is going to last.

B efore heading back toward Kiev, Sean and I first had to see the remote and far-flung Sea of Azov. The western side is Ukrainian, and half of that is Crimean. The eastern shore is all part of southwestern Russia. It is so far east from any place in Europe normal travelers would want to go that it seemed, at least in my mind, more Central Asian than European.

"It almost has to be strange," Sean said, and I agreed. "I want to say that I've been there. Who goes to the Sea of Azov?"

I felt slightly silly, however, for thinking it must be exotic in anything other than name. It's just a large body of water. Right? Water is water. How strange could it be? It wasn't purple or made of Dr. Pepper. Just because hardly any Americans ever see it doesn't mean there has to be anything odd or even interesting about it. I *felt* that it must be unusual, but my head told me it can't be. It's not on another planet. It's just a remote and obscure Russian sea. Visiting would almost certainly be anti-climactic. We still wanted to go, though, on the off chance that our gut feelings were right.

So far, most of what we'd seen had defied expectations, but we weren't wrong this time.

We drove a few hours from Sevastopol and out onto a long narrow spit, certain it would be easy to find the beach since the water was less than a mile from the road. Yet all I could see was a hideous post-industrial wasteland with no way to reach the water on the other side. The sea was just off to our left according to my map, but every street heading that direction was gated and shuttered. Was it possible we drove all the way to the Sea of Azov and would not get to see it? I drove along the desolate road that took us through unspeakable squalor for another half-hour. A sad billboard advertised cheap holidays on that blasted up shore for those who could not afford Yalta.

I was just about to give up when I saw an ungated dirt road branching off to the left. I took the turn and we found ourselves in the creepiest place I had yet seen in the country. Broken glass, barbed wire, crumbling walls, junked automobiles, and garden variety refuse were everywhere. If there were people around, I couldn't see them or hear them. The entire area was derelict and forlorn.

Some dogs detected our presence and barked. I felt a powerful sense that we shouldn't be there. The dearth of other humans added to my sense of uneasiness, but at the same time I didn't want anybody to see us. I'm not sure why, exactly, but a tingling feeling told me we'd be in trouble if anyone did.

A narrow path led to the beach through a thicket of weeds. A wooden sign pounded into the sand showed a camera with a red slash through it. *No pictures.* Why shouldn't anybody take pictures? There was nothing even remotely interesting or apparently sensitive that I could have photographed.

A strong wind came off the sea, whipping the water into a furious lather. Dark rain clouds on the watery horizon headed inland. The beach in both directions was cluttered with the hulking industrial wreckage of a ghost port.

Sean took out his camera.

"Don't," I said.

"But there's nobody here," he said.

All I heard was the wind and the surf.

There seemed to be no one in any direction for miles, so I unzipped my Nikon from its case and took a few pictures.

We stood there in silence and took in the desolate scene for a while.

"You were right," I said, "about the Sea of Azov."

"This is why nobody comes here," Sean said.

We were technically in Europe, but it looked like the nastiest parts of Iraq. The sound of machine-gun fire would not have seemed out of place.

I have never been anywhere that looks and feels more like the rotted dead center of the Soviet Empire. This place was so utterly godforsaken and misery-stricken I had a momentary feeling that the Union of Soviet Socialist Republics had never fallen apart, that, Mordor-like, its malice truly is sleepless, that it's still crushing parts of the world in its totalitarian fist.

The West won the Cold War, but this place experienced none of the springtime of Budapest, Prague, or even of Yalta. This part of Ukraine suffered nothing but ruin. It looked and felt like the end of the world.

Turn the page for a special preview of

Michael J. Totten's

In the Wake of the Surge

Published by Belmont Estate Books

Available now from Barnes and Noble
and Amazon.com

Welcome to Baghdad

Never again will I complain about the inconvenience and discomfort of airports and civilian airline travel delays. You won't either if you hitch a ride with the United States Army from Kuwait to Baghdad in July during a war.

Military planes leave Kuwait every couple of hours for Baghdad International Airport (or BIAP, pronounced *BIE-op*), and the Army's media liaison in Kuwait dropped me off at the airfield so I could take a flight "up."

I waited twelve hours in a metal folding chair in a room full of soldiers who had priority over me for available seats.

At least I had a meal. On the other side of the base a McDonald's and Pizza Hut were tucked inside trailers supplied by Kellogg, Brown, and Root (KBR). KBR seems to have built almost everything here that the military uses for housing and storage. Out of plywood, plastic, and sheet metal, and for exorbitant fees, they construct instant yet aesthetically brutal outposts of America.

I ordered a pizza from a Pakistani employee at the Pizza Hut trailer and paid with American dollars. They don't use coins on the base. They don't even have coins on the base. If your food costs $5.75 and you pay with six dollars you'll get a small round cardboard disk or chit that says "25 cent gift certificate" on it as change.

All night I waited for a flight and was bumped again and again by soldiers on their way to places with names like War Eagle, Victory, and Fallujah. Finally my name was placed on a manifest, and I gathered around a gruff barking sergeant with everyone else.

"I want you all back here in 20 minutes," he bellowed. "First I want you all to go to the bathroom. Then I want to see you standing in front of me with a bottle of water."

Everyone lined up with their gear and marched single file into the plane. I was the only civilian on board, and I felt terribly awkward and out of place. I also strangely felt a little like I was in the army myself.

The plane was windowless and as loud as 100 lawn mowers. I crammed pink foam plugs into my ears, strapped on my body armor, and seat-belted myself into the side of the plane like everyone else.

"Hang your bags on the hooks!" barked the sergeant. "Hang them all the way up!"

"Don't fall asleep!" the soldier next to me shouted over the roar. "When you see the rest of us grab our helmets, put yours on, too! We'll be beginning the spiral dive into Baghdad!"

"To avoid flying low over hostiles?" I said.

"Something like that!" he shouted.

This was not United Airlines.

The funny thing about the steep corkscrew dive is that I couldn't feel it. Anyone who says that dive is scary, as some journalists do, is talking b.s. You can't feel the turn, nor are there any windows to see out of. It's impossible to tell, as a passenger, if the plane is flying level or banking. I'm not sure how the soldiers knew when to put on their helmets. Perhaps someone signaled. No one could hear anything over the clattering machine roar of the plane through their ear plugs. All the same, though, everyone put their helmets on at the same time, so I did, as well.

The landing was smooth and felt no different from an American Airlines touch down in Los Angeles. When the back of the plane opened up onto the tarmac, light like a hundred suns blinded my darkness-adjusted and dilated eyes. I could barely make out the hazy shape of military aircraft in front of us amidst the pure stunning brilliance.

We dismounted the plane and I stepped into blazing sunshine with my fingers over my eyes.

You know how it feels when you get into a black car on a hot afternoon in July? It's an inferno outside, but inside the car it's even hotter? That's how Iraq feels in the shade. Direct sunlight burns like a blowtorch. If you don't wear a helmet or soft cap the sun will cook your brain. You'll just get headaches at first, but then you'll end up in the hospital.

Getting from BIAP to the IZ (the International Zone, aka the Green Zone) is an adventure all by itself. First you haul your gear to a bus stop that feels like the inside of a broiler. Then you get on the bus and ride for 45 minutes to an army base. Then you get off that bus and wait an hour to catch another bus. Then you get off that bus and wait for an hour to catch yet another bus to yet *another* base. Then you wait in the sun yet again—and by this time you're totally fragged from the heat—and take another damn bus to a helipad.

All this takes hours. You will be no closer to the center of Baghdad than you were when you started, and there are no short cuts, not even for colonels.

Once you make your way to the helipad you will sit in the heat and wait. A Blackhawk will eventually pick your ass up, but if you're a civilian like me, you will fly last.

I waited for my helicopter flight with two other civilians— Willie from Texas and Larry from Florida.

Willie and Larry do construction work for private companies in harsh places like Iraq and Afghanistan. They are both small town individuals with Red State tastes and political views, yet they have a certain worldliness that surpasses that of most people I know. They've seen parts of the world that most in the well-traveled jet set would never dream of setting foot. They aren't allowed to tell me how much money they make, but I know it is many hundreds of thousands of dollars per year.

"You get hooked on making money," Willie said. "You think you can do it for one year or two, then quit, but it's like a drug. Or like when you get one tattoo—all of a sudden you want two tattoos. My wife keeps saying, come on, you can do it for just one more year."

"My wife would hate it if I was out here for years," I said.

"You get vacation," Larry said. "You get more vacation than French people. Twenty one days every four months. And you don't have to pay taxes if you take your vacation outside the U.S. Your wife can meet you in the Bahamas."

A KBR employee who coordinates the Blackhawk flights called our names on the manifest.

"Get your gear, let's go, let's go, let's go!"

Military rules require all Blackhawk passengers to wear long-sleeved shirts in case there's a fire on board. This was the first I'd heard of it, and I hadn't brought anything warm with me to Iraq. Why would I want to do that? It's 120 degrees.

Willie let me borrow an extra sweatshirt. I put that on along with my body armor, my helmet, and my sunglasses. Then I hauled my 100 pounds of gear out to the landing zone and lined up with a dozen or so soldiers. We were ordered to stand there in line while we cooked in the sun. We waited. And waited. And waited. My clothes were drenched as though I had fallen into a pool. That's the army for you. Comfort just isn't a factor. None of the soldiers complain about the heat. I didn't either, at least not in front of them.

Our Blackhawk helicopter was ready.

"Move out!" bellowed the KBR flight coordinator.

Larry, Willie, and I ran behind a line of soldiers toward the Blackhawk.

"Hold up!" said the coordinator.

The Blackhawk pilot lifted off without picking up anyone up.

"Man," said the coordinator as he shook his head. The roar of the chopper rotors quickly receded. "No one was mission critical so they didn't want to give anybody a ride. I do not know what to tell you."

"Fuck!" Willie screamed.

We hauled our gear back to the waiting area and sat. I drank a bottle of water in seconds. The whole thing disappeared inside me as though I hadn't drank anything.

"Last year in Afghanistan," Larry said, "I waited a week for a flight. Choppers flew in and out all day every day. I showed up on the LZ for every flight, had my gear ready, and kept getting bumped. A whole week, just to fly one from place to another. At least I was on the clock. We might be here a while."

We could have walked to the Green Zone in just a couple of hours, but we weren't allowed to.

And we did wait for a while. Not for a week, but for 12 hours. We kept getting bumped by new soldiers who showed up with places to go. Another pilot took off without picking anyone up. I couldn't figure out why he even bothered to land. Dozens of people needed a ride. On another occasion Larry, Willie, and I made it all the way to the helicopter itself before we got kicked for some reason.

I tried to embrace the suck. Willie became increasingly agitated.

"Good thing I don't have my Glock with me!" he yelled when we got bumped the sixth time. "I ought to pour a bottle of water on that electrical board over there and short out the whole frigging place."

After the sun went down the air mercifully cooled to 100 degrees or so. That's a lovely temperature after 120, especially when the sun is no longer shining. Bats flew overhead from a reedy lake a few hundred yards away. There were no bugs. They can't survive the heat in July.

I watched helicopters fly over the city in the distance and launch burning white countermeasure flares to confuse surface-to-air heat-seeking missiles as the pilots flew over hostile parts of the city.

"I read on the Internet that the war costs 60 billion dollars a year," Larry said.

"Well, if it's on the Internet it *must* be true," I said jokingly.

A soldier heard me and swiveled his head.

"Did you just say that?" he said incredulously. "You're with the *media* and you just said that? Man, we ought to throw your ass right out of here."

I laughed, but he was barely just kidding.

Most Americans soldiers and officers I've met in Iraq are not hostile, however. Most ignore me unless I say hello to them first. A few say hello or good morning first and call me "sir." Some are eager to chat. Those who do talk seem to want to know where I'm from. Many of them are from Georgia and Texas.

Larry, Willie, and I finally got on a Blackhawk at two o'clock in the morning (oh-two-hundred in milspeak.) We strapped ourselves into our seats. There was little room on the floor for our gear, so I piled mine up in my lap.

Blackhawk helicopters don't have windows. The sides are open to the air. Fierce hot blasts of wind distorted the shape of my face as we flew fast and low over the rooftops and street lights and palm trees and backyards of the city.

Baghdad is gigantic and sprawling, and it looks much less ramshackle from the air than I expected. Neighborhoods the size of cities-within-a-city are home to millions of people all by themselves. The sheer enormity of the place puts the daily car bomb attacks into perspective. Over time the bombs and IEDs have ravaged the city, but the odds that anyone in particular will be hit by one are pretty small.

Just a few minutes after takeoff we landed on a runway in the Green Zone. The soldiers left in Humvees. Willie, Larry, and I were left at the airbase alone. My two traveling buddies had rides picking them up, but no one was waiting for me, nor would someone show up. I was expected to make my way to CPIC, the press credentialing center, but I didn't know how to do that at 2:30 in the morning. I did not have a phone number to call, nor were they any taxis or busses to take.

"You can sleep tonight at our compound," Larry said, "and find your way to the press office tomorrow when it opens."

I would have been in bad shape if I hadn't met these guys. Wandering around loose on my own in Baghdad, in the middle of the night, hauling 100 pounds of luggage, sleep-deprived, in extreme heat, and with nowhere to sleep, does not put me in my happy place, even if it is in the Green Zone.

A man named Mike Woodley showed up in an SUV to give Larry a ride. He said he could get me a bed at their compound before he realized I did not yet have a military-issued ID badge.

"They won't let you in," he said.

"Can't we just tell them I'm on my way to CPIC to pick up a badge?" I said.

"Doesn't matter," he said. "If you don't have it, the guards will not let you in."

"Is there a hotel I can check into?" I said. "What about the Al Rashid?"

"Al Rashid is in the Red Zone," he said. "And you can't get in there without a badge either."

Actually, the Red Zone is on the other side of the Al-Rashid's security wall, but Mike was right about the hotel guards not letting me in without a security badge. And I needed to get to the press office during business hours to get it.

"What should I do?" I said. I'd be damned if I was going to sleep on the sidewalk in Baghdad.

Mike pondered my options. And he came up with a great one.

"I can get into the embassy with my badge," he said, "and I can get you a temporary badge and a bed."

And that's exactly what he did. He secured me a temporary badge for the embassy annex, and he got me a bed with a pillow and fresh linens. I was one lucky bastard. The embassy annex, and the bed I got to sleep in, was at Saddam Hussein's grand downtown palace. The tyrant is dead. And I got to sleep at his house my first night in his capital. What better welcome to Baghdad could anyone possibly ask for?

Made in the USA
Lexington, KY
27 October 2012